The Lesbian Erotic Dance

BUTCH

FEMME

ANDROGYNY

AND OTHER

RHYTHMS

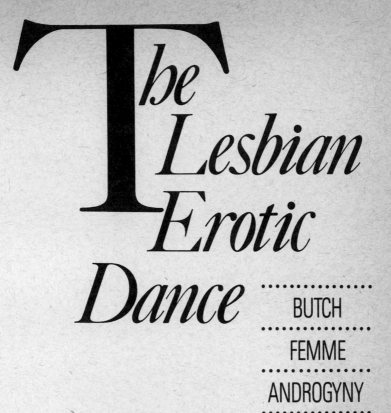

The Lesbian Erotic Dance

BUTCH

FEMME

ANDROGYNY

AND OTHER

RHYTHMS

JoAnn Loulan
with Sherry Thomas

spinsters book company
San Francisco

First Edition
10-9-8-7-6-5-4-3-2-1

Spinsters Book Company
P.O. Box 410687
San Francisco, CA 94141

Cover and Text Design: Pam Wilson Design Studio
Typesetting: Joan Meyers
Production: Georgia Harris, Joan Meyers, Kathleen Wilkenson, Lynn
Witt, Meredith Wood, Kathy Zumski.
Copyediting: Linnea Due

Printed in the U.S.A. on acid-free paper.

Library of Congress Cataloging-in-Publication Data
Loulan, JoAnn Gardner
The lesbian erotic dance: butch, femme, androgyny and other
rhythms/JoAnn Loulan.—1st ed.
p. cm.
ISBN 0-933216-76-9 : $9.95
1.Lesbianism—United States. 2. Archetype (Psychology) 3. Androgyny
(Psychology) I. Title

HQ75.6.U5L68 1990
306.76'63—dc20

90-10177
CIP

By the author
· · · · · · · · · · · · · · · · ·

Period (Volcano Press)

Lesbian Sex

Lesbian Passion: Loving Ourselves and Each Other

ACKNOWLEDGEMENTS

I truly can't believe that yet another book comes to a close. This time, I need to wear my glasses all the time when I'm writing and my shoulder is killing me from computeritis. I've even begun to exercise—me! Well, you know everything changes, that we can all count on.

I have a slew of women to thank for all their help. I'm afraid I'll leave someone out because there have been so many, and the project has gone on for so long. If I leave you out, throw a fit, call me, let me know. I'm really grateful to every woman who had a part in this.

First off, thanks to all the lesbians have helped me learn how to be a lesbian. That is, the women who have come before me, who have written words and music, who told the truth out loud. Thanks to the women who talk to me when I travel, the women who send me letters, the woman who tell another woman her story that eventually gets told to me. I'm feel very lucky that so many lesbians have been willing to share their lives with me.

Right now who is sharing her life with me the most is my editor and publisher, Sherry Thomas. She has been amazing in her ability to work with my words, spinning gold. She has come up with the greatest ideas to keep the text lively: getting the personals ads, putting the "debate" in between each chapter, transcribing the Toronto Tapes that became so invaluable for another voice. Her abilities in both the areas of editing and publishing are remarkable and I am, as always, in her debt.

Designing of the questionnaire, sending them out for comments, getting the fool thing onto the computer (have you ever tried to set all those tabs and had none of them work over and over?), and then starting to distribute them was a task that seemed endless. Mary Alvord, Lynn Murry, Margie Adam, Amy Agigian and those friends I sent them to feedback were all so helpful.

Lynn Murry then took all those little tiny numbers and fed them into her computer. She also, being my neighbor, stopped by at the oddest times to give me support, a new idea, and feedback about what was working and what wasn't.

Mary Alvord, the statistical queen to the lesbian nation, did the analysis of this survey. She has spent endless hours creating these numbers, then endless more hours getting all this to make sense to me. She was patient with calls from how my computer was not acting right (it wasn't plugged in correctly) to what is the "mean?" She would go over things again and again until the light went on inside my head. There is no way this project would be completed without her.

Margie Adam gave me immeasurable support. She didn't agree with me, at least at first, and she helped me clarify what I was saying. She played devil's advocate, debating with me, and making stunning analyses. There were times when I didn't have another thought possible and she would encourage me through loving discourse. Her heart met my heart in this.

Marcia Quackenbush, as in all my projects, helped me to form this one. She read several drafts along the way and gave me critically needed feedback. Her mind works in a way that gives me food for thought, and I loved our philisophical exchanges on the topic. Also honey, thanks for all the support and love.

Carla, Peggy Eva, Karen, Cyndy, and Laurie were all in on the inception, when I said, "I think I'll write a book gang, let's sit down and talk about this and let me take notes." We would talk into the night, at brunch, at the county fair, sitting in someone's living room, at dances. We went on and on. They would tell me stories and I would listen. This was the first group of women I knew (along with Sarie, Georgia and Kerry) that used the words "butch" and "femme" with pride and loving energy. Carla especially helped me understand that I truly was a femme, and proud of it.

Judy Mullins, my sister and comrade, was once again invaluable in her support, love and energy towards this project. My favorite story is when we went to the West Coast Women's Festival to distribute the first 400 questionnaires. From what I understood, my workshop started at ten to eleven. Now, I didn't hear that as from ten o'clock to eleven o'clock, I heard it as ten minutes to eleven. Judy and I discussed this over and over as to what a strange time this was for a festival workshop. I was the emcee that year the night and before my talk and announced it to 3000 women, making fun of the time, like any dyke at a festival could get to something with a time like ten minutes to anything. No one thought I was serious, so no one told me about the real time. Well, Judy and I are driving into the festival area armed with boxes of questionnaires, answer sheets and pencils. As we come over the crest of the hill and can view the whole workshop area, the center field is filled with women at 10:30. We wonder at first who is giving a workshop before mine. Then at the same instant we both scream (as is our nature—when any change occurs—scream): "It's ten to eleven! Not ten minutes to eleven!" We tear down the hill, run out of the car carrying these huge boxes, and when we arrive at the site, Alix Dobkin in her inimitable fashion (happy 50th this year Alix) is leading the group in singing "If it wasn't for the women, women, we would not be waiting, waiting." To the tune of her famous song "If it wasn't for the Women." What a joyous sound, 800 women singing rather than shouting. Alix, I will forever be in your debt. And thank you, Judy, for talking with me for hours afterwards about the fact that I'm human and in a year we'd be laughing about the mistake. You were right. You've also helped me through a hard time and we are sisters forever.

Denise Notzon, hey girl. As usual, you have been there this year when I said "I think I'll write another book", and you said "Go for it!" As my manager, you have always taken me seriously, worked for my best interest and in general been there with your loving support. You are always willing to listen to any problem that gets in the way and have tried to make my travel on the road easy. Thanks for all you do and all you are.

Dee Mosbacher and Nanette Gartrell have a special place in this project. Not only have we had numerous discussions over the years, helped enormously with the statistical presentation, but they have continued to be my cheer-up committee when I have needed it.

Liz Krainer is an academic survivor and has gone through this work with me from a researcher's perspective. She is also a femme, lesbian, feminist with children, an acute mind and a big heart.

Lynn Witt gets special mention here not just because she's my editor's lover (although that alone would qualify for thanks— she was absent a lot, you got phone calls first thing in the morning and last thing at night). But in your own right, you added so much from a butch's perspective.

Jan Zobel, where would I be without you? You have seen me through the craziest of times, always someone I can call at midnight and the day is just beginning for you. The fact that you can make my taxes make sense is a miracle in and of itself, and through all the stressful times I've had you've been there with your shoulder and your kindness.

Marny Hall, as she herself says my "humble mentor", of course helped in many ways to make this project happen. She listened, argued, acted as if I had lost my mind, supported me and in general provoked me by continuously saying she was a femme. The greatest fun was when she came to a butch/femme soiree dressed in drag complete with wig and platform shoes just to prove no one is who you think they are.

There were lots of other ways I gleaned this information about butch/femme. It got to be that I was almost interviewing strangers on my plane trips about what they thought. Margaret Sloan-Hunter, Laura Rifkin, Marylynne Slayen, Lauren Crux, Jill Lessing, Robin Tyler, Jeanne Cordova, and Joan Nestle all were very instrumental in helping me form my ideas about what butch/femme was, how it effected our culture, and what new things could be said.

To Sylvia Villarreal, thanks for the support and love you have given me not to mention helping me figure out what you butches are all about.

Then there were the soirées, gatherings that I held to discuss what was all this was about. I wanted women there who agreed with me, ones who were diametrically opposed to what I thought, and others who would share their feelings about all this. A lot of their comments are included in this text. Some of these women remain anonymous, and have been thanked elsewhere in these notes. Great thanks to all the women who were there, including: Austin, Leslie, Robin, Jane, Sari, Barbara, Carol, Patty, Jaunita, Susan, Lynne, Stasia, Sue B., and Claudia.

Finally, there were all those conversations, stories contributed, loving energy given from Margot, Amy T., Magda, Carol, and Donna. Thanks to all the women who work so hard at Spinsters Book Co.—this project could not have been completed without all the time you spent. I thank you for the part you contribute to women's culture, my work and life.

Juliee Cones Ihrer you know I couldn't do any of this without you. How you take care of me and Gardner is beyond all words. You are part of our family, you are a gift in my life, you are always right there. You and Gardner have a connection that is so valuable to me that I can barely imagine where he would be without you. Thank you so.

Carol and Michael Wagner, my neighbors, my friends. You have been such an important support to me. It's grounding to have you and your family be connected to me and mine.

Gardner, my sweet son, my dear one. Thanks for being in my life, for reminding me what life is really about. It's amazing to watch you. One minute we are in an in-depth conversation about the holocaust, and the next we are making a terrarium with frogs you found in the pond, mud all over the kitchen. Your self is quite a miracle to me. I am so grateful I get to be in on watching your heart, spirit, mind and body grow.

Quan Yin, thank you.

TABLE OF CONTENTS

NOTES

Throughout the text I quote extensively from a panel on Butch/Femme Relationships given at a conference in Toronto (July 1985) entitled "Sex and the State." Deb Edel, Madeline Davis, Jewelle Gomez, Sue Golding, Amber Hollibaugh, Liz Kennedy, Joan Nestle, and Esther Newton all spoke on that panel are quoted in this book by permission. The panel was described as assuming "not only that butch/femme is a reality from the past but also a reality now. All of the people on this panel are involved in some way or another with trying to bridge both a political community and a relationship around butch/femme. This is a discussion about the interior body, not just the history, but the interior system of desire."

Other quotes, mostly anonymous, in the text come from two "soirées" I held to discuss androgyny and butch/femme. The quotes also come from letters that came in with the question-naires and from women at my workshops.

All of the personals ads in Chapter Seven are actual ads which appeared in San Francisco's *Bay Times* between 1984-1990. These ads are used with permission from *Bay Times,* which gave me access to this gold mine of lesbian cultural material.

I also quote from the following books and record:

Another Mother Tongue by Judy Grahn, copyright © 1984, Beacon Press, Boston.

Restricted Country by Joan Nestle, copyright © 1988, Firebrand Books, Ithaca, NY.

Every word
has a charge on it,
either positive
or negative. There is not
a neutral word
in the lesbian community.

CHAPTER ONE

The Erotic Dance

It's the erotic dance. It can be a rhythm, a simple movement, or a swaying in a certain direction. It's her smell or her shape, her eyes, her hair, her stance—an almost chemical attraction. It's a glance, a sideways look, or a full-on, face-to-face stare. It's a hip thing, a swinging foot, a hand lightly touching your knee. It's a chin thrust forward resting on an outstretched palm, a pouty lip, eyes so dark you're pulled into their depths. It's the light brush of breasts on your back, her arm gliding across your belly, your fingers stroking the tips of her hair. It's her ass trying to get your attention, breasts revealed by one less button fastened, her profile as she watches you from the corner of her eye. It's acting as if you don't notice, or mouthing "fuck me" so no one else but she can see. It's moving so your breasts catch her eye, or averting your eyes on the dance floor while you feel the heat of her stare, or actually pressing up against her while talking to someone else. It's holding her ass, cupping her breasts, touching her lips, feeling her hair, rubbing her back, cradling her head between your hands, stroking her thighs with just the sweetest energy.

It's knowing she is willing: curious, terrified, or eager. It's being where you dreamed of or where you never thought you'd be.

It's putting your arms around her, holding her hand in yours, pressing your cheek against hers. It's her leaning her head against your breast, laying your head on her shoulder. It's knowing that her touch is for you, an intention to allow you in, an intention of moving into you. It's that the skin you feel now against your face may be just the beginning of the press of her skin against your whole body. It's that you feel liquid and powerful, wanting and wanted.

The rhythm, the movement, the dance, the momentum towards one another. What is it about that one person that elicits such a stir in your body, such a stir in your mind, eventually, perhaps, such a stir in your heart?

This dance is trying to find a fit. Trying to know when she dips and when you need to bend. This dance is learning her footwork and following along. It's knowing your own pace, listening to your desires. This dance is paying attention to how she wraps herself against you and where exactly your breasts fit together. How you can know each other across all your differences. Of culture, of race, of history, of desire. How you can invite her past your wheelchair so that your skin is soothed. How you can touch her exactly as you want.

You dance with the fear of being close. This fear can fuel you, putting you on the alert that something untoward may happen, pleasures you cannot afford to miss. It may bring you back into your body with a sharp rush or make you float out of your body so as not to feel old pains.

This dance through your life moves with and around the bodies you encounter, the hearts that catch your heart, the eyes that you cannot resist.

The women you pass by, the ones that you cannot leave, the ones that you must leave: what is it that makes you want to dance with one and not another? What is the erotic component that draws you to her? That starts the craving for who she is, for the core of her?

It's the pull of her push, the possibility of being full. This fullness may be as simple as feasting your eyes and ears on the sight and sound of her. It may be that your vagina aches for her to fill it. It may be that your heart is full of delight in her, that your mind hungers for conversations with her. There are so many dances at one time, so many rhythms, that there is no way to take them apart.

It's that those fingers have a way of expressing what you two could do. The fingers move with the lightest touch or take hold as if never to let go. Your wrist is caught and she bears down. Those fingers touch with the simplest communication, a direct line to your heart. We are here is what they say, we are here and attached to someone who wants you. Her nails make a statement on your skin that reaches into your solar plexus.

It is a particular sashay of hips that catches your attention. That hip thing again, only this time with a purpose. You have kissed the woman whose hips you are watching. Your hands know the curve of her waist, the contours of her ass. These hips are round and full, or all flat planes and angles.

It's the surrender to her embrace which you have wished for, an opportunity to give in to her in this simple way. It's finding that you can let go even in your wheelchair, letting her know from the curve of your neck, the ease of your touch, that you are moving with her. It's knowing that just as easily she could be surrendering to you, and yet this time it's you.

It's dancing together again knowing that there is no one else to dance with in this place. You know it and you know she knows it. It's making an excuse to go outside, to move to another room, to be alone, together. She is leading you, which you like, giving in to where she wants to go. Letting her take your hand. Fingertips electric. Liquid fire moving through veins. It's wondering where you are going. Where this is going. It's having a future laid out before you take the first move…or knowing you'll never see her again.

It's that first kiss. The movement of her lips, the parting of her mouth, the feel of the tip of her tongue. It's the wet, the eagerness, the press, the wanting, the ever-present fear of rejection. It's the tasting of her hunger for you. It's the taste of her, the salt, the lipstick, the depth of her supplication. All the kisses you've felt before and kisses like no others. Your mouths devour each other, hungry; then you pull back your tongue, the emptiness as poignant as the fullness a moment before.

It's the beginning of the story. It's how you got privacy, how your friends knew or didn't know, how one of you had a lover or both of you did. It's the story of how you must stop, or can't, or do. This kiss is the beginning of the tale that will become your life together. This first kiss tells so much. It's filled with hope. It's the beginning of the stories in your head about who she is and what she has to offer you.

It's caressing, letting fingers and hands explore a new terrain. It's feeling your way into her skin, discovering the strength in her arms, wanting her to be passive. It's letting her touch you back, or not letting her touch you, or both touching with equal intensity. Infinite possibilities—in this moment, you have no history together, no limits. It's letting this connection give her the message, *I am here.*

It's knowing you are free to do anything you want, or knowing you must make excuses later, or that you will tell the truth to your current lover. It's making yourself stop before there is damage beyond repair. It's not making yourself stop for reasons you will try to invent later. It's being open to this and not stopping even if you should. It's the thrill of being right there at this moment that fills you with promise, or fantasy, or excuses about why it really is okay.

It's that she's been your lover for years, but you see her again, sharp and clear. You remember the thrill when you met her, and you see that she keeps changing: the future is unknown. She has a new tie on, loose around her neck, or she tosses her head, leaning seductively against the wall. It's as if you are kissing for the first time, only it's the first time again.

It's getting on the bus together, or following each other in your cars, or walking, fairly running, wheeling to get there. Or already being there in your own home that you have shared with her for years. It's wanting to look cool, or having given up altogether. It's wishing that you were further along in therapy, or had therapy that day, or were having therapy the next day, or never had therapy. It's wishing your mind would shut off because any second now it's going to ruin things and you just want your body to lead you. It's being so grateful when she pauses for a moment and moves to kiss you again, so that your heart misses a beat and you are thinking of nothing except those lips, her thighs, those fingers, the scent of her skin.

You take her to your bed, or onto the couch, the carpet, anywhere at all. It's getting the nerve to tell her that you need her to move your limbs so that you can be pain-free. It's letting her know that you have a colostomy bag, that you have had a mastectomy, that you have chronic back pain or herpes, that you don't have orgasms with partners, or are still recovering from childhood abuse. It's trying to decide if you should bring any of this up now or whether you two will ever get that far, or if she'll still want to be with you. It's trying to decide if you should just stop things at this point so that you'll never have to reveal any of this—or anything about yourself at all. It's that your mind is back saying all kinds of things that interfere with the messages of your body, the language of your heart.

It's trying to decide if you should let her undress you. It's wanting to strip for her slowly, flaunting your big breasts and full thighs. It's wanting to be in control because it thrills you. It's wanting to be in control because it scares you not to be. It's wanting to be passive even though good lesbians aren't, because that thrills you.

It's leaning back and watching as she slowly unbuttons her blouse, black silk and lace beneath. She reaches up slowly to unclasp her necklace, her arms stretching, her breasts taut as she leans in towards you. You feel her nipples standing up to your touch. You want to suck hard on her breast, to take the nipple between your teeth, but you hold back not wanting to come on too strong. Or you don't hold back and she arches her breast towards your mouth—inviting. When you pull away, there's a dark circle of wetness and her nipple seems to pierce the thin fabric.

It's letting her touch you, deciding to see what she does if you give her no clue. It's wanting to go anywhere she'll take you, to be completely taken. It's knowing you can only hold on for so long before you have to touch her. You get excited and you want her to feel what you feel. Or you get excited and stop monitoring it all and there is nothing but sensation.

It's touching her nipple and your fingertip tracing the flat of her chest where her other breast used to be. It's imagining what she feels when you caress her, knowing she is so vulnerable. You are touching the smoothness of her chest, the fine lines of her scars, letting your fingers and hand explore.

It's wanting her to suck you and touch you, getting so weak you can no longer stand, but being sure if you make any move-ment at all or talk about it, the whole energy will change and you will have ruined it. It's wondering how she feels about your mastectomy, that place that is now so familiar to you. You feel self-conscious but love how she touches you. Or it's that she has both your breasts in her hands and you wonder if she thinks your nipples are too little or too big or too hairy. It's getting your mind to take a vacation and leave this scene to your nerve endings.

It's that you are wet and longing for her. Then you are terrified, wishing you had never remembered the abuse, afraid it will ruin this time too. You cannot decide if you should have told her beforehand, or if you should just stop her if something is too hard—and what deal was it you made in therapy anyway? It's your brain—it's back, knocking at your skull, confusing memories with feelings. You remember this is fear and that you can breathe and get back into your skin. You remind yourself how good this feels, how safe you have made your life, that she is not the perpetrator, that this is your lover here, now.

It's your knees turning liquid and barely holding you up. It's wanting to be done with the rest of these clothes and yet wanting the build-up of taking them off piece by piece. You open her blouse, button by button. You know she wants you too. You unfasten her bra and slip your hand under the cup before you lift it over her arms. You slide your hand over her breast, lightly touching, then putting on more pressure, then more. You take her nipple between your finger and thumb, wondering does she like it pinched, does she like it twisted, asking her to tell you what she wants.

It's awkwardly bending down, lifting her bra over her shoulders and taking her breast fully in your hands. It's that electric charge as your tongue meets her skin, that thrill and challenge. You explore her nipple, watching it pucker and rise, discovering how much of her breast fits into your hand. You need to hold her other breast, urgently cupping both now in your hands, your mouth sucking hungrily.

It's that you stand back from her, out of reach. You unzip your pants and turn away as you slide them down your hips, revealing lace pants against your coppery skin. You kick off your shoes and step out of your pants, turning to face her. The lace at your crotch is wet through, and you watch her slow smile as she takes you in.

It's that she has laid back for you, allowing you to make your way to her. Her appreciation makes your wanting stronger. You kneel above her, still just out of reach, provocative. You slip her jeans down around her hips ever so slowly. You wrap your fingers around the waistband, feeling her skin, the thrust of her hips, pulling her pants down, further revealing her underpants hiding her vulva. You want to linger, and slowly you run your finger over her clit, teasing her, promising more. Then even more slowly, laughing now, you untie one shoe, pull her sock off and wait.

It's that you're not sure how it happened that she is undressing you and you are letting her. But you are begging her, so turned on you cannot believe it, especially because it has been so long between the two of you.

It's that you pull one pants leg off and then the other, figuring out how to get her legs out, worrying that you might hurt her. It's that her legs don't work the way yours do. You don't expect them to have such weight; you really do expect her to move them, to give you some help here. And then you realize over and over that really and truly she can't move her legs like you can. You turn your energy back to your excitement, not worrying, just remembering that you are playing with a body different from yours.

It's that you are wrapping your legs around her, pulling her towards you. You feel your underpants sticking wetly to your pounding clitoris. You want her mouth on you faster than she is moving and you want to let her feel the energy that has you on fire. You want her fingers inside you and you feel no patience—it's not impatience, it's wanting on a level that you rarely feel. She lifts your hips and pulls your underwear off, her eyes smiling. It's that her body up so close to yours, her silk against your naked body is making you feel alternately faint and conscious, intensely present and soaring out into the universe. This proximity is testing your ability to not just pull her face between your legs. It's that she is resisting you ever so slightly to let you know she is on your beam, that she is moving into you in the same rhythm, with just the smallest resistance that makes you know she is with you and jazzed just like you are. The dance from the floor moves to the dance on the bed, ever so rhythmic, ever so slow, ever so exciting. It's that this is the first time you have been with her, or that it's an old dance, masterful in its nuances, in what you expect from each other.

It's that she has her legs wrapped around you and you are trying your best to slow everything down, to drive her over the edge, to keep your equilibrium, to turn her on. You push back against her legs, meeting her halfway. It's that she picked you up on the dance floor, seducing you ever so slowly, leaving you shaken and wide open, and now you want to take over. It's that being passive was so enticing that you want her to have the pleasure of such passion. You want to move on her the way you want to and on your time. As you go to put your tongue on her, you are already remembering the taste of cunt and wanting it again.

You both want this, both of you are moving forward with such energy that if it could be harnessed, it would provide enough electricity for a small town in central Illinois. It's that you haven't a thought in your head except what your tongue wants to do: to lick, to explore, to move in and out. You begin to tell her what you want to do to her, rather than doing it right away. Her legs pull tighter and you resist harder as you tell her in words what you plan to do. Her sounds of desire excite you more. It's that you wonder if you could keep this up for a week and then you decide you must. Laughing, you tell her you won't stop. Touch your tongue to me now, she begs you, take me now, and you give in.

It's that your tongue tastes her salty skin and you want a tongue so wide that you can cover her whole vulva. You try to take all of her in your mouth. You find her clitoris, uncertain at first and then there it is. You tease it with your tongue, moving firmly, quickly, and then you stop, just resting there. Slowly, so she can see, you lick your thumb. While stroking her clit with your thumb in a steady rhythm, you begin to suck just above the hood. Sucking and stroking, sucking and stroking.

It's that you feel her touch you with her tongue. You wonder what this looks like, and you imagine yourself watching, which makes you even more excited, watching this woman eat you, watching, filling up your eyes, wanting her, wanting her to consume you. It's that you want to meld like this so that this pleasure never goes away, so that she never goes away. You make a pact with yourself that you won't marry her, that you won't move in—it's your brain. But not for long; you can barely stand the pressure of her tongue, too insistent it seems but you let her, you give in, and suddenly she stops. She is teasing, and it is doing exactly what she wanted it to do—you are wild with desire.

It's that you want to put your fingers inside her but you hesitate a minute more. It's that you have to figure out how to hold yourself up, keep your thumb on her clit, and yet get your fingers inside. Or you don't know whether to start with two fingers or three—how tight she'll hold you, how loose she'll be. You slowly touch her vagina, stroking the lips that open to you. She is wet and warm and more than surrendered to you. You slowly enter with just the tips of your fingers, stroking in and out, just there at the opening. Teasing and tantalizing her, hoping she'll beg. It's that you explore ever so slowly the minute details of her skin inside, making your way into her wet and taut vagina that you know so well. Or you reach inside for the first time, memorizing with fingertips the familiar and the new. This sacred space has been laid out before you, and you approach it once more, this special gift that has been given, freely.

It's that your fingers slide in and out, moving like a wave and wanting her to feel your desire, your wanting her. She responds by spreading out her legs, letting go, letting you in, drawing you in. She is murmuring and you cannot make out the words, but you know they are singing a song to you of the dance your hand is doing. You put another finger inside her, feeling the map she has within, wanting to make your way to her cervix. You arch your fingers against the front wall of her vagina, and feel it swelling, rising.

It's that your fingers are inside her and you are moving swiftly and turning your fingers as you go in and out, your hand doing a dance. Your hand opens her with its special moves, this dance that makes your heart open up. It's that at any moment she may want to turn you over to receive her whole hand. It's that you don't always know where this is going.

It's that you don't know if she will come or not come; if she wants it deeper, or faster. All of this is a surprise and any of it is changeable. There is no one in charge even if it appears that one is making all the decisions. She is always in on letting you make the decisions, you are in this together. Though she wants you to tell her what to do, it's her acceptance that makes this possible.

It's that she is letting you in further and further. Your fingers disappear inside her. Her skin is getting dry and you lick her clit, her lips, your fingers; you taste all of her flavors. Sliding in again, you forget your concern, then you feel her dryness again. You ask tentatively where her lubricant is, if she has any, remembering that you have some in your purse in the living room. Or you didn't bring any and she doesn't have any. Then you remember cooking oil, thank the goddess for cooking oil. You pull yourself away and dart into the kitchen searching her cupboard, bringing it back and warming some in your palms. You watch her watching you cover one finger, and another, and another. You slide your way into her. She has waited, legs wide, not patient. Her vagina opens to you more; you feel her pulse against your hand, and wonder how you have gone so long since you were last inside a woman.

It's that you are lying on your back letting her inside. You sink into the pleasure beyond words or thought, the lifting of your soul, the joy of this process. She beats wildly against your vagina, a drum, you are all feeling, only feeling.

It's that she reaches down to stop you, wanting you in another way. She pulls your now-soaking underwear down around your knees and tells you to kneel above her, your legs open. She begins to lick you. You hold onto the bed post, balancing there, wistfully feeling your wet fingers, your desire for her, so willing to allow her between your legs. She is licking and sucking and holding onto your ass with a determination that makes you wonder who it was who started this after all.

It's that she is quite strong in her expression of desire for you. You love to have your ass acknowledged. She continues to suck until you don't think you can stand anymore. Your knees give way, then she stops and turns you on your stomach, leaving your lace underwear dangling on one leg. She begins to stroke your ass in a way that makes your heart skip a beat. It's that she is there in that forbidden place, wanting your flesh. She caresses you, runs her fingers in your crack, feels the skin between your folds in a way that is driving you over the edge. You see her slide lubricant over one finger, two, three. You want to put up a bigger fight, just to make this last longer but you can't; you surrender. She can do what she wants.

It's that she has given in so easily when just a moment ago the steps you were doing together were such a different tango. She is letting go to your lead, she is dancing with you in the way you want. You are sure she is sent from above to help you get over that lover who walked out on you, or to get you back to feeling since all the information about the sexual abuse has surfaced, or just to give you a good evening after this period of hard times.

It's that you wonder if playing with her ass might be too forward, but she seems to love it and so do you. It was watching this ass on the dance floor, watching this ass sashay across the room—it was watching this ass, big and round and full that started all this in the first place. You are surprised to find that the skin between her ass is so dark, such a beautiful color like that smooth, dark madrone bark that you love so well. The lips of her vulva, the tight pucker of her asshole is such a bright pink, like a beacon in the darkness of her skin, showing you the way to her, to her center, to her pleasure. You want to comment but you think it might make her self-conscious.

You tell her on purpose. That beacon of pink light in the ocean of her round, soft madrone skin caused you to step up your pace to her and you wanted to tell her, you needed to tell her. She responds by spreading her legs wider, wanting you to see the ever-brighter light, to find your way. You move your tongue between her legs, licking back and forth, up and down, hesitating at this opening and that. You wonder if moving on her from behind was all right, because it thrills you so. But watching her, you have no doubts. She is lying, her arms above her head gripping the bed, one breast showing beneath her camisole, her legs wide, her ass expectant.

It's that your ass is such a pleasure zone for you, to have someone pay such attention to it just made you more excited. Your asshole is purple and mauve against your pink white skin; it's dark brown edged with pink against your golden skin; it's rose and pearl against your dark brown skin. She is really looking, she is delighting in your self, your flesh. It's the whole reason you figure the goddess and your ancestors gave you an ass this big, to get some attention, to create a stir, to pleasure yourself and the eyes and hands of others. You have used this ass when you walk across a room. When you dance, you turn around so your partner can feast upon it. You stroke it a lot when you masturbate, but oh, to have someone rubbing it and sliding into you there. Forbidden, exciting. "Yes," this is right and good, exactly what you want, and you want her to know it.

It's her murmuring "yes" that makes you practically beside yourself. That simple word seems to express all you could want of surrender. No time to wonder now, you quickly turn back to the business at hand, so to speak, before your mind takes over completely. It's so sneaky, this mind of yours that so easily detours, pursuing words instead of women.

You change your pattern. You take your mouth from between her legs and slide your whole body along her back, rubbing your breasts against her skin in a way that drives you wild with desire. Your breasts are a direct conduit to your clitoris.

It's that you want to take the vibrator and masturbate while you fuck her. You took her hand away from your vagina before you "came" (not that you come easily without a vibrator anyway), but that was in some other part of this dance. You are on a mission. You reach one hand under her now, stroking her clit, as you enter her vagina and her ass at the same time. Her vagina holds tight, you can barely get two fingers inside, but her ass opens wide as though it could take your whole hand.

It's that you are up on your elbow, swaying back and forth, just enough to tease your own nipples while you are going in and out of her. You want to dive deep inside her, so deep that you can feel her cervix, feel the walls inside her expand to your touch. With your other hand, you rub her clitoris, rhythmic and steady while your thumb presses against the walls of her ass, pulling her to you.

It's that she comes while you are inside her, her vagina spasming against your fingers, her body convulsing in a way that makes you feel almost as though you were coming too, and it fills you with joy. She seems to be asking for more, so you turn her over onto her back, and dive into her breasts, big and beautiful or slim and pendulous. It's trying to keep your fingers inside her, turn her over, put your mouth to her breasts and not fall on top of her. She is moaning with delight, seeming only to want more of you.

You worry that you take too much, but you really do want to come again and again. And as she is in your vagina, she really does seem to be asking more from you. It will be her turn again, just for now you want it all, you want all the attention. Will she mind, does she think I'm selfish, you wonder. Your mind is right there for just such an idle moment as this. You stop thinking, feeling the insistence of her movements, you figure this is a woman who likes what she is doing. You come again with her nipples firmly positioned on top of your breasts, with her fingers pushing hard now inside your vagina and with her tongue searching for yours in the dark of your mouth.

It's that you float, beyond body, beyond words, only sensation, each cell dancing now, alive. You think you will never move again, but in minutes you are moving your hands towards her vagina to finish what you began.

It's that you reach down with her still on top of you and move your hand up to her vagina, opening her. She is so wet in her wanting of you, so turned on by your coming. She whispers that she will need the vibrator to come. It's that you react: but what about me, aren't I good enough? You don't want to hear the hum of electricity, or you want to be the one to make her come, or you want to be able to turn her on in ways that she has never experienced. It's your brain—will it never shut up?

She pulls the vibrator from its hiding place and kneeling over you, moves it to her clitoris, saying, "Fuck me. Now. Please." And you do. You move your other hand up to her breasts, pinching one nipple and then the other.

Your mind wanders to your brief episodes of dancing along the edge between pleasure and pain you and your first lover experimented with. In fact, if she were willing you would pinch her nipples harder.

She gives you no time to think now, as she is coming against the vibrator. Rising on her knees, she rocks against your hand inside, and you push harder, faster, her vagina ballooning out taut like a drum. You play her, ask more from her, your other hand pulling now on her nipple. And she is wanting more, wanting everything, unable to stand one more moment. She flicks the vibrator off, and collapses against you, rubbing against your leg over and over. Insistent mouth seeking mouth, cheek bone to cheek bone. She murmurs now in your ear. And you lay your head on her shoulder right on her collarbone, as you've done for so long, your cheek resting on her breast, drifting, satiated, completely happy.

You start moving slowly down her body with your hands, your short nails making her skin quiver. You maneuver your hips, pressing against her thighs to let her know you are firmly there, up against her. You inch down, your mouth open now to her salty skin, your tongue making a wet line down the middle of her, tracing the fine line of hair on her belly. You slide off to one side, your tongue following the inner edge of one thigh. You aren't going to give it to her so easy. You make your way back up towards her cunt, but not quickly. Your mouth dripping with your saliva, you want to taste her, taste her after she has had the hot flash of her orgasm. You want to get in on that intensity. Your tongue is on its way up her thigh, moving toward her lips now, ever so slowly. Your tongue leading the way, but your whole mouth making a swath of wet across her.

She wants you, but she is too into the experience of her blood pounding in her ears, her skin alive with the prickles of her coming. She is wanting you, floating in and out of that dreamy state that this whole lovemaking has been.

You are on your way. Your tongue searching between her legs, she parting them ever so slightly. You move forward, upward. You are licking the salt off her lips, now off the hood of her clitoris. She moans softly, muted, drawn back from the dream. You can feel her just where you want her. Your lips touch her lips with more than enough pressure. Actually, you are touching so lightly you wonder if she will even notice given the state she is in.

Of course you notice. You're lying in the ecstasy of the moment, her lips on your lips. Her tongue on your clitoris. Nothing could be too much. She presses into you, parts your legs further. You cannot hide anything. She has you right in that moment, on the tip of her tongue. She licks you soft and slow, letting your cream flow into her mouth.

You slowly put your fingers back inside her, one at a time just to feel the throb. She lets you play with her wetness. You take your fingers out and smear her juices on her belly and your breasts. You slowly let your breasts dance up her body, leaving wet tracks on her belly. You stop when you are over her chest, one of your breasts on hers, the other over the flat part of her chest. The energy flows between the three breasts and the phantom breast that longs to be part of the action. You bring your mouth to rest on hers.

The kiss lasts for what seems like a century. Years of women before you kissing like this. The two of you connected in a way that seems to bridge all that fighting you two have been doing for the last two months. The kiss transcends the fact that you two really don't know each other. The kiss allows each of you to fall into the depths of your hearts. This insistent mouth seeking mouth, cheekbone to cheekbone. You snuggle into the safety of her arms. She murmurs in your ear. You lay your head on her shoulder right on her collarbone, as you've done for so long, your cheek resting on her breast, drifting, completely at rest.

CHAPTER TWO

Erotic Archetypes and Lesbianism

Archetypes: Our Common Reality

Jean Shinoda Bolen says archetypes "represent models of being and behaving we recognize from the collective unconscious we all share...an image that determines behavior and emotional responses unconsciously. The collective unconscious is the part of the unconscious that is not individual but universal, with contents and modes of behavior that are more or less the same everywhere and in all individuals. Myths and fairy tales are expressions of archetypes, as are many images and themes in dreams."

There are many, many archetypal images. All peoples, for example, have a collective vision of the virgin, the mother, and the sexually powerful woman. These collectively held unconscious visions allow us to be part of a global culture and give us a common unconscious language. Bolen says these archetypes "influence how we behave and how we react to others."

But archetypes are not fixed in stone. They can be transformed naturally over the course of centuries or can be changed more directly, through awareness, education, and deliberate action. One recent example of collective thought changing is the view of the virgin and the sexually powerful woman. In the 1960s the women's movement started challenging the commonly held view of rape. Before 1965, most people, even many women, believed that women caused their own rapes. Rape was seen as a result of a woman's behavior, the way she dressed, the way she walked, when she went out, and with whom. It was believed that women were "asking for it" if they wore short skirts or went out at night alone.

These beliefs stemmed in part from an unconscious cultural image of woman as seductress—the seductress who "deserves" the retribution of men for her "evil" ways, her attempts to gain male power. Implicit in this view is that women have no power of their own. Yet in the oldest cultures this female power was openly acknowledged; because of women's ability to procreate and raise the young, we were in a literal sense responsible for the culture. Because the power of women was so unattainable by men, they reinterpreted female power as women using their bodies in surreptitious ways to keep men attached. A modern-day variation on that theme is boys being taught that girls will try to trap them sexually so they can force them to get married. Men have manufactured these explanations in a twisted reaction to the archetype that shows women as sexually powerful. Within this reality, men's struggle to overpower women is seen as something that could not be avoided, since women are always seeking to dominate them.

The women's movement analyzed the cultural consequences of this perception that women are more "powerful" than men. We named the subtle and not so subtle ways in which men reacted to women's power by subjugating us. These included creating a moral code that said women had to be married to men to have children. This gave men an emotional and legal hold on women, and a claim to their progeny which let them maintain an essential role in cultural continuity. In a similar manner, men took over religion, calling female power "witchcraft" and making our spiritual activities both illegal and evil.

Eventually, men went so far as to create a culture that allows the raping of women and children and places women in the position—like other oppressed and colonized people—of participating in their own oppression. This complicity ranges from the heinous: the mother not being able to protect her child from a physically or sexually abusive father, to the less divisive: a woman blaming the "other woman" for "taking" her man. Until feminism, we didn't know that these reactions were rooted in a mass delusion aimed at keeping men on top. We agreed with the prevailing view because we too thought that women could be sexually "too powerful." The raped woman, the fallen woman, the woman who "asked for it" were all part of our world view.

After the feminist challenge, this myth crumbled relatively quickly—at least, in some circles. Today, a raped woman is more likely to be considered a victim, the survivor of a man out of control. Abuse of women is acknowledged as a result of a male-dominated culture, an example of woman hatred at its worst. The woman's responsibility has changed significantly in today's collective view. A woman still needs to be careful, not because she is creating her own rape, but because she lives in a society that does not control men and does not protect women. The archetype of evil women seducing men has actually been confronted and is changing.

The archetypes that we all live with day to day are the unconscious at work, and are often part of the matrix of our racism, sexism, classism and heterosexism. The difficulty is trying to decipher what is truth and what is archetype. What has passed as truth is often nothing more than thought-form that has been created for centuries and in fact can and does change.

The public debate brought about by feminism has altered archetypes, or perhaps has recovered archetypes that were buried to accommodate the oppression perpetrated by men. We have seen new archetypal images of working mothers, strong and smart women, and even a mature heroine in a movie every once in a while.

The idea that women can work and have a family in post-war industrialized society is now accepted. Our culture has a long way to go before these two parts of a woman's life are easily connected, but at least we now believe that it is possible. We have vastly expanded the range of possibilities in just one generation, even if we don't yet have well-rounded imagery to go with them.

One of the most difficult aspects of the archetype is its unconscious nature. We are often not aware of the existence of the ideas that oppress us. Our automatic behavior and beliefs can be explored, but only if we recognize them and believe they are important.

Lesbian Archetypes

I believe there are lesbian archetypes, ways that we collectively conceive of lesbians. The most commonly recognized are the concepts of butch and femme and then recently androgyny as well. All three of these bring images and ideas into lesbians' minds that are collectively held visions. There are lesbian behaviors that I would call archetypal as well: moving in together after the first date; bed death after the first couple of years; believing that coming out is dangerous; believing that lesbianism is not a choice but an act of fate, and so on.

If these images and behaviors are collectively held, then so too are our reactions to them. I feel, as well, that these lesbian reactions are too often based on both internal and external homophobia and misogyny. This homophobia has created an atmosphere in which we've buried our language for centuries. Sappho wrote profusely and directly about lesbian eroticism. Her work survived intact for several hundred years after her death, until it, and many other Greek works, were destroyed in the fire that burned the library in Alexandria. What's striking is that in her own day, Sappho felt no inhibition about her words or her feelings. Since that time, scholars and critics have gone to great pains to prove these explicit love poems were not lesbian.

Gertrude Stein in "Miss Fur and Miss Skein" made extremely explicit sexual innuendoes, while never referring directly to these women as lesbian lovers. As Judy Grahn has pointed out, all of Stein's supposedly difficult and obscure language becomes clear when one reads it as coded lesbianism.

As more material is revealed about Eleanor Roosevelt's obvious lesbianism, historians are racing to prove she wasn't one of us either. In *The Life of Lorena Hickok: E.R.'s Friend*, Doris Faber goes so far as to say that Roosevelt's love letters to Lorena were common for women of that era, who often wrote to close women friends that they missed having her cheek next to hers on the bed pillow!

There are profound problems with having a culture that has only been chronicled in language couched so that straight people wouldn't comprehend it, or in language that was so threatening to the straight culture that it was destroyed or censored until all that is left is conjecture or inference. As a result of our history, our lesbian culture has learned to create a coded language, to be ashamed of our language, or to create no language at all.

This lack of language about even the most conscious lesbian activities makes it all but impossible to explain our unconscious lesbian material. Not having a language for our archetypal images has, in fact, reduced our concepts to two-dimensional forms. What is especially disturbing to me is evidence of our stereotypical views of lesbian sexuality.

I believe passionately in this topic, the topic of lesbians proudly talking about our sexual feelings, about our sexual passions, about our sexual selves. I believe that we are used to being silenced, that we have learned all too well how to cover up our needs, our wants, our lives. I believe that we stymie the growth of our culture when we do not delve into the sexual component of that culture. I also believe that we have allowed our fear of male rage to keep us from further upsetting mainstream society. Our female power has a history of being based in sex. In claiming our lesbian sexual selves as separate and distinct from the female sexuality that is enmeshed with men, we become central in our own lives. We are powerful; we are passionate; we are loving women who deserve a language rich in describing our own ways. Butch and femme are not male and female. They are uniquely and powerfully our own.

Lesbians' Fear of Lesbian Sex

The coded and hidden language of our sexual archetypes has its roots in a silence about even our most common activities. There are few words that describe any part of our unique culture. Except for "lover", we cannot even find a word that truly describes our most intimate relationships. The native peoples of what is now called Alaska have 300 words for snow. The fact that we don't have even one word that fully explains this most important of our connections is remarkable. "Lover" hardly covers what a partner, soul mate, heart connection means to us. Many lesbian couples are not actively sexual or have found that sex has become a secondary part of their lives. "Lover" does not say what is really true about our relationships; it connotes a lack of substance, a relationship based primarily on sex. And since "lover" does not describe us, we seek other language. In the survey for this book, 57 percent of lesbians said they use the words "roommate" or "friend" when talking about their mate to non-gay people. We become what we say we are. We stop having sex, and we become roommates and friends. The sexual, erotic, and emotional aspects that create the essential parts of any long-term relationship are too easily lost with "roommate" or "friend."

We have no words that convey long-term relationship to the world at large. We don't have one for use within our own underground. This lack of language is mirrored in our daily realities. We have little evidence of long-term commitment. We pledge our troth and most of us cannot find a way to carry that out. The frustration of this experience is expressed in endless conversations about why we can't have "long-term" relationships. I find this longing wherever I travel. The question is, if we came up with a word that meant long-term partner would that create long-term partners? I'm not saying there's one easy cure; what I do feel is that without the word it's hard to create the concept. How can you support something you may not even believe exists?

Because we don't even have a subculture language to describe our relationships accurately to other lesbians, we verbally create a vague picture. This vagueness is manifested in the culture by short relationships, lack of commitment that weathers hard times, and tremendous expectations every time we enter a new relationship. The problem of our lack of language is compounded when we introduce our mates outside of the lesbian community. "Lover" is perceived by the straight culture as a impolite way to describe one's own partner. "Date", "girlfriend", "fiancee", or "wife" are all considered more appropriate. Describing heterosexual couples as "lovers" is rare. So, when we try to let the straight culture know what the most intimate person in our life means to us, we are faced with giving a long description of all the different roles she plays, shortening our description to one unacceptable word, or choosing a word which downplays her significance, like "girlfriend." Unless we've already established our lesbianism in the conversation, there is no simple way to explain the relationship.

Describing our partners is only the tip of the iceberg when it comes to lesbian silences. We have a long list of unacknowledged taboos. In the past, whenever one of us became specific about lesbian sex in public or in print, there was a great deal of discomfort in the community. One of the most common manifestations was gossip that these women were not really lesbians. When Pat Califia circulated a survey within the lesbian community in San Francisco (later incorporated into *Sapphistry: The Book of Lesbian Sexuality)*, there was a rumor that she was straight. Emily Sisley and Bertha Harris, who wrote *The Joy of Lesbian Sex* in 1977, were thought to be straight as well. I lecture to lesbians throughout the country, have been on television as an out lesbian, write articles and books in which I regularly talk about being a lesbian, and yet there is still a rumor that I am straight. I can't help but wonder why these rumors were circulated about each of us. Why would the lesbian community think only a straight woman would be interested in writing about lesbian sex? Is it assumed that a lesbian would never break rank and talk about what we do sexually? Do lesbians automatically believe that writing about lesbian sex is intrusive and dishonorable?

Historically, lesbians were expected to act in particular ways around sex or they were "not really lesbians." Pat Bond has written that when she came out in the 1950s, one had to perform oral sex to be a lesbian. Yet Judy Grahn, who came out in a similar era but in a different part of the country, explains that only the very brave did oral sex. Nowadays, I think that oral sex is taken for granted (although 30 percent of the lesbians I surveyed for *Lesbian Passion* didn't like or do oral sex). Today, S/M sex, sex with men, dildos, or vibrators—and sex in lots of other arenas—have become the criterion for who is a lesbian and who is not. Whatever this month's deciding factor about who is a lesbian, we are all still voting.

Another way this discomfort evidences itself is that most lesbians distance themselves from any overt sex. The "sex wars" that have raged through our communities for the last twelve years have done more to create silence and shame than anything the Moral Majority has attempted. Lesbians hold conferences, write books and letters to the editor to state that whatever overt sex is being written or talked about has nothing to do with them. With this distancing comes the "us versus them" syndrome in which lesbians begin to divide up between the good ones and the bad ones. Of course, who is good and who is bad simply has to do with which club you belong to. The result is we tend not to tell each other about who we are or what we are thinking. The last thing we tell each other is what we are really doing sexually.

I am going to start by exploring butch and femme as two of our primary sexual archetypes. I believe as well that there are many other lesbian sexual archetypes for which we have not yet created language. Perhaps I begin here because butch and femme resonate strongly for me personally, but I also feel it is essential to healing our community that we begin the discussion with those images we do already have—namely butch and femme. Our sexuality is tied up with our images of ourselves. We don't like what the majority culture has said about our sexuality, and yet we live with a paucity of self-created images as well. I feel it is essential to create a language that we relate to and that speaks to us, beginning with the words we have had for decades. To ignore or eschew this language is to deny our lesbian history and the part it has played in shaping who we are.

Denial of Butch/Femme

Debate always arises whenever the idea of butch/femme is introduced. We were supposed to have given that up long ago. We were supposed to have grown more sophisticated in our analysis. There was tremendous pressure with the advent of feminism to deny and even debase the concept. Yet despite all the efforts at silencing, butch/femme remains an erotic archetype that has become an almost universal symbol to lesbians.

Because of homophobia, misogyny, and self-hatred, the erotic concepts of butch and femme have been rejected by lesbians in the last twenty years. The result is a sexual shame that has us deny two of our most basic erotic visions. This has created a stilted vision of lesbian sexuality. In rejecting such basic concepts, we also froze creativity and the possibility of giving language to others.

Deb Edel, speaking about butch/femme has said, "I'm always wary about the phrase 'into roles.' I hear it as very condescending to ourselves as lesbians. We need to really think about the language that we use in describing our own identity. I feel it is a deep identity, not a 'role' that I 'put on.' "

Joan Nestle continues, "I don't use the word 'roles', because I feel this is an authentic expression of myself.

Within butch/femme, I found freedom rather than restriction. I've grown into myself rather than assumed a posture! When I do this work, I always do it in the name of women we'll never see at meetings like this. They have perhaps died or been so psychologically wounded and scarred that they don't come here. They lost so many homes. Some of them thought with the bright new day of feminism, they would find another home, and they did not. I speak to reverse that shame. Butch women gave me a sense of beauty. And I tell the feminist community as well as everyone else, no one is ever going to make me feel that shame again!"

This rejection of butch/femme, though very public, was only accomplished on a superficial level; on the unconscious level, the concept of butch/femme never died. Today lesbians all over the United States still rate themselves on a butch/femme scale. Lesbians still unconsciously know the difference between a soft butch and a stone butch, a femme-of-center and an aggressive femme—even if they don't admit it on a conscious level. Butch and femme are unique archetypes of our subculture. This uniqueness has great power because it arises from a profound recognition. For twenty years lesbians have been socialized by other lesbians not to engage in identifying with the concepts of butch and femme. We have used new language, worn different clothes, taken up attitudes and activities because we thought we ought to, and still the underlying current has butch and femme firmly in place.

I feel we have not developed a language of eroticism in the lesbian community for complex and interconnected reasons: partly because we have denied a major part of our erotic heritage; partly because we have worked so hard to prove that we are not lesbians *just* because of sex; partly because we live in a culture that is homophobic and misogynist; partly because we never grew up with ways to express our sexual selves; and partly because we continue to deny our lesbian culture and to silence each other.

As Amber Hollibaugh says, "If we're to open up a discussion about butch/femme, it has to be with the understanding that there is a problem in our movement about who's in it, anyway. Who defines the terms of anybody else's erotic system? Who gets to say what's real or bad with anybody else's sexuality? Who has been left out of the debate from the beginning? Those of us that come out of working-class and third world communities are the bridges. We're proof, living proof, that butch/femme is an active system now. We want to reclaim it. I don't any longer want to have to think I have to leave my hometown and leave the kind of women that I grew up with, in order to be a lesbian."

She continues, "You don't exactly choose how you are involved in your own sexuality. You can analyze it, deconstruct it, try to figure out where you are. But it's not the kind of thing you can put on yourself and take off yourself.

"My own fluidity has been within a butch/femme system of desire, rather than with a variety of approaches and diversities to sexuality. One of the issues for me is that butch/femme is an erotic system. It's deeply based in an erotic definition. There's a great variety, even within butch/femme relationships about how they make love and how they see themselves.

"The problem that we have thinking about butch/femme is that the lack of exploration has also meant there was a narrowness about what could be encompassed in those words. Butches couldn't be the receivers of sex; femmes weren't the initiators. Femmes receive and are the passive vessels for the active butch partner. Those kinds of notions truncate a certain kind of exploratory redefinition of sex."

The denial of one of our core sexual images is indicative of a widespread inability to talk freely among ourselves about what we do sexually, what arouses us, and what sexually attracts us. If we had a language of eroticism, I strongly believe we would by now have created a conscious, complex expression of the archetypal sexual images of lesbian sexual experiences. The sex radicals would no longer have to be on the lesbian fringe, because we would all be radical and daring in some aspects of our lives. What do we have to lose?

Making a Deal with the Women's Movement

I find it valuable to look at the time period when butch/
femme became ostracized and androgyny became the vogue. In
the early 1970s, a distinction was made between "old-culture"
lesbians and "new-culture" lesbians. There began to be jokes
about butch/femme women. Androgyny became the norm of the
lesbian nation. Flannel shirts, blue jeans, no makeup, no jewelry
and short hair were all requirements of the club. Effectively, we
became desexualized in our dress codes. It was not clear who was
sleeping with whom. No one stood out by her attire, and if she
did, she was probably accused of being straight.

There was a very vocal and visible radical lesbian culture,
but it is my belief that in the 1970s most of us also made a deal
with straight feminists. We said we would be good if they would
let us be part of their movement. We said we would run their
battered women's shelters but would not be residents who directly
benefit from those programs. We said we would run their rape
crisis lines, their women's buildings, their foundations, their
national organizations. We said we would work for minimal wages
for the betterment of straight women's lives. We even said we
would call our music and our festivals "women's music" and
"women's festivals" when they were really "lesbian music" and
"lesbian festivals."

We also said we would not be affectionate in front of their
funders. We said we would not be out as lesbians on a public level.
In fact, we said we wouldn't even be out to them if they couldn't
handle it. We said we would do this work, and the only thing we
would ask in return was to be part of the feminist movement.

We did this not out of self-hatred, but because we really
believed in the rights of women, in our rights, and we wanted to
do something about it. We wanted to be part of a movement that,
along with the civil rights movement, has radically changed this
country in the last twenty years. We loved women, and we wanted
to be part of women changing the world.

We were told by the straight feminist women that changing
women's lives would filter down to lesbians as well. And there is
truth to that when we are talking about the rights of women:
wages, childcare, pregnancy benefits, health care, and so on
(though childcare and pregnancy leave are relevant to only a small
percentage of lesbians). Today, abortion is the current and most

consuming women's issue—one that almost exclusively applies to straight women. Yet lesbians have shown up in great numbers marching for abortion rights.

The leaders of the straight feminist movement explain that lesbians should be involved with the abortion issue because what we are really protecting is a woman's right to choose. These laws will somehow translate to lesbian rights as well. I just haven't seen that happen. I haven't seen these laws protect the rights of lesbians (except the infinitesimal number of lesbians who need abortions).

Nor have I seen straight women helping us out with our rights. Maybe individual straight women, but not large numbers of straight women. Straight women as a group don't come to our marches, in the same way that large groups of lesbians come to theirs. Straight women en masse don't help us with our lesbian rights campaigns as we have helped en masse with theirs. National organizations don't support openly gay candidates running on a lesbian platform.

The feminist movement has for years tried to separate itself from any hint of being run by lesbians. National women leaders have lived in fear of being accused of lesbianism. They have denied even knowing any lesbians. They have treated us like pariahs in public. They loved us plenty in private because we have been the backbone of the movement. Our partners weren't nagging us to come home and feed them and the kids. Our women partners were right there with us. Our kids were sitting on the floor stuffing envelopes. What straight women did was usurp lesbian energy for their movement.

What straight women also did was to literally love us plenty in private. That is, they had sex with us. They wanted to see what it was like to make love with women in private while denying any connection to lesbians in public. They loved our womanly ways. They told us how wonderful it was making love with women and being around women's energy, but they just couldn't afford the public visibility.

We were supposed to understand. We understood, all right, and in understanding we let our homophobia become more entrenched. Our trusted feminist sisters were woman-identified to the point of having sex with women and taking the energy of women, and then denying us in public to save their heterosexual privilege.

Yet from these same women we took an analysis of our lesbian sexuality. We accepted that our sexuality should be covert and "proper." From the feminist movement we also took the idea that butch/femme was an inherently heterosexual idea, that old-culture lesbians (before 1965) were mimicking male/female relationships.

I don't buy this analysis. I don't believe we were mimicking male/female relationships. I believe butch/femme was a lesbian concept that was brushed away with the mere hint of a suggestion that it was heterosexual. We bought the idea that the whole world is male/female and that we too were trying to fit into that mold. Well, I don't believe it. I don't believe that this lesbian eroticism of butch and femme which each of us has a connection to, which each of us has been made to deny, put down, and be ashamed of has anything to do with boy/girl. I believe it has to do with woman/woman in a way that is unique and powerful. Woman/woman is what is terrifying to the world at large, and sometimes to us as well.

Lesbians Who Don't Pass

Homophobia (the inordinate fear of homosexuality) and misogyny (the hatred of women) are elements of the lesbian culture. They show up in many ways and are inherent any time we discuss butch/femme/androgyny. As I'll cover in more detail in the next chapter, lesbians commonly describe butches as strong, tough, and aggressive, while calling femmes soft, feminine and passive.

Homophobia is particularly present in discussions about butch women. While we start by saying butches are strong, tough and aggressive, we go on to use unflattering words like "diesel dyke." I believe our internal homophobia is aroused by the idea that women are identifiable as lesbians on the street. One of the comments on the 1989 survey was:

"I see a butch dyke in public and I'm embarrassed. I'm staring at her and I see other people staring at her too. I would never want people looking at me that way."

Butch women make us uncomfortable because they remind us of what we aren't supposed to look like. Our stereotype of butch women is so much the opposite of what a woman is supposed to be. Inside ourselves, we still believe we're supposed to look like Donna Reed in the '50s only with a '90s hairstyle. We're supposed to be small, cute, bouncy, and anorexic with big breasts. We're supposed to appear passive, cheerful, and accepting of whatever comes our way. We're not supposed to threaten men or other women.

Women who don't want to, or can't, pass—women who look like what the world expects lesbians to look like—make other lesbians anxious. Too often, we don't want to be with butch lesbians in sensitive situations with people we are not out to. Many women ask their butch lovers to feminize their demeanor to be more presentable in public. I believe that this homophobia is one reason we so consistently deny that the butch end of the scale applies to us.

Women I've interviewed also use words that are equally stereotyped (soft, feminine, passive) to describe femmes. These words alone certainly don't describe most of the women I know who identify as femme. There is a modicum of misogyny when lesbians talk about this end of the scale. Femmes are often seen as the negative stereotype of straight women, lesbians who have sold out to the look that straight men want them to have. Wearing dresses, makeup, high heels or almost any adornment, are all seen as giving in to the pressures of society and make femmes suspect as lesbians.

Internalized homophobia and misogyny are present in our discussions about butch/femme and reinforce our denial that butch/femme really exists outside of silly jokes. Our internalized fears of what the majority culture thinks about lesbians, coupled with fears that lesbians might be ersatz straight women, keep us from creating our own visions of lesbian archetypes.

"When I came into lesbian culture and people were talking about top/bottom, I was appalled because it smacked to me of S/M, and I didn't like it. Then when I started really listening to top and bottom and I started reading about it, what it did was it opened me up; it gave me a kind of richness. I'd like to be able to be both ways. I'm not attracted to some women, though we can be the best of friends; then there's other women who really do attract me. And why is it? I'd like us to be able to play about our richness, the aesthetic, the myth, the homophobia, the history, all of our heritage. If we can play with that, without being afraid of it, it would give us real freedom to be all of our lesbian selves."

I began this chapter with a discussion of archetypes and how they can be changed by social movements. A perverse result of the almost total invisibility of lesbians in mainstream culture is an unparalleled opportunity now to make ourselves visible in precisely the ways we want. Our images, our language, our eroticism, our visions, are ours to create and manifest. If we give free rein to our very real diversity, we have enormous space in which to describe and validate lesbian realities first of all to ourselves, and eventually to the world at large.

THE DEBATE
1

Since sexual debates often rage through our communities, I thought it would be fun to include bits of the discussion here. "The Debate", which appears between chapters, is taken from discussion groups about butch/femme and androgyny, from letters that came in with the questionnaires, and from conversations with friends. It comes from books and articles, from women on my travels, and from women in the audience at the Toronto Sex and the State Conference. This topic is so important and so filled with passion, that every lesbian seems to have some opinion about it.

....

"How do we score ourselves on both butch and femme scales then?"

"One to ten. Top of the scale is ten."

"What does that mean?"

"Well, one to ten femme *and* one to ten butch."

"Everyone here has a butch and a femme side. So take your butch side, and you've got one to ten, where do you put yourself? And then you've got your femme side and you've got one to ten, where do you rate yourself there?"

"Femme, I would say 7, and butch I'd say 5."

"I want something to relate to, like is 10 femme Suzanne Sommers and 10 butch k.d. lang?"

"Part of the problem is that each of us has a different standard for this. And it's relative to who else is in the room—it'd be different if we were all in a room with heterosexual women."

"Really femmy straight women are a lot more femmy than the femmiest of us."

"But aren't we rating this just for dykes?"

"So, where did you rate yourself on both scales?"

"I'd say about 7 and 7."

"And I'd say 9 and 5."

"And I would say then I'm 8 or 9 femme and 5 butch."

"On a good day!"

"Wait a minute, I didn't understand the scale. I want to change mine to 8 femme and 5 butch."

"Rather than 8 butch?"

"Yeah, but you gotta watch her, she drives a truck...she just borrowed that baby."

"Part of identifying as butch stems from a desire to defend, protect, and defy the traditional feminine stereotype. All of these verbs imply a reaction to the world. Being butch to me to a large degree means reacting to the world.

"A large part of identifying as femme stems from a desire to create, empathize and become the woman (femininity and all) inside us. Therefore, identifying as femme is more of an initial action—not passive at all."

"I'd like to nominate the word 'dearun' (pronounced 'dear'n') as a substitute for lover, roommate, etc."

"I think I know what you mean that androgyny equals sexlessness. But I see a real danger of butch/femme (and this is why it is an easily comprehended linguistic shorthand) as being male/female. Speaking personally, I feel I could be much more sexually/sensually receptive to the full range of goddesses as they paraded in front of me rather than butches."

"The traditional butch role is to be more of the provider, more of the one who deals with economics, who deals with the car loans. Women who are upper middle-class or upper-class don't need someone to do that. So I think that sets up a certain kind of tension."

"They don't need anybody to do it because they earn enough money or they have enough experience of moving in the world and have power from a class perspective."

"This can be a real problem for someone like me who really wants to be a provider...what's my role then?"

CHAPTER THREE

Butch, Femme, Androgyny and Our Stereotypes

All people have stereotyped views of groups that they do not know, have had little contact with, or have had difficult experiences with. Knowledge about specific individuals is generalized to the group as a whole and seen as "the way they are." We're aware, of course, of the stereotypical views of women and of lesbians.

Then there is the further phenomenon in which the group itself stereotypes other members of the same group. We're all familiar with examples of this: women who tell you, "Women are their own worst enemies"; lesbians who tell you, "I don't hang out with other lesbians; I just have nothing in common with them." Part of this phenomenon is trying to separate from the group we have been taught to hate and yet which, by birth or need, we are members of. There are many examples of this horizontal hatred in every culture.

Mothers often participate in the subjugation of their daughters. Many women, who have been taught to hate themselves and settle for less than a full life, teach their daughters to do the same. It's not uncommon for women to talk to men about other women in degrading ways to prove themselves separate from their own sex. Women talk about not having women friends because they just don't find other women interesting, as if they themselves are the only female on earth with anything to offer.

On a more daily basis, how many of us participate in horizontal hatred when we join with straight people in making fun of lesbians and gay men, when we wish drag queens wouldn't march in our parade, or are ready to drop through the sidewalk when we meet a punk leather dyke while going to dinner with our parents? How much of the need to "protect" ourselves is trying to fit into a culture from which we are different? How much of our horizontal hatred is trying to fit into a group that in some ways we can never belong to, distancing ourselves from those who really can harbor us?

Rita Mae Brown has referred to this phenomenon as "crabs in a bucket." She described the lesbian community as being like a bucketful of crabs, each pulling back the others who try to escape. Anyone trying to do something different is immediately reprimanded and forced to return to the group way of thinking.

Sometimes, though not usually, horizontal hatred can be a catalyst for change. Because real oppression creates the situations and characteristics we react to, horizontal hatred sometimes expresses our rage at the narrow cultural confines we are allowed. This rage is not really directed at members of the group, but at what the group has settled for. Rejection of "how things are" is especially necessary when a group changes how it operates in the world, how its members see themselves, and how they want to be seen by others.

When the civil rights movement broke out in the 1960s, the younger generation of blacks and whites began to turn on their own families and the beliefs with which they were raised. The rise of the Black Power movement and the rejection of the "Negro" identity was absolutely necessary in the struggle for Afro-American equality. The hatred of the older generation's oppression and racism was key in moving towards a new identity.

This has been true in the feminist movement as well. Women have sometimes turned to their mothers with compassion, but just as often we've expressed real rage at what generations of women have settled for, at the legacy our mothers gave us. Although we knew that the male power structure was really to blame, we felt most betrayed by our own mothers. Trying to get them to understand the necessity of women's liberation meant trying to get them to understand how they personally had been used and abused by men.

I remember arguing with my mother in 1973 about women's wages. She was supporting herself and actually told me she didn't mind doing the same work as a man and getting paid less because "he has a family to support." She couldn't see that women had families to support as well. In her own office there was a woman who, as the sole support of two children, needed as much money as any man, but this was not something my mother could put into her vision of the world. To do so, she would have had to challenge her own way of looking at the world.

Changes in the lesbian community from the late '60s to the '90s have also meant real conflicts between older and younger lesbians about who and how we are in the world. As we have come farther out of our various closets, there has been a tremendous change in how lesbians view society.

Lesbians coming out in the '90s don't realize what all the fuss is about. They come out into a different world than lesbians just a decade earlier. Major news magazines actually have gay people (albeit usually men) on their covers. There are movies with lesbian characters and lesbian and gay political figures. When lesbians who came out with the women's movement react to younger lesbians, it is almost like fighting between mothers and daughters. The lesbian cultural "mothers" are saying "be discreet"; don't dress in such outrageous outfits; don't go around in obvious butch/femme relationships; come out politely.

The young lesbians today are not always as cautious or concerned as lesbians from the '70s and '80s have been. They are out there making clear statements about their sexuality. They are tolerant of bisexuality. If they ascribe to butch/femme imagery, they don't hide it. Those who are into S/M are open about it. There is an outrageous edge to some of their behavior, not unlike the feminism of the '70s. But this time it is outrageous, open behavior about lesbianism.

I remember only a few years ago that saying anything about lesbianism to the media was seen as a terrible breach of the ranks. When I had a baby by insemination in 1982, a local newspaper interviewed me for a story about insemination. Through the lesbian grapevine, I learned that a study group had been set up to discuss whether lesbians should talk to the press about the fact that we were having babies by insemination. The study group was still meeting and hadn't come to any definite statement yet, but I was told that I ought to be more thoughtful. There were some real fears then; lesbians in England had been legally barred from insemination and we weren't sure that couldn't happen here. I have, however, always believed that lesbians should talk with everyone who would listen about our lifestyles so our lives would become less secret.

To the young lesbians today, this whole debate is probably inconceivable. They're used to information about lesbians being readily available. Maybe not in the quantities we would like it, but there has been a profound change from the dearth of information only ten years ago.

The recent controversy over "outing" is an even more radical example of the clash that produces change within a community. Outing targets famous people who hide or deny their homosexuality (and may even have actively worked against gay rights) and exposes them in the media as gay.

Outing can be seen in two different lights. The radicals see it as a way of making our lesbian and gay comrades deal with their sexual orientation for the good of the whole. If the world knew all the famous singers, actors, politicians, business people, and celebrities who are gay they would be amazed and eventually would have to embrace us. Outing is also seen as deserved punishment for those who have maintained power while the out gay community has suffered for its openness, yet made headway for the rights of all gay people.

The people who are in the position of being "outed," of course, find this prospect less than thrilling. Like other oppressed people, they fear losing their power, their families, their source of income if they are brought out. There is also the horizontal hatred that comes from not wanting to be identified with a group with which they have carefully avoided any association. Both sides in the outing controversy become polarized in their rejection of their "own kind."

The problem inherent in horizontal hatred is that there has to be a sense of separation, an "us versus them" categorization that allows one part of the group to ostracize another. Members on both sides charge that the other side is wrong. The group that wants to change feels righteous and justified; the group that wants to keep the status quo feels either bullied or alienated. To polarize members of an oppressed group debilitates the energies of both sides.

For different reasons in different cities all across the country, most lesbians in the last twenty years have felt shut out at one time or another because we didn't fit into the right categories. We've been rejected, or have rejected other lesbians, over monogamy, nonmonogamy, class, S/M, race, role-playing, and goddess knows what else.

The label of "politically correct" became fashionable in the 1970s and applied to what now appears to be a narrow part of the lesbian community. Politically correct lesbians wore a particular outfit. I thought perhaps there were "movement issue" clothes given at the border of politically correct cities. You were not allowed to make much money (an easy requirement for most women who, on the average, earn 63 cents for every dollar earned by men); children were seen as a hindrance; boy children were the enemy in your own home. Pretending the community wasn't racist, sizeist, classist, able-bodiest, or lookist was crucial.

There were also sexually motivated requirements. One of the most prominent was the denial of our sexual differences. Teflon was the medium. Each partner had to initiate sex, each had to make love to the other, each had to go down on the other, each had to like the same things. We were to have no dildos, no S/M, no porn, no sex with men. Each woman in a couple had to dress and look alike.

What was strictly forbidden was the concept of butch/femme. This was "old culture", mimicking heterosexual roles, pandering (in the case of femmes) to the dictates of straight men, embarrassing (in the case of butches) a society we were trying to "come out" into. Many feminist lesbians would have hotly denied that last statement, but I feel it was, and is, so.

A critical expression of our lesbian horizontal hatred has been that we have been afraid to take a stance on our sexuality, except to punish each other for doing it wrong. Not being the same in how much sex we have, the way we practice sex, using S/M practices, wanting to be celibate, practicing monogamy or nonmonogamy—all of these have been cause for separation in our community. This fear of our own sexuality, which I believe is generated not just from the majority oppression, but also by our own internalized homophobia and misogyny, is the obstacle that keeps us from exploring what *is* lesbian eroticism.

One to Ten

The concept of butch/femme is something that I explore when I travel and talk to lesbians throughout the United States. I lecture to lesbian audiences about all different aspects of lesbian sex. When I begin to talk about erotic archetypes in the community, I start with butch/femme/androgyny.

One of the most common discussions centers around the "butch/femme scale." This scale is usually described as a range from one to ten. Lesbians rate themselves or others according to where they fit on this scale. If lesbians have actually thought of it as a scale, they at least recognize the process of evaluating how butch or femme a person is.

When I present the scale, the numbering itself can elicit heated debate. Is the femme end of the scale one or ten? Should femme be a higher number than butch? Should butch be "number one?" Lesbians consider 1 as femme and 10 as butch in some parts of the country, while the reverse is true in others. The placement of the androgynous woman is also of concern. The problem on a one to ten scale is that there is no middle (the true middle would be 5.5). One has to choose either 5 or 6. This is difficult for the many lesbians who want to stick precisely in the middle.

Somehow the middle is supposed to absolve the good feminist lesbian from having any connection to the dreaded identification with butch and femme. If we had other words for the different numbers on the scale perhaps more women would be more willing to wander off the middle. Would we be more adventurous if we said "Okay gang, from now on, 1 is the only femme number, 10 is the only butch number, and 3 means you're politically aggressive and sexually receptive, paint your toenails red but never wear open-toed shoes?" The idea that the scale is a continuum is important. To automatically opt for the middle of the erotic spectrum is probably doing yourself a disservice. There are cases of women who are truly 5.5s, but I believe the incidence is much lower than how we want to or feel we should label ourselves. The animosity here, of course, comes from the false perception that butch/femme is a male/female model.

My intention in polling audiences is to get an understanding of the impact of butch/femme/androgynous images on the lesbian community. I ask the following: "How many women here who have been lesbians for longer than two weeks, have *not* ever rated yourself or been rated by others on a butch/femme scale?" At the most, five percent of the audience raises their hands. That is, in an audience of 500 women, 25 women would raise their hands and say they have never rated themselves on a butch/femme scale.

This is phenomenal in statistical language. When 95 percent of a group has experienced something, it is considered a universal experience. It is very rare for almost 100 percent of any group to have a shared experience. What is even more remarkable is that this phenomenon recurs in lesbian audiences throughout the United States. Consider this yourself: what other scale has every one of your friends rated themselves on? What other scale does everyone of your friends understand when you simply mention it? Class, maybe. But what else?

Next, I ask the audience: "How many lesbians here consider butch and femme to be an important concept in your life?" Less than five percent raise their hands. Once again, 95 percent of the audience has a shared experience. It is universal that lesbians in my audiences find butch and femme unimportant in their lives.

There are probably few universal experiences in any subculture that the group also considers universally unimportant. Lesbians finding a part of their own unique culture to be unimportant concerns me. That would be like saying that every lesbian in the United States knew a mainstream singer was a lesbian but that fact was unimportant to them. It does not seem possible that a concept known to all would be unimportant to all. Why is butch and femme so commonly discussed in our communities? Why has virtually every lesbian been rated?

Further evidence in my mind that butch/femme is archetypal is what happens when I call some member of the group to come up on stage to be rated on the butch/femme scale by the audience. I make sure that the audience is clear which end of the scale is femme, which butch, and that 5 is not really the middle. Once the numbering is established, I ask the audience to respond with clapping when the number that most fits the woman standing beside me is mentioned. The majority of the audience is seeing her for the first time that night. I start to call out the numbers of the scale and the audience members clap when the number called is what they believe fits that woman.

Out of the ten numbers, the audience is usually silent for at least four or five of those numbers. There is light applause for three or four of the numbers on the scale. In sharp contrast, there is a resounding applause for one or two of the numbers that are beside each other on the scale. (For example, 1 through 5 gets no applause, 6 and 7 get slight applause, 8 and 9 get immediate resounding applause, and 10 gets none.)

The fact that the audience is for the most part in agreement indicates to me is that there is a collective opinion about where a woman fits on the butch/femme scale. There is no discussion, no prompting: the woman is just standing there, and the audience has a collective opinion. This happens so consistently in so many different groups and different communities, that I've come to believe that the lesbian community has standards about the butch/femme scale that are unconscious, but distinct.

I decided to do a survey and began distributing it in September of 1989. There were very clear responses when individual lesbians were asked what they think of butch and femme. Many believe butch and femme is important to others but has nothing to do with them. There is shame that butch and femme is from our embarrassing past, and a belief that lesbians back then mimicked heterosexual lifestyles.

Words used to describe butch and femme included: confining, disgusting, outmoded, useless, stereotyped bullshit, extreme labels, superficial.

Lesbians wrote that butch/femme is: a "hetero fantasy about what lesbians are"; "how we internalized straight folks' judgments about us and we think we have to carry it on"; "locking into a concept limits the individual." Others wrote: "We shouldn't identify with one gender or another"; "I don't like labels"; "butch/femme superficially identifies lesbians"; "I hate the words."

In feminist descriptions since the '70s, two women who were in a traditional butch/femme relationship were the ultimate in counterrevolutionary. The change in the concept of butch/femme from what it was thought of in the first half of the century to what it became in the 1970s was quite remarkable.

Madeline Davis and Liz Kennedy have been interviewing lesbians from the bar culture of the '30s, '40s and '50s in Buffalo,

New York. What they've found is probably typical of other urban lesbian communities.

Madeline Davis says, "It wasn't until we had explored the evolution of bar culture that we realized that butch/femme roles were such a tremendously important organizing force in the lives of these women. It was essential to these women's personal lives and also to the organization of their political stance against the straight world. Butch/femme roles created an authentic lesbian sexuality appropriate to a flourishing of an independent lesbian culture. Also, lesbians pursued a rich and fulfilling sex life at a time when sexual subjectivity was not the norm for women. This was also consistent with the creation of a separate lesbian culture. It represented the roots of what we call a *personal political feminism:* women seeking their own pleasure and women seeking to pleasure other women as an essential goal of their lives. Butch/femme was an evolving forum to the resistance of oppression."

Liz Kennedy continues, "Roles were a prepolitical form for the community of the '30s, '40s and '50s. You announce yourself to the public through roles. A femme's ability to pass only occurs when out by one's self; when you go out as a butch/femme couple, you're out. This is very important for people to understand. People have said 'Everyone was so into roles in the '50s, it was so disgusting, I wouldn't be a part of that.' Madeline and I have come to understand this statement as being: 'I couldn't take the abuse that being out as a lesbian in the '50s brought on me.' That is how you had to be in that community in order to be out. That's what it meant. If you fudged at home and your sex wasn't role-defined, that was all right, but to be public, you had to be into those roles. We are looking at the evolution of gay liberation. The public [image] of this community is a critical factor. The Daughters of Bilitis provided the more traditional political forum, [while] the bar community added a lot of guts and energy; combinined together, they exploded into gay liberation."

Amber Hollibaugh carries this analysis into the present when she says, "It's working-class and third world women primarily who are butch/femme now, because they're living it out. When I speak at Gay Pride in New York, one of the things that's always extraordinary to me is the variety of butch/femme women that I never see any other time.

"The kinds of issues that are raised around erotic systems have components in class and race. The problem of defining butch/femme as a viable sexual system [touches] ideas about class and about whether we pass in terms of class. Butch/femme is part of a defiance that didn't allow these women to pass, especially butches. The more they were out, and obviously involved in matters of erotic systems, the more narrow were their options for where they could work and how they'd be treated in their daily life. That included the femmes [who] were with those butches."

When we dismiss roles so blithely, we may minimize the differences between us in terms of class and community. It's easy to impose a middle-class standard in the name of feminism, and to have that imposition obscure deep feelings about identity.

Esther Newton describes this dilemma, "I came out in 1959 in working-class bars. You had to be butch or femme, and people made very negative comments about 'those uptown dykes who [are] ki-ki and don't know what they are.' That was what was accessible, what I could find, and who I was attracted to. I didn't want to be working-class in the money sense, so I reacted against being butch. It took me a long time to come back and find a kind of middle-class way of being butch. I thought the choice was either you could be butch, or you could go to college. You couldn't do both. I didn't come from a working-class background, but having come out that way, I'm very aware of [the] working-class being a bedrock of gay culture. It is a class and gender identity thing for me."

Madeline Davis sums up the real political implications of our butch/femme heritage: "When people discuss butch/femme roles, past and present, they see it as the difference between who washes the car and who washes the dishes. It really is a lot more than that. Butch/femme sexuality is expressed in terms of public presence, dress, and specific erotic expression. It was brave. It was forward-looking, it was monumentally outrageous for the times, and it also provided a framework for a woman's stance against an oppressive society."

It was a tragic misunderstanding of our real history when feminists began to describe butch/femme in narrow and stereotyped ways. Those stereotypes are especially disconcerting given that almost universally, lesbians talk about butch/femme (if only to tease about it) and have engaged in rating themselves and others in some way on a "butch/femme scale." With such a wide usage, one might imagine the delineations would have become more complex and sophisticated over the years. Instead, they have become more narrow and superficial.

How Lesbians See Butch/Femme Now

I did my first butch/femme survey with my colleague, Marny Hall. We surveyed over 800 lesbians, from California, Oregon, and Washington, at a convention in San Francisco. One of the most interesting parts of the survey was when we asked the women to write three words that they would use to describe "butch" and three to describe "femme." They were allowed to choose any three words in the English language; there were no suggested lists. Although many of these women identified with being a butch (25 percent) or femme (20 percent), their concepts of butch and femme were stereotypical and sexist in nature. The most common words to describe butch were: strong, tough, aggressive, masculine. To describe femme: soft, pretty, and passive.

The statistical significance of 800 women choosing any three words and ending up with such agreement is enormous and demonstrates the power of our oppression both as lesbians and as women. Even though half of these women identified themselves with the categories, they still have words for only the most narrow definition of butch and femme.

In 1989-90, I changed the survey and got responses from an additional 589 lesbians across the country. Again, I found the same stereotypical views of butch and femme. To accommodate for the tendency for women to place themselves as a "5" on the one to ten scale, I used a one to nine scale (so the respondents could actually choose the middle).

The following is how these lesbians rated themselves (see Appendix B for more details):

One ("ultimate femme") 2%
Two 5%
Three 14%
Four 16%
Five 26%
Six 19%
Seven 13%
Eight 3%
Nine ("ultimate butch") 2%

When asked how they identified, they replied: butch (nineteen percent); femme (25 percent); androgynous (44 percent); and none of the above (twelve percent). When asked if they *had* to choose between identifying butch or femme, 46 percent said the former, 52 percent the latter. When asked if butch/femme was important to their identity, only five percent thought it very important; 31 percent thought it somewhat important. Not even all of the 44 percent who actively identify as butch/femme thought this was somewhat important to them!

There were other ways the respondents distanced themselves from identifying with butch and femme. While 89 percent said that discussions of butch/femme come up in conversation at least occasionally, only 36 percent said that the idea is somewhat or very important to them.

One of the great debates about butch/femme is the concern that it is mimicking male/female roles. The fear that came out of the '60s was that lesbians didn't have any other way of being and had to play-act what the straight culture did. Someone was the "boy", and someone was the "girl." I feel that this fear has haunted lesbians, and that somewhere in our deepest homophobic selves, we agree that lesbians are an ersatz version of the heterosexual model. This anxiety makes us scared about fantasies

we have about being men, our lovers being men, or an attraction
to a man. Having sex with a man gets a lesbian kicked out of the
club for good—the end.

This knee-jerk response to the majority culture's concept
of lesbianism has been one factor in stopping our own development of lesbian erotic images. The fact that butch and femme
appeared to have something to do with male and female made us
doubt our *own* visions. We abolished our own sense of this unique
lesbian construct. In its place we established our own sexist and
heterosexist image of butch and femme, especially in relationship
to one another.

Jewelle Gomez has a groundbreaking view of relationships: "My sense has been that butch/femme roles in our
community have been condemned by some feminists
because they emulate traditional male/female relationships.
Some feminists say they replicate the repressive patriarchal
mode of interaction. This basic assumption is also its
primary limitation. The assumption that the male/female
dyad is the root source of all human interaction is a real
limitation in looking at butch/femme roles. The male/
female dyad as a source relationship against which all other
relationships must be measured is a complete failing. In
modern society, marriage has been oppressive for women
and men, who then limit themselves by the roles.

"That isn't necessarily the primary relationship in
human relating. I could just as easily say that the mother/
child relationship is a primary dyad against which we should
measure our relationships. It could be student/teacher,
siblings, many different types of dyads.

"Rather than looking at male/female relationships as
the root, we should look at them as a distortion of the natural
order of things—a distortion of the two poles that nature
presents each of us with. Old folks have many sayings which
express this pole-like natural order: 'What goes around,
comes around', 'Opposites attract', 'Up ain't up without
down'; even scientists say, 'For every action there is an
equal and opposite reaction.'

"This has been the underlying principle in Eastern
religions for thousands of years. The principles of the yin

and yang have been basic to philosophy and everyday life in most Eastern, African, and Latin cultures on this planet. But those principles were lost to Europeans when they evolved into Western European puritanical religion. There was no circular action and reaction between life, nature, and the cosmos. And so we forget that there are two sides within individuals, that we can go from one end of the spectrum to the other. It's a natural principle, a natural, psychological, biological, emotional, physiological principle."

If we recognize female dyads as truly significant in lesbian lives, then it becomes clear that butch and femme have nothing to do with male and female. We certainly know this from our own firsthand knowledge—either the women we know who embrace this categorization, or by our own placement on a butch/femme scale. Many factors contribute to the knowledge that our sexuality is not simply polarized into opposition of male at one end, female at the other. Our placement on the butch/femme scale is mobile and can change depending on life circumstances. Our placement changes depending on the partner we are with at any given time. Placement changes depending on what our own vision is of ourselves. Collectively, the lesbian community has beliefs about where women fit on the scale simply by looking at them, without knowing them in the slightest. All of this should give us a clue that we are dealing with a lesbian construct, one which the majority culture doesn't know how to deal with. If we begin to accept that we are talking about something profoundly female, then there's a whole discussion that can emerge about the true nature of woman/woman relating.

Madeline Davis says, "The archetypal lesbian couple—the untouchable stone butch and the femme—is a puzzle of the history of women's sexuality in a culture that perceives women as sexually passive. These butches developed an assertive, aggressive sexual stance, uncommon to women of that period. Inherent in that was the giving of sexual pleasure. These women have also been defined as simply [replicating] heterosexual roles. The male role, which the butch role appears to be [reproducing] on the outside, certainly does *not* define its goal as the giving of sexual pleasure to women. The butch role most essentially does. The femme role, which had been traditionally seen as a passive, accepting role, actually was a much more assertive role. Femme women defined what they wanted and what they needed. They asked for it and taught the butches how to give it to them. They drew them pictures. They were very positive and clear about what they wanted. Once again, this was a tremendous divergence for women at the time to seek out, to know, to be brave enough to know what they wanted. Butch/femme roles certainly turned heterosexuality on its head and on its ear and on its ass."

Two lesbians who attended my workshops have enlarged on this idea, talking about how our relationships actually work. The first said, "I don't think that butch and femme are a lesbian replica of the male and female role. Particularly because we are able to give and take from one another, where it's the men and women who seem to actually be stuck in a role. I'm stereotyping now—not all women and men are like this—of course; but generally they're stuck in their roles. Lesbians trade off their roles. You can be strong and you can be needy. When you're coming home from a long hard day at the job, and you need some comfort and some loving, you can ask for it from your partner and she'll give it to you, whether you are butch or femme. We trade those qualities back and forth, and I don't think it matters one whit whether you're butch or femme."

A butch-identified woman went on to say, "The traditional male/female definition is that the woman is oppressed, that she is submissive, that she's done to—all that stuff that defines a woman's sexuality. Of course, that's the core of the inequality and oppression on the political and other levels too. As for the lesbian sexual role definitions, I think what makes it safe for me is that there isn't that kind of an imbalance between us and there isn't a danger of it. If the woman can be submissive and surrenders and receives, I feel she is in control, not me. I'm not looking to her to satisfy me. I'm looking more to satisfy her and to be satisfied. If she is receptive, I can be aggressive. There is absolutely no way I can express this part of me and get this part of me fulfilled if she wasn't receiving, if she was closed to it, if she felt oppressed. It's really different for me than traditional male stuff, but we get confused because we grew up with men's definitions of femininity and what being feminine is. But for lesbians it's just really different."

Labeling Butches and Femmes

Because gender identity is so conflicted among many lesbians, I decided to include a section in my survey that would reflect how we lesbians currently view ourselves in relation to traditional sex roles, using an already established scale that showed the cultural views about male, female and androgynous characteristics. I also wanted to see if lesbians had stereotypical views of butch and femme lesbians, given our ideas that these lesbians were mimicking male/female models. I wanted a scale that had been established by a feminist in the world of statistics. I chose Sandra Bem's Sex Role Inventory (BSRI), even though it was created back in the mid-'70s, because it showed the sexist and stereotypical views of sex roles in our culture. Bem was able to identify a long list of human characteristics as "male", "female", or "androgynous" *in the eyes of traditional mainstream culture*.

The idea that we relate the concept of butch to maleness and the concept of femme to femaleness in *relationship* to heterosexuality became clear in the answers to this survey. Over and over, exclusively "male" characteristics were applied to butches and exclusively "female" characteristics to femmes. What really shocked me is that we still use the sexist language of the 1950s to describe ourselves today. Everyone knows some lesbians who identify butch or femme, and to reduce these complex and different women to such basic stereotypes denies the reality of our own experience.

In my survey, I asked each lesbian to describe *herself* on a scale of one (never or almost never true) to seven (always or almost always true) using a list of 60 characteristics in the BSRI. Each was also asked to choose three of the characteristics that *most* described "butch", "androgynous", and "femme." I wanted to know how these women themselves perceived butches, femmes, and androgynous women. It's possible that these lesbians may instead have given what they feel are the common stereotypes of butch/femme/androgyny, though this is not what they were asked to do.

According to this survey, femmes (just like traditional females in Bem's analysis) are more likely to be: yielding, cheerful, shy, affectionate, flatterable, feminine, sympathetic, sensitive to the needs of others, understanding, compassionate, eager to soothe hurt feelings, soft-spoken, warm, tender, gullible, childlike, does not use harsh language, loves children, gentle. Femmes were also the most: conscientious, theatrical, inefficient, and tactful (all traditionally androgynous), as well as analytical (traditionally male).

Butches (just like traditional males, according to Bem) are more likely to be: athletic, assertive, strong personality, forceful, has leadership abilities, dominant, masculine, aggressive, acts as a leader, competitive. Butches are also seen as: moody and jealous (both thought of as androgynous) and loyal (their only "female" trait).

Androgynous women are described (like androgynous people in Bem's list) as: happy, unpredictable, reliable, truthful, secretive, sincere, likeable, solemn, friendly, adaptable, unsystematic, conventional. Androgynous women are also viewed as having very positive "male" characteristics: self-reliant, defends own beliefs, independent, willing to take risks, self-sufficient, willing to take a stand, individualistic, and ambitious. There are *no* "female" characteristics selected for androgynous women in this survey.

What Does All This Stereotyping Mean?

The majority culture certainly assumes that butch is male and femme is female (in a heterosexual sense). This can be excused as oppression, prejudice, lack of knowledge and sexist belief that all couples exist only within the heterosexual male/female model. However, how do we account for the reality that as an oppressed group, we ourselves also adopt the stereotyped view?

It should be no surprise that we lesbians take on the opinion of the majority culture as well. This is reflected in our internal homophobia that keeps us from coming out to our neighbors, children, families. Somehow we have bought the idea that our lesbianism is shameful and should be hidden. Still, I thought this would be different when it came to defining our own sexual, affectional images within our own culture. So far, the majority culture has beaten us to the punch and we have adopted their views as to what lesbians really are about.

The concepts the lesbians in this survey have of butch and femme reflect an intensely sexist image. Butches are most identified with "male" characteristics; femmes are most identified with "female" characteristics; and androgynous women are seen as mostly "androgynous" with an additional large smattering of positive "male" characteristics.

I don't want to imply that women are not self-reliant, independent, and so on, or that these characteristics belong to men. What the BSRI scale does is to describe mainstream assumptions about sex roles, assumptions which lesbians seem not to question when it comes to the stereotypes that apply to our culture.

I may be pushing a point here, but I believe it is sexist when the androgynous group is not seen as having even one "female" characteristic. Since the majority of these 589 lesbians see themselves as androgynous, it's striking that they kept such distance from the traditional "female" characteristics. I do feel that lesbians often believe traditional female characteristics are beneath us. I'm concerned that androgynous women didn't get high marks for being affectionate, sympathetic, loyal, understanding or compassionate (all very positive "female" words).

The information on the butch characteristics is equally disturbing. How is it that a lesbian population would imbue butches with all "male" characteristics except one of the positive female characteristics (loyal) and two androgynous characteristics, neither one particularly positive (moody and jealous)? Do we really know this kind of stereotyped woman? Or is it that we really don't allow ourselves to consider the complexity and diversity of the women we actually know, relying instead on straight cultural stereotypes to describe something that is lesbian?

Four androgynous characteristics were associated with femmes in this survey. Two were negative (theatrical and inefficient) and two were positive (conscientious and tactful). Assigning the former to femmes I see as sexist. The latter two were a pleasant surprise—though hardly indicative of the power of femmes.

In fact, many of us know butches who are helpful, femmes who are ambitious, and androgynous women who love children; yet in this survey, each received zero votes for having those characteristics.

It is difficult to believe that we are unwilling to use our own knowledge about women who fit in these three groups to break the stereotypical vision that butches just want to be men, femmes are lesbians who would really like to be with men, and androgynous lesbians are the saviors, the guiding lights who have all the cool characteristics.

This vision is so narrow that there is little room for us to develop our *own* sense of what butch, femme, and androgynous lesbians are, what we believe the delineations mean, and what the women who fit each of the numbers on the one to ten scale are really like. What *is* the difference between a 6 and 8; a 3 and 5; a 1 and 10? What is the meaning of butch and femme? Who are truly androgynous women? Why is it that we judge ourselves in the same way the majority culture does? And why is it that a universal concept in our community is thought of as universally unimportant?

. . . .

One woman who attended the Toronto conference spoke about transforming identity: "This year for the first time my nine-year-old and twelve-year-old kids saw me wearing a dress. My nine-year-old asked what it was called. I came out into the feminist movement and this year for the first time I learned that I can say I am a born-again femme! I had to confront my woman hating. A lot of what we've done in feminism has been to hate the very stuff that's part and parcel of being female. We don't have to do that anymore!"

. . . .

Instead of using mainstream stereotypes as a catalyst for change within our own community—turning the images inside out and on their heads, as gay men have often done and as some young lesbians are beginning to do—we too often are willing to be our own cultural police. We limit not just the conduct of others, but our own awareness and imagination.

Somewhere along the road to our own liberation, we also took a curious detour. We embraced many of the characteristics so long denied to women, and became more powerful in the world. But in the process, we seem to have left behind a truly positive vision of what it is to be female. We rejected not only our mothers, but their gifts within ourselves as well. This truncated view of our achievements and of our possibilities also limits the flourishing of our culture. If we take other dyads, in Jewelle Gomez's words, as our source, then what kind of complex lesbian culture would begin to emerge?

THE DEBATE
2

"I think butch/femme doesn't exist outside of the male/female framework. It's our conditioning. I have a split. I find myself attracted to more masculine or butch women, yet, intellectually, I can't relate to it."

"But are you attracted to women who are more femme than you?"

"Well, see, if I look at the women that I have been with, I would have to say no. If I were to just line them all up, they're all butchy women."

"But your feminist rhetoric says, oh no, I could be attracted to anybody."

"Yeah, but when I think about it—it evaporates."

"When you tell the truth—"

"When I'm acting on it, then I think that it's part of my conditioning, part of my own sort of self-hatred, to not react to the more feminine looking woman."

"It's so individual, isn't it? Because I'm attracted both to more butchy women and women more femme than me."

"Here we go again, what is butch and femme? I don't see them as masculine and feminine."

"I agree, I don't see butch and femme as male and female."

"You should see some of the men I know!"

"I think that in the male/female sense having power is more identified with feeling like you are in control. But if you're a lesbian, to me, you already have chosen that you don't want to play that part and don't want to submit to a man. To me, you are already exercising a power if you are on the lesbian side of it, no matter what position you are in, cause you're not with men. That's why I think it's all an act. That's why I think the butch/femme thing with lesbians is an act, because it's pretending to be submissive."

"For a long time, what femme has meant has been very pejorative."

"Right."

"It's an imitation of a heterosexual woman."

"Yes."

"And it is not."

"And it's our job to start beginning to turn that around, and say that femme is a homosexual lesbian term."

"Absolutely."

"And that we embrace it, and that it's a strong dynamic lesbian woman who can be strong, competent, do things, get things done, and be successful in her job, do all the things that—"

"What happens if you're weak and not good at your job?"

"If a femme is also being strong, then how do you define a butch?"

"I was putting on a new toilet seat—should be easy right—just two screws—of course not. So I'm under the toilet trying to get these goddamed fucking corroded screws loose. My young son is watching all this. I say 'It's sure a bitch being butch.' He looks at me in confusion and says 'Mom, I thought your girlfriend was butch.' It lives with us or we just live it and it takes the children to show us it exists."

CHAPTER FOUR

The Androgynous Imperative

Since the second wave of feminism (the first having been the suffragists), the lesbian community has held an ideal of androgyny. There has been an unspoken dress and behavior code that (until the mid-'80s) went unchallenged for nearly twenty years. Hair was short. Clothing was uniform: jeans, hiking boots, running shoes, Birkenstocks, T-shirts, flannel shirts, baseball jackets, down jackets, baggy walking shorts, and athletic clothes. No adornment. No barrettes, no jewelry (well, maybe simple rings or a small gold chain necklace), no makeup, no hose, no high heels, no skirts, no dresses, no scarves. Minor exceptions were allowed for work, but women who wore anything more traditionally feminine than dressy pant suits were expected to defend their outfits.

There were other rules that didn't relate to dress, but did relate to the lesbian-feminist culture. Some were permanent rules, some went in and out with the fashion. The two most permanent rules were no sex with men and no confusion or ambivalence about your lesbian identity. The trends included: monogamy, nonmonogamy, separatism, insemination with a known or unknown donor, being friendly with men, therapy or no therapy, telling the public about our culture, staying isolated and thus safer, coming out, pulling others out of the closet, and so on.

There was a purpose in all of this at the beginning of our movement, as we proudly began to be visible and to tell the world that we were lesbians. We were determined to let others know. We also wanted to let each other know, to find each other and be found. We wanted lesbians everywhere to know that we were lesbians too. We quickly developed cultural signals to say who we were. We wore two women's symbols entwined in every conceivable manner; we cut our hair; we listened to women's music (which we always knew was lesbian music); we wore "dyke" clothes. We held hands in public, we kissed each other in front of strangers, we slept in motel rooms and didn't bother to mess up the extra bed. We set a lesbian erotic standard by wearing androgynous clothes, one that was challenging at the time.

Our androgynous ways made a statement, and they also gave us a special kind of power. The world couldn't categorize us. We determined who we were—no one else did. We weren't going to follow the fashion trends. Year after year we'd be there in our blue jeans, T-shirts, tennis shoes, changing clothes only in response to the weather. We wanted safe, functional clothing that would serve us, not men or the fashion industry. Most of all, we didn't want to give in to our parents' and society's expectations of us. We were dykes and that was it.

But there was also a large segment of the lesbian population that never liked the androgynous movement. These women were embarrassed by the "masculine nature" of the clothing. There was a great deal of homophobia in reaction to the style, the attitude, the visibility. It is of course absurd to assume any clothing belongs to one sex or the other, especially functional, practical clothes, to which everyone has a right.

This negative attitude only fueled the fire of the androgynous lesbians. It was considered "politically incorrect" not to subscribe to what became the androgynous imperative, of which dress was only the most obvious manifestation. Lesbians who wanted to wear other clothing were derided and brought back into the fold—or they vanished into lesbian obscurity. Lesbians who legitimately wanted to wear whatever they wanted were lumped into the same category as the homophobic lesbians. Anything that was outside the norm was seen as a threat to the lesbian movement. Many women went along because they wanted to belong to the club.

There was a particular snobbery about the whole manner of androgynous dress. Lesbians who did not subscribe were outsiders. They were derided as trying to "pass," wanting the privileges of looking straight along with the pleasures of loving women. They were accused of not understanding the importance of the politics involved, the oppression of women, and how the traditional dress of women reflected that oppression. If a woman felt she had to dress for work, she was questioned about the job and how important it was to make a statement. Making money was already suspect, and dressing in a way that was too traditional in order to make that money was definitely questionable behavior.

I remember being taught by my first lesbian lover how and where to buy used flannel shirts. She also took me to buy my first pair of Levi's. At the time, there were no jeans fashioned to women's shapes, and I definitely had (and still have) large hips, a small waist, and thighs that are proportionately much larger than the bottom part of my legs. I bought men's Levi's that would fit over my hips and thighs. This, of course, meant the waist was huge and I would have to belt it in severely. I'm only five foot three, and getting Levi's the right width meant getting them way too long. They always needed hemming. The flannel shirts had arms that were too long so the cuffs were rolled up at least two times. If I got flannel shirts with arms the right length, they never were large enough to be buttoned over my breasts. Luckily, Birkenstocks were made in my size, and I still had hiking boots from having lived in Colorado. (Why people needed hiking boots in the quite mild climate of Northern California was beyond me.) I did know a requirement when I saw one though, and I gladly traded in all my former clothes (except the boots) for lesbian regulation gear. I wanted to be in the club.

I was in graduate school at the time and was taking a psychology class in which I was sure the teacher's assistant was a lesbian. She wore lesbian-approved garb. The class was huge, and I tried to get her attention by wearing my clothes religiously and asking pertinent questions about her study on rhesus monkeys and how males were not part of the domestic scene of raising offspring. She seemed not to notice me, which pushed me to go further in my quest to be part of the recognizable lesbian nation. I cut my hair even shorter, which only served to make me look like a teenager with a fuzzy head.

The truly wondrous part for me was that men stopped coming on to me. It was glorious. I walked across campus without drawing any attention to myself. I became invisible, which thrilled me. No more looks from men that seemed to undress me. No more innuendoes or outright solicitations for my attention. This was a relief and made moving about in the world suddenly much more simple.

There were times when a group of us wearing lesbian androgynous regulation clothing were harassed by unaccompanied males. (This is how I refer to any group of men who do not have female companions with them. Even one female traveling with a group of men civilizes them somehow, and I'm not as afraid.) The great part about this attire is that you felt stronger than society meant you to be; I remember yelling back at a group of men who were harassing me and my lover outside a known lesbian club. Though not trained in martial arts, I never stopped to consider that this behavior was not exactly safe.

I believed taking up space was my prerogative, and I did it all the time. This really did have something to do with the clothing. I was separate from men. I didn't belong to them or with them. I was with women and my style of dress proved that. It was obvious that I wasn't straight and therefore, they should stay away from me.

This form of dressing really did allow me more freedom and helped to form my analysis on a gut level. Separating myself from the ownership men always thought they had over me, and being able to do this with an external statement brought a release that cannot be explained. You just have to feel it yourself.

There was also the powerful knowledge that androgynous dressing separated me from the ways my parents had always intended I dress, which was, of course, symbolic of who they also thought I should be. I was more my own person. No one in my family dressed like me. Though no one had told me overtly that women don't dress like this, I knew that they didn't expect me to do it. In those days, "single" daughters still belonged to their parents. Dressing differently reminded me that I was different, that I was a lesbian. Even if I wasn't out to some members of my family, this attire would subconsciously give them the message. Questions about boyfriends stopped.

One of my radical lesbian professors in graduate school asked me if I really liked the barrettes I wore in my hair. She wondered if I had ever considered that they convey passivity. Well, actually, I hadn't, but indeed I did consider it then. She seemed to know what she was talking about, and I wanted to belong since I was just coming out. I got rid of my barrettes, my dresses, my makeup, and jewelry. In that class, we discussed at great length the connections between breast cancer and woman hatred, rape and the invasive techniques of the military in the United States, and we also discussed how dressing in a particular manner made a statement about power or powerlessness. I was proud at the time to trade in clothes I now interpreted as a sign of weakness for those that meant I was strong.

Of course, those clothes did not make me a lesbian, and conversely, wearing other kinds of clothes did not make me straight. But I didn't realize then that I joined many others in feeling betrayed by lesbians who didn't heed the party line. I always thought they were trying to be "other", and not part of "us." I argued vehemently with lesbians who said, "None of those androgynous women look like me." I explained it was just their homophobia that they needed to resolve. It never occurred to me that perhaps there was homophobia among the ranks of the androgynous.

In speaking of this period, Jewelle Gomez says, "I think the fear and anger that butch/femme has created among some feminists isn't rooted in anything having to do with being politically correct. It presents a fearful choice to people. All movements go through phases where they have to demand uniformity. That's why members of armies wear the same uniform, so they can recognize each other. The choice to explore these varying poles in ourselves opens up a chance to envision yourself in different configurations and boxes. Most people want you to be in a box, stay in that box, and be recognizable."

Everything Is Equal

How did we change from becoming more empowered to enforcing androgyny as the lesbian norm? How did it become the imperative?

Along with our dress being the same, we were also supposed to be equal in all things. Differences in power were not meant to be part of our lives. This showed up in ways that were both beneficial and detrimental. The androgynous movement made rules to govern our behaviors, actions and activities.

As I make these bold generalizations, we need to remember that this was not the norm for every lesbian. I'm speaking about the visible lesbians who came to lesbian and women's cultural events, those we call "the community." These feminist women saw androgyny as the trademark of lesbianism.

I feel the main impetus behind the androgynous imperative was that we were becoming an organized and recognizable group of women with a strong and collective vision. We agreed with each other and that was obvious by the fact that we looked alike. We needed an identification that allowed us to be a group, since in fact lesbians are quite diverse; much of the time the only thing we have in common is our love of women.

Seeing each other in public or private gatherings, as strangers on the street, our lesbian regulation look said, "Hey, I'm a sister too," and brought instant recognition. We weren't alone. Together we had a movement that bound us. We were in a club, and being able to know immediately who else was in the club was reassuring.

The problem was that we came to believe that certain specific codes were necessary *to be* a lesbian: not only rules of dress, but also dealings with children, money, race, class, women's art, what books to read, which movies and television shows to watch, what sexual activities to engage in.... Our righteous stance that lesbianism was superior to heterosexuality spilled over into a righteous stance that everyone had to act and look the same. This wasn't published in the lesbian press. It wasn't something that anyone checked on; it was simply done through peer pressure.

"I think there's less pressure today to be one or the other (butch/femme), but I think there is more pressure to not identify that way. Ten years ago, there was a lot of pressure to be male-identified in how you looked and in how you acted. Women who looked feminine were put down. Now that everyone is more secure, and is dressing differently, there's a whole different attitude, but we were supposed to dress more male-identified and yet call ourselves woman-identified. It was very crazy-making; I got shit all the time. Twelve years ago, I didn't look much different than now. I would dress really nice and I wore jewelry and makeup and I collected shit from the flannel shirt crowd on a regular basis. Yet at the same time, the very butch women were the ones coming onto me and wanting to be sexual with me, yet putting me down at the same time because I looked too feminine. It was very crazy-making and I think there is still some of that that goes on."

No Heroes in the Amazon Nation

Back then, the peer pressure seemed to be for a righteous cause. You see, there was a whole new day dawning. The goddess had chose us for a special task, that of claiming space for women to be. What was especially thrilling was that it seemed like spontaneous combustion. No one person, no one group, no one city was responsible for what was happening.

Lesbian communities were a phenomena that emerged suddenly. Everywhere lesbians were becoming visible. Lesbians began to form groups to study class and race. Almost instantly, there was a new way to think. We opened bookstores and coffeehouses, invented festivals, thousands cheered touring musicians, and political debates flourished. In San Francisco, Minneapolis, Chicago, Los Angeles, and New York, lesbians were coming out in record numbers. When I came out in 1975, there was already a way to dress, a way to act and a way of analyzing the culture. I had no idea that these rules didn't exist in 1973. In fact, they almost didn't exist in 1974.

There seemed to be no leaders and those who fancied themselves leaders were called out. If you wanted to lead, you fell from grace. Lesbian musicians were expected to mingle with the audience after a performance; if they didn't, they were called elitist or accused of star tripping. We didn't know it at the time, of course, but the truth was some were more equal than others. There were those who enjoyed special privileges, there really were leaders, and there was some form of direction from elite cliques in each community. As long as these "ruling" women were in favor, they were able to get away with it, but once they made a wrong turn, they were called elitist, and another group took their place.

It was at this time of spontaneous combustion, the big bang theory, during the time of the hidden leaders, that we were taught to fear power imbalances. This was the beginning of the belief in lesbian culture that no one should have more power than anyone else. If they did, we'd get rid of them, humiliate them, or refuse to use their resources. This came from having been used and abused by a male culture, even by the leftist movement.

We were actually creating what seemed like another gender. There was no way to be a woman and be who we were being. We couldn't be women in the ways that we had been taught women behaved. We didn't want to claim the traditional values assigned to women in our society. We wanted our own place. We saw ourselves as part of the "women's movement", but we already knew that mainstream feminism did not want our version of womanhood. We scorned our straight feminist sisters for pandering to men. The fact that some of them thought their men were "feminists" sent us into paroxysms of laughter. A feminist *man?* That heterosexual women called themselves feminist was almost as ludicrous. "Feminism is the theory, lesbianism the practice" was our battle cry.

Some of us decided the only way to really practice lesbian-feminism was to isolate ourselves from men. This movement was dubbed "separatist." That title implies that we were separate, when in fact what we most wanted was to have power in our own lives. The idea was that the male-dominated portion of the population had the problem, not us. We were setting out to create a world not unlike Sappho's on her island, where she began a learning center for women because the powerful males in the universities had decided not to teach women any longer.

Many of us passed into our androgynous identity by going through a separatist phase. We renounced all dealings and inter- actions with men. We sought solitude from them, rejoicing in "women-only space." If at all possible, the women who embraced this movement learned trades, started women's businesses, or found jobs that didn't involve men. A network was established of woman-only land. We expunged "man" and "men" from the ending of the words woman and women, calling ourselves womyn, or wimmin. The number of spellings of these words became legion. Seeing "wimmin" on a flyer about an event always indicated that the philosophy of equality, sameness, and androgyny was honored in these spaces.

This was a way for us to learn what women would do if they did not have to be involved with men, to see what would happen if we didn't have to vie for a place in conversations and allow ourselves the freedom of not having to explain things that other women automatically understood. And we didn't really want to do what women had been taught to do. We wanted to separate ourselves from the culturally imposed expectations of women. Many of us believed that there was no way to be ourselves and act the way women were supposed to act. This was especially true when it came to motherhood.

The lesbian culture in the "old days" had dealt with the question of children. You didn't have them. If you had them, you sent them somewhere else to live. There was no place for them in a "deviant" community. Many women cherished the thought that they were moving into a community that was not going to have to deal with children. However, the new wave of '70s lesbians had a more radical view of mothering: it was seen as enslavement of the mother.

In the early days of separatism, this idea of motherhood as enslavement went so far as to sacrifice mothers. Children were not welcome at gatherings of lesbians. Boy children were absolutely forbidden in separatist space. Actually, boy children were not welcome at most lesbian gatherings.

Women who had had children by heterosexual unions were suspect. Those of us who didn't have children thought that any minute now when these women quit being mad at their ex-husbands they would find a nice man and settle down. It was a terribly condescending view of these women who often had to sacrifice everything, even their children, to come out.

Minnie Bruce Pratt writes about losing her children because of her lesbianism in her recent book, *Crimes Against Nature:*

"If I had been more ashamed, if I had not
wanted the world. If I had hid my lust,
I might not have lost them."

Some women were actually forced by other lesbians to give up their children to prove their loyalty to the lesbian-feminist movement. A woman I know had a young son and daughter when she came out in the '60s. Her ex-husband was actually supportive of her change, so he was not fighting her for custody of their children. The lesbian collective that she settled into insisted she give up all ties to her children, then reluctantly agreed that she could keep her daughter, still in diapers. She severed all ties with her son, a separation that lasted over ten years.

It is difficult to believe that lesbians really demanded that of each other, or that desperate mothers paid the price. Yet it seemed that in some cases survival in a new life required giving up your children. The heterosexual culture believed it, but so did the lesbian culture. In retrospect, in the '90s, who remembers why we had to exact such a price for a membership card?

It wasn't until the mid-'70s that childcare at public events even became an issue. Artificial insemination wasn't happening on any level until the late '70s or early '80s. I remember being in New York the year my baby was born (1982), and the lesbians there were astonished that I had actually had him by insemination with a gay male donor. In fact, at that time the only negative responses I had about having a baby were from my family of origin and from other lesbians, the former because of the prejudice the child would have to put up with, the latter because I was wasting my lesbian energy having a baby. Raising children was seen as an extension of the subservience of women.

· ·
· ·

Alix Dobkin has a wonderful song from 1980 called "Just Like a Woman," with the following verse:
"Isn't it just like a woman to raise a little boy
train him for the privileges she does not enjoy
and when everything is due to him
her duty is endless mothering,
it's depressing, but it's just like a woman."
· ·

Eliminating the "Isms"

One of the most positive aspects of our efforts to make everything equal was our struggle to equalize power in relationship to class and race. Gradually we came to see that the culture of the United States was based not only on a male standard that excluded women, but also on a white and middle-class standard that left out people who were poor or of color. Though the lesbian community was proud of purging "male" standards, it became increasingly clear that lesbian standards were decidedly white and middle-class.

Class analysis began in study groups and at women's events, and to some extent, had positive results. Lesbians of all class backgrounds came together to work on projects and thus became part of one another's social groups. Interacting at many levels helped to educate all of us. Women were not judged by their designer clothes (especially since we weren't allowed to wear any). This allowed everyone in the community to look the same and be treated more equally. Education was not the ticket to power in our community, giving all women a more equal footing than was often afforded in the majority culture.

Women with money began to see what statements like "I have no money" really meant, learning that when poor women said "I have no money," it meant they really had no money. When women with money said the same thing, it meant: "I spent my money on clothes this week," or "I haven't gotten to the bank today," or "I paid all my bills on time so I have to wait until I get paid again to get some more money," or "I don't have as much money as I'd like to have." Women who had been raised middle-class began to understand what it was like to have been raised without food or proper shelter and how that had resulted in a lack of access to the culture in general.

Working-class women had a say in how lesbian organizations ran. Sometimes, though not often, there was a space during which middle-class women shut up and listened to the poor and working-class experience. The advent of the sliding scale made it possible for women with less money to attend cultural events. The fact that sliding scales became the norm, instead of a resented charity, was a statement about the ways in which poor women brought their different currency of exchange to the lesbian community.

Some of the solutions to class differences raised their own problems. The analysis often was shallow and too simplistic. Money became evil and an anathema to the community. The most widely practiced of these solutions was "downward mobility." It became an important part of the androgynous movement. No one was to have any more money than anyone else. Women who were raised middle-class or above conspicuously demonstrated a lack of possessions or material power. Women were criticized openly and surreptiously for having any claims to wealth or perceived wealth. There was tremendous peer pressure to act as if your family had few or no financial resources. Telling the truth about having money was seen as bragging or being oppressive. Women denounced their family's money (except when they needed it). Wealthy women were openly criticized for having money (yet depended upon to keep organizations running). Conversely, being poor was revered. Working-class women held elevated status simply because of class (except when they were secretly criticized for their spending habits—"She would have more money if she didn't spend so much on blah, blah, blah").

This spirit of equality was certainly an honorable one. Money ceased to be the primary source of power in the community. But instead of figuring out how those differences could work for the good of the whole community, we reversed the standards. Since we said being poor was the only way to be, we lost many resources for our community. Women turned away from careers that could have contributed to the whole. Many women with money were hounded out of the visible community and took their resources with them. Poor women were objectified, their experiences co-opted, and their culture sanitized by middle-class women. In effect, our struggle to become multiclass backfired into nothing more than one more "right" way of being, one that didn't reflect the true nature of our differences.

The struggle to become a multiracial movement was fraught with even more difficulties, though making room for women of color to voice their anger at the white culture was certainly overdue. The lesbian movement flowered with the active contribution of minority cultures. Our record companies, performers, magazines, and book publishers expanded to include multicultural experiences. Women from all racial groups approached this process with wariness and hope, gradually and with difficulty making our lesbian movement more deep and inclusive.

However, the androgynous imperative also required smoothing of differences on all fronts, which was particularly problematical in the case of race. Accusations of racism abounded, with all white women wanting to be relieved of that epithet. Any separation one could muster from racist constructs was displayed proudly—major proof being that you knew other women who were more racist, and you could call them on it.

Women of color, on the other hand, were encouraged to be racist. There was a patronizing quality to white women confessing in public that all white women deserved to be punished for the crimes of centuries of white domination. Some white women embraced the ideal that the beliefs of any woman of color were more valuable than those they knew to be true themselves. The goal of changing our culture to become multiracial was distorted into a simplistic version that too often was used to divide the troops into the "good women" and the "bad women."

And Then There Were The Therapists

The fact that the androgynous imperative dictated no power differences distorted other areas as well. The role of the therapist in the community is a classic example of our intolerance of imbalances.

During the '60s and '70s there was an upsurge in the role of therapy in the leftist liberal communities in general, but nowhere did therapy become so universal as in the lesbian community. It may be hard for young lesbians to believe, but there was a time when everyone did not have hot and cold running individual and couples therapists. In a fast culture with everyone so busy, lesbians so intertwined, religion reviled, and our pain so great, the "wise therapist" has become a community institution.

But there was a time in the '70s when the word therapist was written in graffiti as: "the/rapist." This came from a history of women being victims of psychiatric assault. Women were the majority of the patients, men the majority of the practitioners. Women's problems were treated with drugs, men's problems were treated with respect. Mothers were the cause of all psychological problems of their children. Women were seen in psychological terms as masochistic and hysterical. Lesbians were treated in traditional therapy as sick and immature.

It was not until the middle of the '70s that feminist therapy became a reality. *Women* began to build a new definition of women's problems. Oppression by men, the feminization of poverty, and the total responsibility of childraising were seen as the real reason women had psychological distress in the world. This was the time when lesbianism became redefined as a sexual orientation, not an illness.

The influence of feminism brought the idea that not only was the practitioner of the past a threat to women, but that the true feminist therapist should have no more power than her client. The therapist was just another member of the community and should receive no deferential treatment.

This was certainly a positive idea; however, the androgynous ideal that lesbian therapists had no more power than their lesbian clients led to real problems of boundaries. Many therapists became friends, landlords, employers, acquaintances, even lovers with their clients. Being a therapist to a good friend's lover seemed to be no problem. Seeing in therapy two lovers and each of their ex-lovers, and maybe even someone's current affair, was a regular practice for therapists. If one could be friends with two lovers and their ex-lovers and the current affair, why not be their therapist as well? This extreme arrogance led to all kinds of problems. It was almost impossible to feel deep trust for someone who was also listening to your lover's side of every issue. There was little likelihood for a small circle to be helped by someone simply becoming part of the circle. Worst of all, becoming lovers with a client was incestuous.

Separation is necessary to do effective therapy. This doesn't mean that the therapist is all-powerful, but the therapist does have more power than the client in this arena, not unlike a car mechanic who has power over someone who knows nothing about cars. Unlike car repair, which can be learned, one cannot learn to be objective about oneself. Though there are certainly other paths to self-healing, the role of the therapist is unique. That power needs to be used in an honorable and respectful way. For the therapist to deny that her power exists is to abuse her role, not unlike neglectful parents who insist their children raise themselves.

Power imbalances that come from professional status, income, and class privilege have surfaced increasingly in recent years. Yet we have no feminist framework in which to understand and negotiate those differences. Our rhetoric still represents us as all equal, and our movement has faltered more than it has changed.

Sexually Equal or Sexually Limited

Another area that has been powerfully (no pun intended) affected by the androgynous imperative is sex. The concept that partners should be equal in sex is important in a world set up to make women inferior. Teaching one another what we each liked sexually was part of the ideal of equality. The expectation that both partners are responsible for initiating sex is a liberating one. No one has to have the burden, no one has to be responsible for any given aspect of lovemaking.

Herein lies the rub: why should each of us in a lover partnership be responsible for everything? There is tremendous pressure for both women in a couple to do and like the same kinds of sex acts. There is pressure for each to initiate the same amount. There is concern that one cannot be more dominant than the other. If one woman in the partnership is being more aggressive, she is feared to be "male." This is simply not true; two women being together sexually is a lesbian experience. Within this paradigm are many configurations. Each woman does not have to do what the other does. Each woman does not have to initiate sex the same amount to have it be true lesbian love. The expectation that we each become powerful and equal in exactly the same way may not be possible.

There is a certain stiffness to the idea that both partners will want to have sex spontaneously and at the same time. We're different. It's possible we won't want sex at the same time; in fact more often than not, we don't. This doesn't mean we should look for another partner. It means we are two individuals with different needs and different timing.

I believe that we have subjected sex to the same often unrealistic constraints that we've foisted upon other important parts of our lives. The lesbian who subscribes to the androgynous imperative idealizes a relationship that has no differences in power. As women we are taught to be acquiescent and adapting. We merge in ways that make us feel comfortable. I feel the androgynous movement appeals to our sense as women that difference is intolerable.

There is no way that some people don't have more power than others. There is no conceivable way to keep a sexual relationship power-free. There is no way to keep a relationship of any sort power-free. The fact that there are two people exchanging energy means that they are passing power back and forth. (Whatever your concerns about S/M, I feel that the extreme reaction to lesbians engaging in S/M exemplifies our concern about the acting out of any lesbian power exchanges.)

I believe there is an ideal within us that we can each be as strong and as vulnerable as the other. This isn't likely to be true in most aspects of a relationship. However, two women can strive to understand the differences in power between them, and to account for that in their dealings with one another. The idea that everything will be equal—ideas, friends, money, power in the world, sexual desires, or practices—can be a source of anxiety that really isn't necessary.

Of course, now there's a new generation of lesbians for whom the rules are completely different. And even for those of us who came out through the women's movement, more has changed than not. Many of us have gone back to school or gotten professional or corporate jobs; we're as likely to talk about the price of houses and the cost of health care as about the latest lesbian imperative. Not that the '80s have been a steady march back to middle-class bliss; we live in the midst of Reagan/Bush repression and a very real erosion of our rights and opportunities as women and as people of color. To many of us, our communities seem fractured, and we wonder where we've gone or they've gone.

For women who moved back into the mainstream, the women's community becomes even more precious as a safe and familiar world.

One corporate dyke said, "I'm uncomfortable with all this butch/femme stuff, and it's because I don't want to be made to feel wrong in this community because it is too goddamn uncomfortable everywhere else. I don't want to find out there isn't a word for me here, because there sure isn't one for me out there where I live and work. Maybe it's because I work in a straight world, and I'm not out in that world. I don't want my lesbian culture messed with. You know, it's sacrosanct. It's where I come home to, where I know what things are, what they mean. If we examine and change the current meaning of these words butch and femme in our community—is there nowhere that's home? You play with that for a while, people get betrayed. I know I don't belong where I spend most of my life now. So I don't even want to question, I don't want to even interfere for a second with anything that gives me the idea that I don't belong with lesbians."

When I explained so much about the androgynous dress code, it may have sounded as if it occurred in another century and it certainly may have seemed trivial. Dress and personal style have probably changed more quickly and easily in the '90s than deeper changes of sexuality or identity. But all of these changes come in the context of our histories, and bring with them all we've learned about being dykes.

A femme friend of mine said to me the other day: "I've been putting together a dress-up box for my five-year-old niece. A hard hat and ties, a feather boa, slinky dresses, and flowered straw hat. And I remembered how much I loved dressing up as a little girl. It sounds insane, but when I started wearing pink again, not all that long ago, I really worried what my dyke friends would say. Even now I wear what I would call 'tailored femme'—though some flowery chintzes are creeping in. For a whole bunch of complicated reasons, I doubt I'll ever wear skirts or dresses again, but I miss them. Here I am over 40 years old, and I'm just beginning to know my own tastes and style."

In the lesbian community in general, there is still tremendous attraction to the androgynous ideal and a lot of pressure to conform. Recently, I was at a professional conference for psychotherapists, and I asked the audience to rate a volunteer on the butch/femme scale. Despite resistance to the whole idea of butch/femme, the audience very clearly voted her an 8. Afterwards, I overheard one of her friends telling the woman who had volunteered that she was *not* an 8, that if the audience had really known her, they'd have known she was a 5! The friend was a missionary from the lesbian androgynous imperative, saying "To belong to this club, you have to fit into the middle."

The next day, this newly out lesbian had the number "8" proudly displayed on her name tag; at least for the moment, she had not succumbed to the pressure. Yet how quickly the group closes ranks to eliminate extremes and find a universal common ground where we can feel more comfortable. Perhaps I was so struck by the woman walking proudly with her "8" name tag because the worst censors are usually inside ourselves. An unquestioning adherence to the lesbian rules is just as damaging to us as following our childhood socialization would be. And those internalized rules are so subtle that they can limit possibilities before they've even formed. Androgyny has its place in our culture, but only if there's also room for each of us to be truly ourselves. As an imperative—as a set of rules that flattens all differences and ignores real power imbalances—it has outlived its usefulness.

THE DEBATE
3

"I just don't see the world as butch and femme. I don't want to be called an aggressive woman; I'm myself, I'm strong, I guess I just don't want to be seen on those terms."

"I think there's a dichotomy getting set up—if you identify with a role, does that mean that you're not going to be integrated as a holistic person? I can be feminine, masculine, androgynous. Both, either. Have it all, be loved, take in love. I don't think that resonating with the term butch or femme necessarily negates that. I mean, I say that I'm butch, but I'm a cupcake. I'd like to be given to as much as I want to give. Androgyny is, of course, my goal."

"That's why I'm wondering if we're coming out of a butch/femme tradition, and we're going towards something else where those words won't mean anything and we'll be more self-defined. I'm not saying that we should or that we will, but I'm just asking the question, are we using those terms out of a respect for our tradition that ceases to have meaning at some point?"

"Is there something inherently real about those roles?"

"Right. That's what I want to know."

"Well, it's very inherent to me as a lesbian. I don't have a problem with it."

"It sounds like there's a real dichotomy between those of us who hold on to that concept of butch and femme and feel that it's very much akin to claiming our dykeness and our lesbianism. And at the other end of the spectrum, there's those of us who feel it's the same thing as male and female. And we both have real strong feelings."

"People are responding to a lot of things. What do I do with the feelings that I have, the aesthetic feelings that I have about a beautiful man walking down the street. Does that make me less of a lesbian, do I not fit onto the spectrum?"

"A lot of lesbians think that."

"On that continuum though, if you are very femme or very butch, it seems to me, you see the roles much more clearly than those of us in the middle."

"But I think that it depends on how you define it. I have friends who are middle femme. Now they're comfortable with what that means and they are very role-identified. They tend to go for femmes and butches. They have a wider range. I sometimes go for femmes."

"Come on."

"I think the idea of femmes with femmes is kind of exciting."

What other words would you us as an alternative characterization?

I hate the word used in Texas—'fluff'—I use jock, sporty, handsome or fashionable—Houston, Tex.

Androgyny—Mound (really!), Minn.

Id rather just be called my name—Ore.

I'm in a relationship with a woman who's in relationship with her self, her truth, and her own love—Mill Valley, Calif.

Frou-frou for the femmes/Tough for the butches—N.Y.

hors d'oeuvre/dessert—Calif.

I dunno—Miamisburg, Ohio

Expressive/instrumental—Calif.

Beings of light—Eugene, Ore.

Brown bears/koala bears—Ore.

Roses/Cubbies—Seaview, Wash.

Yin/yang—frees the concept from the heterosexual model—Houston, Tex.

Yin/yang—polarity is the name of the game. I'm not sure that the artificially induced butch/femme role is the alpha and omega—Tigard, Ore.

Hu-Womyn—"hu" meaning goddess/spirit/purity—Portland, Ore.

Swan/lion—animals characterize people—Reseda, Calif.

P.L.U.—People Like Us—not too butch or femme, but themselves!—Grand Island, Neb.

Strength/Grace—Salinas, Calif.

Dykey—I think both butch and femme lesbians can be dykey—confident, proud, feisty about loving women—Albuquerque, N.M.

People—barf on polarity concepts—Denver, Col.

"When there's something that divides the community, then a lot of times we'll want to talk away the differences and then we talk away our richness."

"Talk away our personhood."

"Exactly. Disempower that person. You know, I want to go stand in a closet by myself so I don't get hurt. And then I hurt my own fucking feelings. I have to be in that closet and then I have to shut up."

"I don't like the use of the term 'androgyny.' It implies a mix of male and female. The next step is the implication of different psychological characteristics or gender roles for male and female. It is useful for the patriarchy to conceptualize this dichotomy, as it justifies labor division and oppression of women. By continuing to use the term 'androgyny', we are continuing to give that dichotomy meaning even as we try to transcend it.

"I don't think of butch and femme as connected with gender roles. If anything, I tend to think of 'butch' and 'androgynous' as synonymous. Is there another way that we can talk about that half-way or mixed point between butch and femme, without using the term 'androgynous?' "

"If I would be rated on the butch/femme scale, I would be judged anywhere from a 2 to a 9 depending on my dress, hair style, accessories, posture, pursing of lips, way I used my eyes, the tilt of my head and shoulders, how far apart I spread my feet, hand movements and all other body language. There's a lot of gray area between 1 and 10.

"You expressed a concern that feminists became critical of butch/femme roles and caused a great deal of damage, that feminists mock the naturalness and diversity of lesbian sexuality. I remember the time of great criticism in some circles of feminists—and lesbian-separatists. These movements allowed me to become empowered. I no longer had to cater to men's likes, needs, images—I could create my own. I shudder when you spoke against feminists. I know we need to create dialogue, clarify, talk about mistakes. But I don't remember heterosexual feminists criticizing lesbian butch/femmes. I remember lesbian-feminists talking about role playing as a mimicry of heterosexual oppressive relationships."

CHAPTER FIVE

Femmes Aren't Wimps

Femme—what is it about this word that has so unnerved us? What does it mean to identify as a femme? What does it mean when a friend acts as if she doesn't know what this word means? What happens when a lesbian tries hard not to identify as a femme so she can fit in better—so she will not be questioned on her politics?

It's amazing that we have such a full, unique culture with so few words to describe it. Of course, there're lots of reasons for this that I've already discussed. What I'm speaking of particularly here is not just the silence about our culture in general, but the even greater vacuum we have to describe our sexuality, sexual energy, or eroticism. How we view our sexual selves suffers greatly from the emptiness of our images. Attempts to describe lesbian eroticism often become two-dimensional, flat, hollow.

As I set out to write I can't help feeling that there's a way we do ourselves a disservice by even trying to put this information down on paper. How can any of us write about something so trivialized, so misunderstood? I believe we must, because we really have little choice. Our sexuality is being scrutinized and judged in every legislature and courtroom in the United States. More than ever, we need to give our own names to our culture, create our own contexts.

Acknowledging that femmes have an important role in our sexual culture is crucial. The concept, if not the language, has been with us from the earliest lesbian literature to the present.

Since the onset of feminism, the word femme has become almost an anathema to our culture. To the feminist theorist, "femme" is the same as "feminine", synonymous with the most stereotypical images of the heterosexual female. I believe we don't just stop there, but in fact we see femmes in relationship to heterosexual males. Some lesbians believe that femmes would be with men, except for some fluke, and that femme lesbians are women who have been lovers with men at different stages of their sexual lives. There is also a belief that these women are likely to "go back to men" at some point, betraying the lesbian sisterhood.

I wish it were unnecessary to point out how homophobic these ideas are. To describe, even in an unconscious way, a lesbian in relation to men is like comparing apples and prunes. What has lesbian energy to do with men? To link femmes and men, or femmes and straight women, is to deny their lesbian identities. As one woman said, "Butch/femme is the reverse of the straight relationship. Butches want to give and femmes want to receive."

As I said earlier, in our first survey, Marny Hall and I asked over 800 lesbians to describe femmes. The same stereotypical words appeared over and over: soft, feminine, passive, makeup, and pretty. This was from a group of whom twenty percent identified themselves as femme. Think of a specific femme lesbian right now, and ask yourself truthfully if you would describe her as someone who is soft, feminine, passive, wears makeup, and is pretty.

The connotation of these words strung together is almost frightening. Are we Donna Reed, Harriet Nelson? There aren't even straight women on television sit-coms who fit all these characteristics—especially the soft and passive parts. Give me a hint. Who came up with this truncated image? The heartbreak is that this was not a cross-section of people in 1950; this was a group of lesbians in 1988. Where is the impact of our own experience? What about what we know to be true? How does it happen that what we know is real is absolutely discounted?

One woman at the Toronto conference said, "I've always had a basic knowledge that I was femme. Yet there have been times when things about me scared me. Being too brash, forward, taking leadership. I'm not a shy, retiring flower. So am I really a femme? When I came out into S/M it was okay to be a femme on the bottom. When I was on top, I was in trouble. It took a long time to figure out that being on top and being butch were not the same thing. I could remain a femme and still be on top."

Discounting actual experiences is classic in the field of psychology. What the conscious mind knows now often can't compete with the persistent strength of the unconscious material from youth. These early messages overshadow what we experience in the here and now. For example, a woman who was abandoned as a child may not be able to tolerate her partner engaging in separate activities. Now, this has nothing to do with the partner actually abandoning her. It has nothing to do with the partner wanting to get out of the relationship. However, the woman may experience the same anxiety she felt when her mother did not care for her, when her mother stayed away for days at a time, was passed out from alcohol, or actually said how much of a burden her daughter was to her. The woman still fears that those closest to her will abandon her. When the old feelings are stimulated, the woman cannot differentiate between the traumas of the past and the reality of the present.

It's been my experience as a therapist that no matter how often the partner returns as scheduled or tries to accommodate the woman's fears, none of it counts. The woman herself has to find ways to cope with her anxiety. She must work with herself to remember that this partner is not her mother and will likely not behave as her mother did. This partner wants to be with her. Her fears of abandonment are old and inappropriate. This process of relearning takes time and energy. One has to be committed to making the change. In fact, the anxiety has to be debilitating enough in the present to make one *want* to change, since change is the last thing most people want to do.

Our imprinting in a lesbian-hating culture is no less powerful than our unconscious material from youth. Because we live in a homophobic society, we have all had imprinting about lesbianism and the evils of a non-heterosexual life. And unlike gay men, who at least have a visible culture, we often are eerily invisible as well. Every time a lesbian discovers who she is, she has to reinvent the wheel.

This cloak of secrecy surrounds our eroticism as well. Our sexual selves are defined in relationship to heterosexuals even though our sexual energy is different. The truth is that sex between women is really different from sex between women and men.

Learning to celebrate these differences has been a cornerstone of our movement. But it's also been frightening. It means coming out; it means talking frankly with our lovers about what we like sexually; it means reminding the straight culture, even in this time of repression, that our sex is different. It means admitting our sex is hot and sometimes not so hot. We need make no apologies about our sexual activities, yet we commonly hide them, are frightened by others' reactions to them, or don't have sex at all.

We know so little about our sexual attitudes or our sexual constructs, that when we describe other lesbians, we usually resort to the images already implanted in our minds. And in these images, femme lesbians are seen somehow as the ultimate example of the heterosexual woman who has gone astray. Perhaps she was abused once too often or had a terrible father. We all know the reasons we have been given for why women choose other women. It's never that there are women who want to be with women, who are absolutely lesbian. It's never that we have our own symbols, our own ways, our own deep attractions.

A Femme Heritage

Femme lesbians are given little room in the lesbian-feminist community to create an open identity that is strongly lesbian—powerful, vibrant, and far from passive. Femme lesbians have to struggle to claim space within the lesbian erotic circle. Although femme energy is firmly here, the prejudiced belief of the unconscious that femme lesbians are really straight women in disguise seems to override the conscious experience.

Perhaps the most painful part of our femme-hating is the direct correlation it has to woman hating. How has it happened that we've lost touch with positive characteristics of women? When the feminist movement began, there was a lot of flurry about the thrill of being woman-identified. In twenty years, the concept of women changed so drastically that the world changed with it. In the lesbian community, these changes coincided with the Stonewall Riots that forever changed the face of the gay movement as well. Dykes and faggots fought back on the streets of New York against policemen who were trying to arrest and hassle us one more time.

As our identity as dykes continued to emerge, our confusion deepened about what aspects of being female were worth keeping. With the arrogance of a new movement and ignorance of our own history, we dismissed the lesbian images of the past. Being an out, feminist lesbian seemed to offer so much more than before; we were reinventing how to be ourselves.

In the process, one of the unfortunate things that happened was that our strengths as women were devalued by our new movement. Something about the feminine became abhorrent. We weren't allowed to adorn ourselves even for other women. We weren't allowed to have children since it would interfere with our political work. We weren't supposed to wear dresses because they were the symbol of passivity. Even kindness, nurturing, mercy, and consideration became suspect. Our vision narrowed, and short hair, muscles, and confrontation were the standard of the day.

Somehow there wasn't room for the image of a strong femme lesbian. Yet, even in our lesbian history, it was the bar dykes and bar faggots who fought for gay rights the night of Stonewall. Faggot queens started the riot, and femme lesbians with their butch lovers rebelled as well. And for several decades before Stonewall, as Liz Kennedy pointed out the bar community was the "guts and the energy that exploded into gay liberation."

It was not the theorists who were fighting in the streets in 1969. The people who started the gay rights movement got lost in the reams of rhetoric that followed. Feminist lesbian intellectuals took over the reins and never looked back. Practically overnight, the femme image was no longer acceptable. We got out of the bars, into the streets, and suddenly there was no place for femmes and butches. No credit was given to them for catalyzing the movement. Once butches and femmes were no longer acceptable, their images faded from the sight of those who wrote and created theory, the rest of us began to fashion our lesbian identities with a significant part of our culture rendered invisible.

Femmes were especially affected. Dismissed as heterosexual clones, if they weren't with their butches, they weren't even *seen* as lesbian. That's an interesting concept in itself, not unlike how heterosexual women have been treated as if they have no identity apart from their husbands. Needless to say, this is completely offensive to femmes. A femme has always been recognizable to many lesbians, even in jeans and T-shirts, nude, standing on her head, or using a jackhammer. But because our concept of femme is so immersed in high heels and dresses, the depth of her real images is lost to culture, which has remanded femme to the back rooms of dingy bars in the '50s.

Femmes are women like Alice B. Toklas, Virginia Woolf, Eleanor Roosevelt, Natalie Barney, Margaret Anderson, Sappho—hardly a crew that we remember for their high heels and makeup. Hardly a gang that we would call passive. These women and others who never became famous were lost to femme history because people thought they were heterosexual, or because lesbians refused to call them femme. These women hung around with the most butch women in town, and in their own right were powerful and creative.

As Joan Nestle says, "When lesbian feminists and straight feminists told me 'You can't talk about that, you're reactionary, you're patriarchal,' I just want to say that for me, before there was feminism there were butches. Butches made me feel beautiful. They let me know my womanness was all right. They took my big hips, my fatness, my awkwardness, and they gave me back myself! I was always independent. I'd been taking care of myself since I was thirteen years old. It had nothing to do with the woman doing for me what I could do for myself. It had to do with a woman doing for me what in some ways I *couldn't* do for myself, which was to make me feel beautiful. And that's something I'll spend a lifetime saying thank you for."

Passing and Hiding

There is a great deal of pain within our community associated with the notion that femmes can "pass." We seem to believe passing is a necessity for work or child custody cases, or it is seen as treasonous to the lesbian nation.

There is a myth in the lesbian community that femmes are glad to pass, want to pass, and breathe a sigh of relief when they do pass. The idea that femmes do not want to be seen as lesbians is incredibly simplistic. Certainly there are times when all of us feel relieved not to be recognized as lesbians. We can move more easily through the world. In the survey in this book, two-thirds of the femmes thought they always passed. But their reactions to passing were ambivalent, with more of them believing they were living a lie than feeling relieved.

Passing makes you feel like you have bugs crawling under your skin. Femmes who pass against their will hate how they are treated—like unattached heterosexual women. Femmes who purposefully pass pay a high emotional price for concealing who they really are. The question of passing has such negative connotations that we almost have no way of talking about its impact on our community. We really don't know what it means to us to pass, or how it impacts our self esteem. We have a completely unfounded belief that passing solves all our problems. On the contrary, it sets up a constant reminder that we aren't who we seem to be to the rest of the world. We are invisibly passing through a sea of heterosexuals, lost to the world, living in a shadowland.

In my current survey, I asked whether the femmes (who comprised one-fifth of the sample) saw butch/femme as being linked to heterosexual male/female models. Half of them said 'somewhat', and another third said 'yes.' There was a strong fifth who said that it 'did not.' If we could divine the reasoning behind that "somewhat" category, it might tell us a lot about ourselves.

Following Jean Bolen's images, I also asked the femmes which goddess they most identified with and which most personified their most recent lover. The largest group (36 percent) saw themselves as Aphrodite, the goddess of love and beauty, governing a woman's enjoyment of love, sexuality, and - sensuality. 41 percent of the femmes saw their most recent lover as Artemis, the goddess of the hunt and moon—the independent, achievement-oriented feminine spirit. Each of the other goddesses got at least some votes, showing that femmes are diverse in their identities and choice of lovers.

Judy Grahn, in her wonderful book *Another Mother Tongue*, writes that "femme derives from femina (in French), 'woman' more literally 'who gives suck' or 'who nourishes.' " Grahn goes on to say that of course we don't see the word "homme", which is French for man, opposite femme in our descriptions. She says: "Gay characteristics...are far more original to the Gay underground culture than they are imitative of the above-ground heterosexual culture."

In putting "butch" opposite "femme" we create a distinctly lesbian erotic stance. It's my belief that we have so limited ourselves with the stereotyped definition of femme that we are unwilling to explore the complexities of our sexuality.

Sue Golding said, "I'm afraid that we're trying to dichotomize ourselves. 'Where do I fit butch, or where do I fit femme?' The '80s has made me rethink things in a complicated way. It is gender-bending times two. For me, it's less of a psychological thing than it is about irony and sex. The rigidity of the categories has been expanding because they are *living* categories. It's living right now, because we are making it happen."

Instead of trying to explore the complexities of our sexuality, however, we tend to stick to rigid stereotypes. Not unlike straight women interpreting what lesbians do, the new feminist lesbian of the '70s interpreted what butch/femmes were doing, as if they knew. Did anyone even bother to ask? There seemed to be a tremendous need to put down the existing butch/femme women, many of whom were working-class lesbians and lesbians of color, while at the same time putting on a pedestal the upper-class famous butch/femmes like Gertrude Stein and Alice B. Toklas, Natalie Barney and Romaine Brooks.

Since I didn't come out until 1975, I was a member of the feminist community that was rewriting history. Butch/femme women scared me. I learned that they were the outcasts; the ones who were unenlightened. Not unlike young lesbians today who are quickly reminded that they should be a "5" on the one to ten scale, I was taught that butch/femme women were those who would be left behind. They were not of us, they were "other." We were blazing on ahead with a vision they could not possibly understand.

But now the questions begin. How did we explain many of our cultural heroes? Take Judy Grahn and Pat Parker, both poets, writers, visionaries, and theorists of the lesbian community. They were as butch as anything. They were acceptable as long as we didn't mention that they were butch. And if *they* talked about it, I either didn't understand, ignored it, or denied it.

The heartbreak for me in looking back on those years is that I denied my femme self. I was told to change my clothing, my hair, and my stance if I was going to be a "real" lesbian, and I did just that. All the while I felt there was something wrong with me, rather like living in a huge cardboard box that would make me acceptable to my peers. I denied the fact that I too was part of the group that was being thrown out with yesterday's newspapers.

The women of the '50s either faded into the background, or they took on the new interpretation of their culture and, not unlike me, denied that they were ever part of it. If they acknowledged having been butch/femme, they admitted that they had updated their thinking and the new vision was the one they wanted to embrace.

Femmes were particularly despised in the lesbian-feminist movement. Within our community, butch has a much higher value than femme does. Those of us who were femme were quick to hide anything that might differentiate us. We learned how to change the oil in our cars, walk in "strong" ways, dress in ways that conformed. Yet femmes have kept part of their self esteem intact; almost all of them (80 percent) in this survey said they were comfortable, or even very comfortable, with being called femme. Less than one-fifth said they were uncomfortable. However, half of the femmes felt that androgyny was more highly valued in the lesbian community.

One example of a hidden butch/femme dynamic is in women's (lesbian) music. At that time, women's music was one of the most influential aspects of our lesbian culture. The most well-known lesbian musicians were Cris Williamson, Meg Christian, Margie Adam, and Alix Dobkin. Though they may disagree with me, in my opinion all of these women were on the butch side of androgynous. When I sat there as a fan, I would look at them and identify with their music, but not personally with their energy. We dressed alike, we all had short hair, we all had similar visions about the women's community, but I also saw them as other than me in certain subtle sexual ways. This difference was a very positive source of attraction.

Later, along came Holly Near. When she first started singing to women's (lesbian) audiences, she had long hair, wore skirts, and had a male accompanist. After the famous Women on Wheels concerts in 1975, she cut her hair, started wearing pants, and found a lesbian pianist. When she did this, I was certainly relieved. I had suspected, as had many others, that she was really a straight girl trying to make money from lesbians. When she came out publicly as a lesbian, we all breathed a collective sigh of relief.

I think it important to note that she got a standing ovation at the Michigan Women's Music Festival when she came out. She was the only musician I remember who received such a response for coming out. We were excited that a straight woman had come over to our side. However, now I believe our response had something to do with Holly being a femme. Now, she may not see herself as a femme, but the difference between her sexual energy and that of the first four I mentioned puts her definitely on the femme side of center.

The fact is that femmes have to declare themselves; they have to prove themselves in certain ways that androgynous or butch women don't—they are already in the club. Lesbians already see androgynous or butch women as role models, as acceptable images, that is, if they're not too butch.

I identified with Holly Near more than the other musicians; I recognized a similar sexual energy. I never fantasized about being lovers with her, as I had with all the others. When she conformed to the "right" dress, just as I had, it reinforced my femme capitulation to the androgynous imperative. And this made me happy. Looking back, I see I co-opted myself. But it was so necessary, so important to belong, that I was willing to do anything, including getting rid of the female accoutrements that made me feel good, that made me feel pretty, that made me feel sexually attractive, and that made me feel connected with my real self.

Interestingly, I was doing exactly as I had been taught to do as a woman in our culture. I was told that I should make myself pretty and presentable. In feminism, I was told to make myself presentable as a dyke, so I quit doing what for me felt pretty. I felt guilty about any transgression from the androgynous norm. At parties at a friend's house who still wore makeup, I'd sometimes allow myself to put it on, all the while making fun of myself. I secretly felt I looked pretty, and I found that other women responded to me. I didn't talk about that part of me; it was a betrayal of all I had learned about being a lesbian.

A friend of mine, Laura Rifkin, describes herself as a "high femme" and speaks movingly about growing up as a dyke femme girl. "In my experience, women who really identify around roles find it very liberating. It's a form of naming, just as we all found it very validating to name that we are lesbians, or name our class, or name our racial stuff. That naming was a liberating force that became a focus of how I view reality or know that what's important to me is seen. When I started to understand and identify with being a femme, it was also very liberating for me.

"Now, I did not grow up having a butch experience as a girl; I did grow up a femme lesbian. And I think that that's a reality that's not been named a whole lot in our lesbian culture or given a voice. I wasn't the tomboy; I wasn't a number of things that we've said 'this is what growing up lesbian is.' But I was a little lesbian femme.

"I'm very strong and very aggressive, and very assertive, and dominating, which is all top stuff to me, femme stuff. I see myself as a 'high femme.' This is a cultural term for me, I've used it for years and years. I'd be like a 9 or 10 on that femme scale. I like dressing feminine, not always, but I like that. I like looking a certain way. I'm very attracted to a butch woman, that does it for me.

"To me as a high femme, it's intrinsically comfortable to identify as femme. I have friends who are lower on that scale and it doesn't mean so much to them. But to me, it's personally meaningful. Growing up as a real strong aggressive femme girl, there's no voice for me in the lesbian movement. There isn't. You know, I'm invisible. It's like, if you're not a butch, if you don't look butch, if you don't act butch, you must be straight. You're going to go straight once you are out. My reality has been invisible for a long time. At the same time, I also didn't suffer certain oppressions that a lot of my lovers have suffered. I pass. But passing was very painful because I didn't feel straight. I was a femme girl, okay, but I wasn't straight, and nobody ever thought I was straight who was straight themselves. They knew I was different because I was a lesbian.

"When I was growing up, I didn't wear makeup; I didn't shave my legs; I didn't wear dresses; I wasn't interested in any of those things. So, it's only as a lesbian where I feel the safety within my own culture to express those things, where I can do that."

Femme Sex

The kind of sexual energy I felt for the (to me) butch members of the androgynous women's music scene is key to understanding different nuances in lesbian sexuality. If we apply stereotypes to femmes in general, we certainly apply them to our visions of femme sex.

Joan Nestle (in *A Restricted Country*) says: "In bed, the erotic implications of the total relationship only became clearer. My hands and lips did what felt comfortable for me to do. I did not limit my sexual responses because I was a femme. I went down on my lovers to catch them in my mouth and to celebrate their strength, their caring for me."

This femme sexual energy does not mean that femmes don't initiate, have limitations, only want to be made love to, or don't want to make love to their partners. Often, quite the opposite is true. The range of what femmes actually do sexually is as varied as all the women in the lesbian nation. The difficulty comes from trying to define what makes femme sexual energy different from that of androgynous, butch, or other women on the lesbian continuum.

In fact, in this survey, all four of the groups (femmes, butches, androgynous, and none of the above) had extremely similar answers about sex. This included: how often they initiated sex, how often they responded to their lover initiating, entered their lover's vagina and anus, used a dildo, had orgasms, had lovers who had orgasms, gave and received oral sex. Femmes were more likely to have started consensual sex with girls and women earlier in their lives (more before the age of ten). They were also more likely to enter their lover's vagina during sex than any of the three other groups. Femme sexuality may be a stance, but it's not a prescribed set of actions or activities.

Jewelle Gomez says, "I think a really interesting way to try to place yourself is to figure out what your fantasy is, and where you place yourself within a fantasy. A lot of us are terribly afraid of our own fantasies and try to proscribe them and make them correct. But I think if you look at your basic and big fantasies, and where you put yourself in them, they will tell you a lot about your hungers and your powers."

A butch friend of mine swears when she is in a lover relationship that she is androgynous (even though her lovers are femme in my humble opinion). But when she is single, she declares her butchness. She says that all she has to do is go to a lesbian gathering and look butch and aloof, and the femme women will initiate everything else. This is how she always finds her next lover.

Another woman's comment gives the femme side of that story: "Most butches that I've experienced have played hard-to-get, or like 'maybe I'm interested', kind of nonchalant. And that hooks into what I feel is a natural aggressive part of myself. I mean, if I'm attracted, I will go for it. But I'm always the one who has initiated the relationships or the affairs, or whatever. I have never had a butch come on to me who was going to follow through with it, you know. I've been flirted with at parties and stuff like that, but they never mean it. I mean, they never go for it. I'm always the one."

Sue Golding describes another version of this femme aggression. "The other day I was on this couch with this very femme, very beautiful woman. She said she didn't want to have sex, she didn't want to do it. So I said, 'Fine, you know, it's fine.' Then she proceeded to seduce me. I was very impressed and so I talked to my resident femme who I go talk to about these things. I asked her could she explain this. The woman laughed at me. She said 'You just picked a good femme!' "

Sue Golding has also said, "There are all different kinds of femmes. There are submissive femmes, dominant femmes, bitch-femmes—which is a sexual term." If we think of femme sexuality as being truly fluid, not limited in either specific activities or in stance, then what does define some of the essential pull that draws femme and butch to each other?

Deb Edel has described that powerful force. "I call that balance between butch and femme as butch power and femme hunger. I'm talking about sexuality specifically. Not general life presentations. I sense that there is a great difference in sexuality, in sexual need, in sexual expression between butches and femmes."

And Joan Nestle goes on to develop that image. "I always knew that I was a femme and that I was hungry. I was insatiable. Temporarily insatiable—sometimes for only very short periods of time. When I met a butch there was something in them that something in me knew. We came together with some kind of basic, prehistoric foreknowledge of each other. Somehow psychological, spiritual, physical also. Very ultimately physical. I could fall apart with some-one like that. I could trust myself to them. They would be able to make it happen, take care of me. They had the power to do that, I had the hunger to let them. And probably always will."

Another woman from Toronto continues, "Butches imagine themselves in a movie scene as the man kissing the woman. But for me, where could I imagine myself? If I didn't want to be the man kissing the woman, but I didn't want to kiss the man either, who did I want to kiss? I want to see that hunger for me from a woman. A butch woman is a woman who recognizes that and gives it to me. I want to be the woman a woman always wanted. I want to be that powerful inside a sexual system that's mine. To see her desire for me, that extraordinary power that she'll take it, gives me my sexual hunger. I need the dynamic in order to have sexuality. I think there's a whole lot of variety out there about butch power and femme hunger. I think of all the women I went home with, who for some reason it just didn't work, didn't click, didn't move. Did they have another way of imagining that power and that hunger? But it's an extraordinarily erotic idea. When I walk into a group, I use it all the time. I want to know who's going to look. I want to know whether I can hook into that in some way that's deeply queer."

One of the ironies of hunger is that it has a power all its own. And that's the power of femme sexuality.

Doing It or Getting Done To

When I was in Los Angeles in 1989, I talked with Robin Tyler and Jeanne Cordova. (Both are quite confirmed butches, although Jeanne has recently begun carrying a purse. Somehow, the way she flings it makes me think this is an experiment gone too far.) They have a theory that each woman likes to initiate and receive sex to a differing degree. They suggest that lesbians could rate themselves according to how often they prefer to be made love to (e.g., 60 percent); versus how often they like to make love to their partner (40 percent, in this case). This could relieve a major source of tension in relationships. (Perhaps we should do that before we get together so that we are compatible. But I suspect we'd prefer to leave it to guesswork and then torture each other for not being all we want.) Robin and Jeanne feel that each woman has different preferences in this regard, not necessarily divided between butches and femmes, and this spectrum of initiation/receptivity has an equally profound impact on relationships.

I think this issue of receptivity is so taboo in the lesbian community that if we talk about it at all, we do so only in the privacy of our own bedrooms. We are all supposed to be the same sexually. We're supposed to give and receive equally, and if we don't, we're betraying our feminist roots. I think we also have this fear that if we like to make love to our partner more than we like to be made love to, we are being male. Some women are stigmatized for not being able to be vulnerable enough to receive. Conversely, if we like to receive love-making more than give it, we fear we are hopelessly female. I suspect these women's partners take this as a personal affront, rather than simply a preference. No matter how much we want to be equal, for many lesbians this isn't the case. If we were able to tell the truth about what we want, our sexual lives could be so enhanced. Imagine knowing what you want all the time. Imagine the possibilities in any given moment if you know exactly what you want.

The vulnerability is different, but equally present, whether you are making love to someone or receiving their love-making. Some women feel more vulnerable being made love to and others feel more vulnerable when they are making love to their partner. This openness can be present for both partners.

There is a special vulnerability in trying to please another sexually. You approach her in different ways; she may or may not respond to you. And if you are the receptive partner, you are acutely aware that your partner is trying to please you. You are vulnerable in a more passive position, even if you are active in your acceptance of pleasure.

It can't be said often enough that these poles do not necessarily fall along butch/femme lines. I believe different women feel more in control, and thus more comfortable, in one position or the other. You are not always in control because you are making love to someone; in fact, the two of you share a control of the sexual scene. Even in S/M, the surrender is planned, whether verbally or nonverbally. The woman who "gives in" controls the scene. No surrender, no scene. Being able to be vulnerable to the excitement of either position is the real gift, whether you are making love to your partner or whether you are receiving your partner.

This scale of desire is a visceral one, deep inside oneself. As one woman at Toronto said, "I tend to see things very tactilely. When I think of someone's body, I think of touching it, pulling on it, tweaking it, slobbering all over it.

I don't actually discount the reverse, it's just that I don't think of it that way until afterwards, until I've been all over this body."

Femme Energy

So what then is the difference in energy for femme women? I know that I know a femme lesbian when I see one. And I know that it has nothing to do with our estrogen versus androgen levels. A femme lesbian doctor friend of mine once did a research project on the androgen levels of women to see if there was any difference between straight women and lesbians. She also wanted to tell her lesbian friends if there was a difference between femme and butch lesbians. Years later, her butch partner was still reporting the results with surprise and a bit of disgust: her femme lover had almost identical androgen levels to her.

So if there is no difference in our initiating, no difference in what we do (there are even femmes who specialize in strap-on dildos—just check out *Susie Sexpert's Lesbian Sex World),* no difference in our hormones, why is it that I can tell a femme or a butch from across the room?

Femmes possess a certain type of energy. I like to swish around in my skirts. I even like to swish around in my jeans. If panty hose weren't such a drag and I didn't get cold, I'd probably wear skirts all the time. I love to wear earrings that catch others' attention. Oh yeah, I know I also like to wear them for myself, but the truth is that I wear them for others to see. I don't wear earrings around my house if I'm not going out. Lesbians who are more evolved might, but I don't.

When I solicit attention from others, there is a difference between the femmes, who are checking out my style to see what they might try too, and the butches who are attracted to the display, who enjoy the presentation. Not that the femmes I see don't please me in their presentation. But I'm looking at them like a sister, feeling in some deep way we are the same. I'm enjoying a narcissistic pleasure. When I am enjoying the display of a butch, I'm appreciating as an observer of the "other." When I am attracted to a butch woman, I want to get into her skin— literally. I want to know her in the carnal sense. I already know my femme sisters. There is a mystery about the butch woman that I crave being in on, a way of relating to her body, to animal instincts different from my own.

It's not just butch dress. It's the stance. There is something about that bend at the hip in a nonchalant way that makes me weak-kneed. There is something about taking up physical space, something about being in her body in a way that I just don't do, and it's not just because I have no earth in my chart.

There is a valence difference between the femme and the butch. Valence is "the degree of combining power, ...of attractiveness, an individual, activity, or object possesses." There is a valence difference between each of the numbers on the butch/ femme scale. I think that valence is what attracts us or repels us from one another.

Each of us has the capacity to "combine" with another. There's an almost chemical interaction that is a combination of many things: height, weight, race, age, body type, astrological sign, eye color or shape, hair, brains, sensitivity, class, creativity, and sexual energies. I am certainly not attracted to every butch, but in the women I am attracted to, it's their butch energy that draws me to them, even if they themselves would identify as an androgynous woman.

I asked the lesbians who answered my survey to choose any three words to describe what attracts them to butches, femmes, and androgynous women. I specifically asked femmes to report what they found erotic about butches. The most frequently mentioned (34 percent) aspect was that butches are strong. The other most common aspects that femmes found attractive in butches were: assertiveness, confidence, independence, and self-confidence.

How do I describe this energy, this femme energy? A certain lightness, a certain sparkle, a certain interest in every single little detail about what my best friend said to that person she met in the grocery store. A connection to gossip columns filled with people I don't know and will never meet. I don't think it's just because of my co-dependency that I enjoy collecting data about people I don't know, famous or not. I find that most femme women I meet want to talk about all the dirt they've ever heard.

Then there's that certain way of enticing a lover. Presenting myself as available in particular ways that match up with her ways of approaching. Not in a passive way at all. In fact, it's about as active as a woman can get. I am active in my pursuit of my lover.

Though it's much too easily reduced to stereotypes, a lot of femmes I talked with described femme energy in terms of connecting with "the other." If we remember that these poles of difference are happening among women, within the realm of women's connectedness, then the differences these lesbians describe may be a positive source of attraction to someone who is *not* just like themselves.

In this survey, I asked women to categorize their activities while in a couple. Would they most likely be the initiator, the responder, or would it depend upon the situation? The femmes were the most likely to initiate cleaning and decorating the house, doing childcare, organizing social activities, and doing the actual socializing. Wouldn't you just know it, right when we thought we'd trounced those stereotypes of "femmes as heterosexual women." So there you have it: femmes really don't work on their cars (but who does these days?). Fourteen percent of femmes did say they were more likely to initiate car repairs. And at least they said they didn't initiate cooking most of the time. It's important to note that almost half of the femmes said it would depend on the situation whether they intiated *any* of these activities. These activities are not set in stone for all femmes. However, looking at what makes femmes different can be a source of empowerment.

One couple talked to me about the dynamics between them.

"My experience is that femmes tend to really want to talk about the relationship. We like to process, we want to talk about things, we want to share our feelings. And butches are more likely to say 'Why don't you give it time, honey, and see how it goes?' Of course, I've known butches who are talkers, but it's less fluid.

"I rely on my butch lover to ultimately take care of me, since I would spill my emotions all over everyone and let them know everything in great detail. I know that somehow, ultimately she's going to manage to put me back together. She's going to make boundaries and limits; I think she kind of does the boundary caretaking in our relationship...and I don't think she relies on me to do the same thing."

"I don't. And I should say that that is comfortable for me, because it's not comfortable for me to be focused on it that way. I'm not nearly as open as I'd want to be. I tend to be more stuck or keep things inside. But one of the things that makes butch/femme different from masculine/feminine, is that it's a much more complex thing. As a butch, I'm pragmatic *and* nurturing."

Amber Hollibaugh talks about trying to form a Femme Group in New York City, and what they ran into.

"How do femmes define themselves? Society has created a place for femmes to be, because we were supposed to be femmes—be nurturing. We didn't have to learn to accept that, we had to learn to accept it as feminists! Women are also taught to talk more and to share, to rely on a woman-to-woman system of support. The reason I don't think the 'femme group' worked as a group is that whatever came up in the meeting, I had already been on the phone to all the members the week before. Because I already use them as friends. We were in the habit of communicating, defining ourselves, exploring what we meant on a crisis-to-crisis, event-to-event basis. When we began to meet around those same issues, we found it was almost ridiculous because we were already sharing all those things.

"There was a real problem trying to form a femme group like the butch group. It was hard to figure out who was a femme, how to approach people, since often it isn't even something you can tell. Especially in the lesbian-feminist community. The most unlikely people have come up to me and said: 'Oh god, I'm a femme, it's so incredible to meet another femme!' I would not have picked them out as femmes. It's not such a simple thing as being able to identify someone. It's about how one imagines oneself inside. Finding a lover then to make that work is a very intricate thing. My lover was approached to join the 'B-Group' and was dumbfounded. She had never perceived of herself as a butch. To me, she is the personification of a butch. But inside she doesn't see herself or her behavior that way.

"In my experience, many more butches are involved with each other than are femmes to femmes. It's still very hard for butches to get together, but it's much more rare to ever see femme-femme couples, or to even hear that discussion among femmes. Whereas, I'd see butches and all of a sudden there'd be some very heavy sexual thing happening between them. I've only been involved in one relationship with another femme and it lasted for two weeks! We really could not figure out how to give each other what we wanted from a lover. Even though we were powerfully attracted to something about the other, it just didn't work for us."

What 589 Lesbians Think About Femmes

Given the complex vibrancy of this femme energy, when I look at the descriptions of femmes in the two surveys, I'm still amazed. I guess one might perceive feminine, pretty, and soft as not too negative, but combined with passive and wears makeup, it's almost hard to believe that the respondents were lesbians and not straight people from the bible belt.

As I already discussed, when I asked lesbians on my latest survey to list three attributes from the Bem Inventory to describe femmes, the list is not particularly offensive (although there are some uncomfortable attributes given to femmes that were not given to either butches or androgynous women). What is disarming is what is absent. I'm really offended at how we *don't* see femmes. I almost expected to see someone write in "hysterical", "needs smelling salts at political debates", or "not capable of voting because they can't think."

We have pushed femme from our world, ignored our erotic energy, and many times acted as if there are no differences between lesbians, that we are all the same. Nothing could be further from the truth. And nothing could be more painful than trying to stop being who we are. This is the time for us to reclaim what we have tried to repress and to develop language that fits us today. This is the time for lesbians to be lesbians. Those of us who know we're femmes can re-emerge from our closets and let the world know the '90s version of femme eroticism. There *is* such a thing as an assertive, aggressive, soft, angry, nurturing, loving, exciting, sexual, powerful, squishy femme.

"There is an aesthetic thing that goes on in butch/femme energy, and a sexual thing—it's cultural and historical—"

"And it's a social thing—"

"Then there's myths that we have—"

"I have this idea about the myths, if we would say what the myths are, what we mean by butch and femme, without having to apply it to ourselves or say 'I'm femme,' then I think we can figure out what it means in our culture."

"I definitely think there are myths about what those roles are about. I don't think I can name them out loud; it would be hard for me to put into a sentence 'this is what a femme is,' but I know what a femme is."

"Exactly, you know it."

"And I know a butch when I see one."

"That's right. And I know one when I see one."

"You are a butch-o-meter."

"You're not limited by being a butch or a femme, but I bet you know what that means to you."

"You're saying butch and femme is about sex."

"Yeah."

We don't have a specific definition of what a femme is, but in fact, we have so many words to define it, to talk about it, you can't get us to shut up."

"Good titles for the book: 'Femmes in Demand', 'Butches in Retreat', 'The Armored Butch', 'Femme Not Straight.' "

You know how you said femmes are oppressed in the lesbian community? Well femmes are also in demand. I've been at parties where there's a lot of butches around and they are looking for femmes."

"Yeah, the femme's the one who gets the butch into the position where sex is going to happen."

"When I hear a woman talk who has really claimed butch and femme and named it—I think it's thrilling! I don't care what the fuck it is. It doesn't matter to me. To hear a femme talk and take pride gives me pride in my lesbianism. Because I don't identify in the same way with those roles doesn't in any way negate the fact that butch and femme is alive and well, obviously, we wouldn't have hours of discussion if it weren't valid in our community."

"Just because we name and define something doesn't mean we have to invalidate anything else."

"I think that's where we get in a polarized, male kind of thinking. If we name it, then we all have to define ourselves as it, and therefore there's no more room."

"Or if you don't define yourself as what has been defined, then you're not okay. If you don't have a definition for yourself then you're lost."

"We went around the room, rating ourselves, and rating each other. For those of us who were more femme, when we got a higher butch vote, we felt great. But those butches who got a femme vote—"

"Uh-oh"

"—they were freaked out."

"That's about woman hatred."

"Absolutely."

"When we were doing it, I got mad that you got higher butch scores than I did."

"She got furious."

"Not because I minded getting my scores, but I was mad that you got higher scores because they clearly didn't know who you were. And other women got mad about their lovers getting 'better' or more butch scores than they thought they should, or than they themselves got."

"Femmes are strong. Femmes are lesbians. Femmes are aggressive. Femmes are competant."

"You can count on them."

CHAPTER SIX

Butches Are Women Too

The butch lesbian often enjoys a certain type of power within our community. The old-fashioned butch brought a vision of strength and a particular ability to take up space—usually reserved by men—that was appealing to those of us in the androgynous movement. "Androgynous" appearance was more typical of the traditional butch than it was of the traditional femme. Even today, butch lesbians enjoy a certain kind of honor in the community; they represent "real" dykes.

Butches, however, are often the specific target of homophobic attacks from the world at large. They have been the brunt of jokes about bull-daggers, biker dykes, bar dykes, etc., and are the ones most likely to take the heat of the heterosexual community. Many heterosexuals believe stereotypical butches are the only lesbians; meanwhile homophobes charge that butches drive testosterone-poisoned young men to batter women in the street or that butches are to blame for forcing sweet young things into lesbianism. These lesbians, heterosexuals believe, are the ones that run away with the neighbor's wife. Just as I was finishing this book, a nationally syndicated "news" story reported that Margaret Court (a former tennis pro) had accused Martina Navratilova of corrupting innocent young girls on the tennis circuit. This took place only one week after Navratilova won her record ninth Wimbledon singles title. To homophobes, butches are the picture of femaleness gone awry, women who are not truly women. And if they're not "feminine", then they must be trying to be men.

The survey reported in this book showed that fifteen percent of the lesbians identified as butch. When these women were asked how they felt about being called butch, two-thirds felt comfortable, or very comfortable, in spite of the homophobia coming their way. Over half the women in the survey who identified as androgynous were uncomfortable or very uncomfortable being called butches. This percentage didn't change much when the androgynous women were asked how they liked being called femme. There was an equal distaste.

As a good lesbian, I would like to believe that our community does not believe these stereotypical images of butches and in fact denounces them at every turn. However, I have heard too many comments from lesbians who characterize butches in the same manner as straight society. I've actually heard lesbians say: "Why do they have to dress like men? They give us a bad name." Or "They should stay away from straight women, they have no business messing with them." In February of 1988, I was on the Oprah Winfrey Show with six other lesbians. Three of the women were newly out, having left long-time heterosexual relationships. The other three were separatist lesbians. The entire show centered on how the separatist lesbians hated men. No matter how much these women stated that lesbianism was about loving women, not hating men, the audience and Oprah were uninterested. This reaction was to be expected, but as I traveled around the country afterwards, I found that the reactions from lesbians were all too similar.

"Why did those women go on national television and look so unkempt?" The truth was the women had on clean, pressed clothes. They were in T-shirts and jeans with tennis shoes. Other comments included: "Why did that one separatist put her feet on the chair? She was just rude." "You were the best thing on the show. My mother watched it and didn't even know you were a lesbian." "I liked the lesbians who had just come out, but those other ones who hated men, I just couldn't stand them."

These are just a sample of the comments, and there were many others. It was painful to hear our own homophobia in these statements. The speakers assumed I would agree, probably because I went on the program dressed in a skirt. It didn't hurt that I'm femme and able to pass as straight. Now, I didn't pass on the show: in fact, I was quite clear that I'm a lesbian. They showed my books *Lesbian Sex* and *Lesbian Passion* on the screen. I too said that lesbianism had nothing to do with men and that, in fact, straight women may have more problems with men because they are intimately connected to men in a way lesbians are not. My views were remarkably similar to those of the separatists.

One might say I got away with little criticism because I wasn't a separatist, but I think it's because I went on national television looking like the daughter every mother wants. I looked different from a stereotypical lesbian. Heterosexuals and homosexuals alike were pleased with my appearance. It's when I analyze this that I get so sad. Why is it that we too want lesbians to look like everyone else? So heterosexuals will like us? Why is it that when butches or the butch-of-center lesbians get on national television, even lesbians are afraid of what these women represent?

When we talk from real experience, we can touch both the pains and the joys of being lesbians out in the world. Yet, when we talk about butches, sometimes we don't draw on real experience. Instead, we put "butch" into the category of "other." We rarely acknowledge the power, sexuality, and inherent womanness of butches. Even in our own community, these women are separated out and seen as something other than what we have been taught women should be. Some of the comments women wrote on my survey included:

"The idea of butch lesbians actually makes me sick. How do they get that way?"

"Butch women in the past were not anything like lesbians today, we are prettier."

"I don't know, I just can't relate to that wanting to look like a man trip."

Much of this criticism has a superior tone that raises an ugly specter. Esther Newton talks about the complex intertwining of class and identity. "I don't come from a working-class background, but having come out in working-class bars, I'm very aware of the working-class being a bedrock of gay culture. Those are the people who could be

out, and were out, and [who] took the shit. And that's a part
of me. Class and gender identity is a very big question. And
there's a tremendously strong relationship between the two
to this day."

As I said earlier, when asked to describe butch lesbians, the
women in my survey said: strong, tough, aggressive, masculine.
Just as with the words to describe femme, the separate words
(save for the "masculine" epithet) are not a problem. But all four
words together give me a picture of a linebacker for the 49ers, not
a lesbian. Yet we continue in our own community to talk about
butch in this framework. We assume butches are associated with
"male."

Judy Grahn in *Another Mother Tongue* writes: "...the butch is,
ceremonially speaking, Puck. Cross-dressing is a magical function,
and the butch is the equivalent of the traditional cross-dresser
who may also become a magical/shaman of the tribe. She is the
one who cross-dresses, becomes a hunter or a soothsayer or a
prophet or the first woman in a formerly all-male occupation. She
keeps the idea of biological destiny untenable." The idea that
butch women "cross-dress" and resemble men would be accepted
without argument. But adding to it the notion that this kind of
dress on a woman is powerful, revolutionary, and, in fact, spiritual
would raise the hackles of many lesbians. Unfortunately, there is
almost no way for us to get past our own homophobia and our
submersion in a male-dominated culture to see these clothes in a
neutral manner. The idea that butch women could indeed be
"Puck"—a character who is magical and spiritual—is hard for us
to comprehend.

I remember my first lover remarking, "Who said these were
men's clothes?" What an enormous impact that simple statement
had not only on my ideas of dress, but also on my growing
conviction that women could do, wear, or say anything they
wanted. I'm convinced that butch lesbians helped change the
face of womanhood while being told they were debasing it.

As the '70s and '80s progressed, there were many dyke
styles that became totally acceptable for all women. Pants—yes,
there really was a time when women didn't wear pants everywhere—ties, bolos, double-breasted suit coats, pantsuits, work
boots, big black shoes with thick soles, crew cut or buzzed hair,

muscle T's, one earring, the "natural look" (no makeup, no hair spray), not carrying a purse, tennis shoes for everyday wear, tuxedos for formal wear. This list goes on, too many to name.

During this time, the jobs women held, the subjects women studied in school, the ways in which women began to decide consciously if they wanted children or not, the concept that women could function on their own and be independent of men—all of these were influenced strongly by the butch lesbian who did drive a truck, became an auto mechanic or a carpenter, studied math or science, didn't want children, felt totally fulfilled without men, wore what she wanted, and was independent within the patriarchal culture.

There were certainly straight women who did these things, but it was the butch lesbian who was the critical mass for the walls around women to topple. Once we openly were choosing women as lovers, once we were freeing ourselves from the bonds of male oppression, once we were taking care of our own, women everywhere could take courage.

The lesbians who were the most visible and took the most heat showed the rest of us the way. The result of this new freedom was that while many of us wanted the goodies, we also wanted to make ourselves acceptable to the majority culture as well. To do this, we had to separate ourselves from the butch—we had to make her "other."

Six years ago, a butch friend of mine became pregnant by insemination. During her eighth month, she got a pink maternity top that had "butches can wear pink" printed on it. It was a great spoof, funny precisely because wearing pink and being pregnant was *not* traditionally expected of a butch. We expect that butch women wear pants and short hair, and maybe their lovers get pregnant, but not them. We have a whole set of expectations for the butch lesbian.

In the July/August 1979 issue of *The Lesbian Tide*, there was the first of a two-part series on butch/femme. That issue quotes a woman named Marianne who identifies as a butch:
"...on a very deep level many butches are confused about the fact and don't like the reality that their bodies are female.... ...Here you are growing up this tiny child dyke subconsciously emulating the male figures in your

household for some ten years and then you hit puberty and find yourself taking on a body that clashes with your self-perception as a left-over tomboy. It's enough to rattle your adolescent development profoundly. Being an adolescent butch without feminism—that is, after you've discovered that you are a woman, but before you've understood that you can be a woman and not like boys—it's hard to know just what you are."

There have been times in my life when I would have said, "Hey, this is a reaction to what we think butch women are supposed to be; this is what we have been taught." I would have been quick to say: "Just wait a minute, butch women aren't confused about gender. We made this up." The woman with the pink maternity shirt also felt that all her life she had identified with men and had somehow been betrayed by growing up to be a girl. It took her awhile to figure out that she could be with girls. She also wanted to be a mother and figuring out how to do *that* was not an easy task for her.

In fact, I have been talking with butch women who say that they always wanted to have children but knew they didn't want to be mothers. This is very confusing to them. These women said they really wanted to do the "father" role and didn't know how to voice that desire. The result for many was that they cut themselves off from the idea of having children. In my survey three percent of the women overall said they played a "fathering" role in their children's lives. When broken down by identity, six percent of the butch women play this role. These are very small numbers, but consider that these numbers correspond to a question we were never allowed to ask. We aren't supposed to want to fit any of the roles that men commonly do, much less remake those roles in dyke fashion. I wonder how many other configurations we might have within our chosen families and our community if we allowed ourselves to make choices that are gender-free.

The Girls and The Boys

In my son's elementary school there are several young girls who look like future dykes of America. They dress the way the boys dress. They play sports the way the boys play: with a sense that they are going on from here to be athletes, not in the more casual way that girls are now expected to play soccer or other sports.

My son is at the age eight when boys and girls do not mix socially. However, there seem to be certain exceptions, especially for one young girl who is much more in the boy culture than the girl culture. When I ask how come she gets to be a part of the boy scene, he says to me, "She's not like a girl, Mom. She does boy things." Now interestingly, there are many girls in that school who "do boy things," but I know what he is talking about. She is not "of" the girls, and girls are not her companions, except the other girls who are in the boy category.

This story is one I have heard from butch lesbians for years. They grew up not being "of" the girls, but in addition, at a certain point in their lives, they were also not "of" the boys. They may have been kicked out by the boys, or been told by grownups that girls weren't supposed to play rough, or they may have decided themselves that their boy companions were too different. Whatever reason, the alienation these baby butches felt was often tremendous. If they didn't have a group of girls like them, they were left out of both the clubs.

As one butch lesbian told me: "I was the best baseball player in our neighborhood. The boys always wanted me on their team. I was better than my brothers. Then when we all got old enough to play Little League, I wasn't allowed because I was a girl. I used to hang on the Cyclone fence and cry because I couldn't play. The boys quit asking me to play in the neighborhood too. I was left in the dust."

When these women figured out that girls were going to be their love objects, it may or may not have helped. As a butch woman once told me:

"Once I discovered that I actually was fantasizing in a sexual way about the girl who sat beside me at school, I was thrilled. The problem was, I was just as freaked out that I wasn't supposed to be doing this. While she became the vessel for my sexual feelings, I knew I couldn't take her to the prom or anything. So on one hand I was happy, and on the other I felt even more isolated."

Deb Edel describes her emerging butch identity. "I came out about 1970 into a lesbian-feminist world. I looked very different than now. Yet I knew in myself that there was something that made me very different emotionally than many of the women around me. There was a manner, a style, a feeling inside myself. When I heard the word 'butch', it was an act of coming home. I'd found a place and a name, a label, an identity that in some ways was as strong and as total to me as the word lesbian. I was the one growing up who wanted to be James Dean, when my friends all wanted to have affairs with James Dean. I was the one who wanted to be Montgomery Clift. Now it's interesting to me that I chose two clearly gay-identified men. Even as a child I knew I was different. "

The problem is not that butch women are men or want to be men. The problem is that as adolescents there is no other way of being. And similarly, when we talk about butches now, our socialization encourages us to assign people to categories that already exist in the culture. So we start thinking of butch/femme as male/female rather than as a distinctly lesbian cultural phenomenon.

The Stone Butch

Our stuck images of both butch and femme lesbians causes us problems on many fronts. It's time to update our ideas. Since we don't expect women today to act as they did in the 1950s, and we are furious when men act in ways that reflect that era, why would we expect butch lesbians to continue to portray an inaccurate stereotype of the '50s? Of course some women find this a soothing fantasy. Many lesbians have told me that they liked it better in the '50s because everything seemed clear then. In fact, a woman quoted in the *Lesbian Tide* article stated:

"Old gays...see roles as stabilizing relationships.... When roles are undefined there tends to be psychic, emotional and sexual confusion, which results in a confused relationship...."

In the same issue, another woman who identifies as femme discussed her perception of the "stone" butch sexuality: "...it seems to me that butches like to make love to other women but they do not like, want, or enjoy having women make love to them.... For them, giving up control seems to be the key problem. They have a concept that weakness is involved."

Instead of stigmatizing the butches of the '50s, we might be able to learn something from them in the sexual arena. The most notable characteristic of the so-called "stone butch" women was that they exclusively made love to their partners. That is, their partners did not make love to them. It's very unpopular today to announce that this is how you want to conduct your sex life. Yet, women still do. Without the categorizations of the '50s, we don't have a term that acknowledges this desire and makes it acceptable. Instead, we make it into something pathological instead of a genuine preference.

As a sex therapist and educator, I know this is something that many women secretly wish for—making love to a woman is all they want to do. Having a partner make love to them does not feel nearly as good. There is, in fact, a powerful sexuality that can build up between the active partner and the receptive one. Honoring these differences can help keep a sexual relationship exciting over time.

In the femme chapter I talked about having a scale of initiating/receptivity that's separate from a butch/femme scale. What the "stone butch" concept offers us is a butch twist on all this. A butch filled with desire, a butch with style and technique, loving an insatiably hungry femme generates a powerful sexual force. Lesbians often feel guilty about not wanting total equality in the sexual arena. We are unwilling to explore the possibility that while some women may want almost exclusively to be made love to, others prefer to make love to their partners. It's my belief that as lesbians we have been so oppressed, both by our own community and the homophobic world that surrounds us, and we are so frightened of being seen as male-identified, sick, or wrong, that we have become unwilling to tell the truth about our sexuality. What results is a distortion of the richness of lesbian sex. Our sex lives become two-dimensional, with many rules to keep us within the bounds of current favor. Instead of this lock-step march, we can choose a rich world of erotic possibilities.

Myth and Reality

When we describe butches as tough, strong and aggressive, there is both myth and reality going on. Like all stereotypes, ours are fashioned with some truth. The problem arises when we take those truths and make them rigid realities. This is a common problem when any outside group tries to define a culture it doesn't understand. While it's true that butch lesbians may have grown up more identified with boys than with girls, given the choices available, this was a reasonable response.

In fact, when asked which activities they initiate most in a couple, the butches said: paying bills, working in the yard and on the car, and dancing. Sounds a little like Dad to me. But they also saw themselves as more likely to initiate cooking. One-third to one-half of the butches did say that they did these activities depending on the situation (as well as other activities such as decorating or cleaning the house, doing childcare, etc.) That so many lesbians said it "depended on the situation" shows the fluid nature of lesbians, no matter what their identity.

To generalize from that and say that all butches act like men, dress like men, want to make love to women like men, is an extreme exaggeration. Butch lesbians are, after all, women with their own unique connection to other women—one that men simply cannot have.

Esther Newton describes a group that began meeting in New York City in 1984. "In the beginning, we referred to it as the 'B-Group' because most of us had too much trouble saying the word 'butch.' It was a very difficult identity to come to terms with for many of us. It's all white, with working-, middle-, and upper middle-class women. We have an age spread from 20s to 40s. We have some who are old gay, who came out prefeminist movement, and some who are new gay.

"I joined the group to have support to come out as a butch, to come to terms with that identity and the conflict between that and dominant lesbian-feminist ideology. We found we had a lack of social skills, we didn't have anyone there to kind of mediate and make small talk. Most of us had difficulties talking about our feelings, talking personally.

"We tend to have topics. A primary one is 'What is butch?' 'Am I butch enough to be in this group?' There's a whole list of becauses: I wasn't gay before the movement. I'm not tall enough. You're butcher than I am. What is butch, a way of dressing? A way you feel inside? Sex? That's been the biggest topic. Are there internal problems to being butch? Over-control? Do you wish you could cry more? Another is passing as a man, since two of the women in the group can pass and do very frequently.

"Another topic is 'who are you attracted to?' Most are attracted to femmes, but some are also attracted to butches, which has been the hardest part of the discussion. A big topic, naturally, has been femmes...and indulging in some bitching about femmes and feminism."

Butch Power

There is a certain energy about butch lesbians that I feel is denied because of the taboos about "maleness" in the post-'70s lesbian movement. We have so few ways of describing butch energy that we keep calling it "male" when it's not.

Judy Grahn addresses the issue of butch haircuts: "The heterosexual male model is by no means the only factor involved in the mannerisms of butch women. There is a tradition, for instance, of short-cropped hair for Western women that is not connected to the short haircuts of men.... Though I had believed for years that American dikes wore short hair in direct imitation of men and as an aggressive rejection of the perception of 'femaleness' as a form of slavery, I saw for myself how waves of extreme hair-cropping took place in the Lesbian feminist movement at a time when the styles for men's hair had been long for years. The women were cutting their hair to become dikes, not to imitate men."

We are too quick to believe that certain clothes, hairstyles, and mannerisms belong to men. We have forgotten that many tribal people dress alike regardless of gender, and that many cultures are nonsexist in their approach to tasks. In trying to alleviate our sexism, we need to stop accepting Western gender assumptions as givens.

Liz Kennedy carries this idea further. "Recently I read a paper by Tricia Franzen comparing images of women in *Ebony* and *Life* magazines between 1945 and 1950. What became clear is that the dominant image of heterosexuality, which implies that women don't care about sex, is really class-based and white. *Ebony* had some very powerful articles about sex, talking about women's fulfillment. *Life* really had no image of women's sexuality, only about men controlling everything. I think it's really important we remember those class and ethnic differences."

And Jewelle Gomez adds, "Taking the overlay of butch/femme relationships, the black community has had a difficult and conflicting experience. Black people have tended to emulate American white society and at the same time disavow our connection to it. So trying to get to how we feel about butch/femme and how we express it has not yet gone back to any kind of root Eastern or African philosophical perspective. Instead, it's been based in white, middle-class, feminist theory that has been totally inadequate at this point."

A butch friend of mine, Jill Lessing, describes the shifts in her identity that came about because of that feminist theory. "I came out in 1954 and there was this fear of 'Oh my god, I have to choose.' In those days, you were supposed to choose one side or the other. And it was very tyrannizing. What is frightening to me now is that the tyranny goes the other way. We've gone so far to liberalize it. Now there is no such thing as butch or femme, and that becomes a tyranny in itself. There's a danger of 'everybody is everything.' You know, everybody *isn't* everything.

Everyone has different ways, styles and rhythms, things that turn them on, and things that move them.

"I guess what I'm saying is that the role is something that I claimed as an early coming out dyke. *I claimed it.* And then I disclaimed it, discounted it. I put it down and backed way up, and my highest goal was to become androgynous. I wanted the best of all possible worlds. I very much wanted that for myself. That process helped me find a place of synthesis inside that was very helpful to me. Now I'm in a place where I can reclaim the old parts of the butchiness of me that I like. They're not the places of the oppressor that were put on me, they're parts of me that I just truly like about myself.

"I dress fairly butchy. I like the fact that I can want to be friends with or want to date a woman, and I can let her know that I'm available and aggressive and assertive, and then sit back and wait. See if she picks up on that. I like that part of me. I like courting. I like being the courter. I like to do more of the stereotypical things—stereotypically butch things. Not male. I draw a distinction between male and female and butch and femme. I don't think that femmes are trying to be imitation heterosexual feminine women. I think femme dykes are largely misunderstood; they are strong dykes, strong in their lesbian identity. They are pooh-poohed and put down by our culture a lot. A femme to me is a person who feels really good about identifying with other women. It's great; I feel, 'Ah-hah, I can relax now.' "

For many, many women, being butch is a core identity, not something that changes at will. As Esther Newton says, "What's frustrating to me is the new trend to say: 'You know, gee, I like to wear my jack boots one night and my high heels the next. Gee, I can express all these parts of me, it's kind of camp.' I can't switch around, it's very difficult. Most of the time I don't want to. We've been living with a long history of people saying: 'But you should do everything!' Well actually, the first edition was that there are no roles, there's nothing. Now it's becoming I like to do this, dress up and camp; you're better if you can do all these different roles. For some of us it's not that at all! Some of us want to go deeper and deeper into one thing, and that's just as good."

There is a sexual energy that butch lesbians give off. A turn of the hip, some nonchalance, the dip of a shoulder, an attitude, an air of assurance. Why is it that femme women say they can tell a butch woman from thirty feet? What Deb Edel has called "butch power/femme hunger" is a profound part of this energy. As she says, "For me, being butch is a lot about sex. It's the whole thing of who has which end of the dildo. It's about power. It's about protectiveness. It's about strength. It's about technique." Another woman at a butch/femme discussion said, "For me, it's about the attraction of being different. I have friends who I think are very attractive, but I don't read them sexually. I've never considered myself a butch. But I realized that if there's a continuum from 0 to 10, let's say I'm a 7 on the continuum and I have a friend, and she's a 7 too—I don't read her sexually. But if she's a 9 butch and I'm a 7, then I can have some sexual interest. I realized that there was sort of an interchange—though I'd never use the words femme and butch."

I can sexually abandon myself to a butch lesbian. I can acknowledge a willingness to give myself up, to allow for a strength different from mine. Maybe she has a sexual agenda that I don't, maybe she knows a special secret to turn me on. She might not—it depends on the lover—but I have this fantasy that she does. My sexual energy connects up to a butch's sexual energy to make a circle. It's not that I haven't had and don't have sex with lesbians other than butches. But butch women, the ones 7 and above on the scale, have a way of enticing me that others don't. Now I like, enjoy and even delight in the sexual energy of women in the 5 and 6 range too, but there is probably no way that someone below 5 would even turn my head. There is that magic number cut-off. Don't ask me why my sexual adrenaline level goes up as the numbers go up. It just does.

As one woman said to me, "For me, being butch seems to be the way we present ourselves, do ourselves, and those are the first clues we give out about who we are. It may not be the totality of who we are, but it's the first sentence that's read."

Butch energy catches my attention. It's a stance in the world, taking up space in a particular way that says "I get to be here." Feet firmly planted, hips not fluid, a structure to hold on to, no matter what body size. Taking authority over mechanical things, figuring them out. How? Don't ask me. Just being there with a certain knowing that I don't have access to, and not because I can't learn or haven't got power. My power is different. The butch erotic statement is immediately recognizable to me, no matter what the garb, or the job, or the accent, or the race, or the class. It's a presence I enjoy, delight in, want to be around. A presence I cannot emulate, and have no desire to. A presence I can match and stand firm with. A thrill.

As Joan Nestle says in *A Restricted Country*, the issue is not that butch women are acting "as men." Our own paucity of language is "a testimony to the lack of erotic categories in straight culture." She goes on to say, "Part of this responsibility [of the butch] was sexual expertise. In the 1950s this courage to feel comfortable with arousing another woman became a political act...."

That is still true today. While it's still unfashionable in many circles to show that obvious butch self, arousing another woman is the same no matter what the rules of the day prescribe. That sexual energy is there, no matter what others want us to do with it.

Butch Eroticism

I wanted to know what butches find attractive. What is it that makes a butch woman attracted to another lesbian? What kind of self-image do they have? When asked how they saw themselves in relationship to the goddess, the largest group of butches (36 percent) saw themselves as Artemis. Their most recent lovers (29 percent) fit the description of Aphrodite. This was exactly the opposite of the femmes (see the previous chapter). It's impossible for us to get away from the fact that butches and femmes are in opposition. This doesn't mean that they are completely different, only that there is an opposing force in the other that each finds to be an erotic turn-on.

Almost half the butches in the survey said they were primarily attracted to femmes, who to them were: beautiful, gentle, sexual/sexy, and sensual. They also liked femmes' clothes. The most common answer (25 percent of respondents) was an attraction to the softness of the femme. None of these characteristics (clothes, softness) were even listed by the femmes to describe their attraction to butches. Well, all right, there was one femme out of 589 who said her attraction to butches was beauty and clothes; two more said sexual/sexy; and three said sensual. It's just that these words are two to twenty times more likely to show up as something butches find erotic.

Looking at the word most used by femmes—strong—and the word most used by butches—soft—to describe what is erotic to them, I think we've stumbled on a hidden but real truth about lesbian sexuality. When I compare this to the survey I did with Marny Hall in 1988, there seems to be no way around it. The same words—strong and soft—also showed up as the most frequently chosen to describe butch and femme. I think we need to develop a female vision through which we can understand these attractions.

Sue Golding discusses the range of butch sexuality. "I think a lot of butches actually identify more with hermaphroditism. They see themselves as being male and female, and want to gender fuck. Looking like a gay man, which is a whole other thing than a straight man. I think there are several types of butches. There's baby butch, butch-butch, bull dyke, aggressive butch, submissive butch, femme-butch."

There are other aspects of butches and their attractions as well. Robin Tyler once described herself as a "faggot butch." She found herself attracted to other butch women, not exclusively, but usually. So did one-fourth of the butch women in my survey. Robin has said in her routine that she has seen more ceilings than Michelangelo, referring, of course, to taking the receptive sexual position. Anyone who knows Robin or has seen her perform knows her as the quintessential 9 or 10.

Butches are attracted to other butches, but the dynamic is different. I've heard this force described as a profound connection to self: an acknowledgement of one's own power that energizes both partners, knowing what to do and how to do it because the energy is the same, not different.

This may come as a surprise to some women because we expect our stereotypes to prove true. We expect butch women to only go with femmes. It's important not to limit our ideas when discussing our sexual proclivities. Whenever we try to do that, we'll immediately find exceptions to every rule.

"I could look at a classically beautiful butch woman and find her beautiful, and I would be attracted to that woman. I would not immediately turn off to that. I've changed a lot. It's not a static thing for me—that's a real important thing for me to say because it used to be very static."

Butch Images

Two of the most common stereotypes are the butch who is only attracted to straight women and the butch who likes to wear and use a dildo. Okay, you say, now this is really stretching my limits. How can you say this is not male-identified in some way? How can you say that lesbians who go after straight women are not homophobic, or trying to be men? How can you say that dildos are not an experience of male sexuality?

Well, in exactly the same way that I say that lesbians who like penetration are not heterosexual. By now we've realized that lesbian sexuality can be expressed in countless ways. There are lesbians who have fantasies of being a man or of their lover being a man. I don't think these lesbians are trying to be men or that they would rather be with a man. Given how bombarded we are with heterosexual images and power, it would be surprising if we *didn't* sometimes have those fantasies.

As for myself, I'm grateful that some lesbians like to bring straight women out. Like a lot of other lesbians, I did identify as straight at one time. My first lover didn't exactly come and drag me out of a straight scene; I was definitely flirting with the lesbian culture. But I'm sure glad she took the initiative. Many lesbians avoid bringing someone out—in part for fear that she might go back to men, but more often perhaps because of an unwillingness to deal with the emotional turmoil of a woman newly introduced to lesbianism.

There are, however, women who are willing to take this challenge, who find it exciting. It's not that they say, "You know, I think I'll go after a straight woman tonight." It's that this element of discovery is what turns them on.

The dildo question appears more difficult. And when a dildo is used with a harness...I know this is a problematical leap for some women to make—understanding that dildos, while a male image for some women, can still be lesbian-identified, even for those who like to pretend that they are men when they have a dildo strapped on, or that their lover is a man when they are receiving the dildo. The reality is they can take the dildo off. There isn't a man in that bed: not a man's attitudes, experience, power, or assumptions.

There are also many lesbians for whom wearing a dildo has nothing to do with male fantasies, but is simply a way to stimulate their lover's vagina while doing something else with their fingers and mouths. For some women, this is the most comfortable way for a lover to enter their vagina. For others, this is the way they can enter someone's ass without anxiety.

In the survey, one-third of the women used dildos. There was essentially no difference in dildo use between the femmes, butches, androgynous women, or those who didn't identify with any of the categories. They all equally used dildos on their lovers or had their lovers use them on them. In fact, femmes and the women who didn't see themselves in any category were the *most* likely to penetrate their lover's vagina.

This is *female* sexuality, two women, making love, having fun, being vulnerable, playing with a toy that is convenient and even has the added cachet of being taboo. Hiding the dildo from friends, giving it a name, having an array of them, only letting certain partners know that you use them—all of this is something that gives any sexual toy a thrill.

The simplest truth about the dildo is that it has a shape that fits smoothly into a vagina. Many women trade it back and forth (after washing it off) and use it to pleasure one another. Lesbians are now manufacturing dildos for lesbians, in the shape of fingers, dolphins, diving women, even dildos in lavender silicon to express our unique lesbian selves

. . . .

> "When I came to North America in 1974, I was immediately educated about what was politically correct. One of the first things I did, which I still regret, was throw out my dildo."

. . . .

I'm tired of lesbians being compared to men because the majority culture can't think of any other way to define women who love women. I'm tired of hearing that what we wear, how we act, and the ways we move prove that we are or wish we were men. And I would like to see lesbians give up the idea that certain lesbian sexual activities are male. A lesbian said to me recently: "Why do lesbians think I'm into being a man? I'm a woman and filled with woman juice, energized with my affection for women. To say I'm male because of my appearance or the way I have sex...I don't get it."

There's a wide repertoire of butch feelings, actions and sexual activities, there could be as many as there are butches. Being cut off from homosexual role models keeps us from learning to live our lives in a lesbian framework. Denying over and over again who we are makes it much more difficult to create an identity that fits.

Martina Navratilova is so striking because it's so very rare to find a positive butch lesbian role model. During our formative years, we had to live with shame, fear, and anxiety about being different from other girls. The butch lesbian had to figure out who and how to be. She had to learn to conform enough to get by and yet she knew she could never be that person she was pretending to be.

Now is the time to start really describing ourselves, to come out of the mental closet that has kept us from telling ourselves the truth, that has kept us from telling others who we are. Butch women defy the world. They are not passive women or overbearing men. I hope in the coming years we will celebrate butch power in all its diversity. I hope we will fully experience who we are and let the world know, so that little girls who do "boy" things can find out that indeed they are being girls too. Many of them are butch lesbian girls. Let's make sure they know there is a place for them in the world.

As adult butch women we have much to be proud of as well. We have energy that is both sexual and powerful. We have a way of moving in the world that attracts other lesbians. Because we are women, we can synthesize strength with loving, assertiveness with giving. We can bring our complex talents and inclinations to all aspects of our lives.

The nature of being a child is in finding similarities. As we grow older, we learn to tell the differences between things. As a lesbian community, it's time now to grow older, to discover our differences and savor them.

A lesbian friend, who has recently embraced the butch identity from which she had run her whole life, gave me a clue as to why butches have more difficulty than femmes sharing their experiences.

"The culture gave me two choices: female or male. If I'm not like the other females, there is something wrong with me, because obviously I'm a girl. You begin to feel that *you* are wrong and bad. I think it's a bit like sexually abused children before the '80s. They grew up with television, books, and movies that only showed them grown-ups being good to children. So the child decides 'It must all be my fault, adults don't do these horrible things. It didn't happen to me, I must have made it up.'

"In much the same way, there I was surrounded by my stuffed animals (and two dolls which I had mysteriously named with my lover and her sister's names—two women I wouldn't meet for another 35 years!) So I'm trying to figure out—if I'm not like my mom, I must be like my dad. Only I'm not like my dad. If your fundamental experience of your identity is something you're not supposed to be, then nobody better find out. There is heavy punishment when it slips out.

"When I was about ten, my mom came home really excited and asked 'Who's your favorite literary character?' Her face fell at my choice, Davey Crockett. I had been invited to a party where we had to dress up as our favorite character. She sent me there as Heidi.

"I felt I had this horrible secret, that I must be a man in a woman's body. This was the time when Christine Jorgensen, the first transsexual, got to be famous. It became a vague permanent anxiety. I was in this gang at thirteen, and I was the only girl. The boys had titles like Prince or King, and I wanted to be Duke, not Duchess. If you're pretty sure you're not a girl and yet you know you are, after a certain point, there is no one to play with. I spent a lot of my life reading about boys and being isolated. I had so much existential panic, and there was nothing to be done and no one to tell."

For many butch lesbians, childhood brings the pain of having a deep secret and never being able to tell anyone. It's common to feel that you belong to neither sex, and that there must be something really wrong with you. Thinking about this has made me look at how different it is for femmes. Femmes at least grow up knowing they are girls, liking girl things, and having fun with other girls. They have lots of companions and some role models.

Since girls are taught not be sexual, there are fewer complications for femmes in childhood. You play with dolls and with other girls, you learn how to dress and to act like the other girls. There is less shame, less conflict. The problems come once you begin to identify sexual feelings. You are being abandoned by all your girlfriends, but you're not able to get into boys. Or else, you get into boys and know it isn't right. For femmes, there are many years of childhood when you don't have a secret, when you fit in just fine. Femmes come into adolescence at least with a gender-appropriate sense of self.

To grow up butch is to have no words or images for that way of being a woman. You have no gender-appropriate sense of self, though you know you're supposed to have one. And you can't tell anyone that you don't. This is extremely painful. Living like this teaches you how to keep who you are to yourself, to keep your true nature under wraps. It makes easy sociability an unfamiliar experience.

This was shown further in conversations with another butch friend of mine who told me that one of the great aspects about being butch to her was, "The mystery, the intrigue about who I am. This is around all kinds of things, like power and butch sexuality and just who I am in general. Part of the stance is not talking about what may be going through my head. The women I'm interested in wonder what I do, who I am. It's part of the sexual excitement.

"I adapt and react to who I'm trying to pursue. I don't reveal myself until I feel secure. The intrigue is part of the fun. It's also part of the survival. It's scary to be a butch woman because of the homophobia in our community.

"The last thing I was told by my mother when I was walking out the door at seventeen to join the Navy was, 'Don't let those bulldaggers get you and don't come back a bulldagger.' This was a problem since I knew perfectly well that I was joining the Navy to find the 'bulldaggers' and to become one. Of course, I found them, and they taught me how to be a butch. I watched how they moved their hands, how they talked to women. They taught me how to pursue a woman. They taught me how to be a female who makes it with women, and who loves women.

"Butch energy is this overtly powerful woman energy. Butch women aren't begging for crumbs from the heterosexual world like some lesbians do. We can't fake looking like the traditional woman. We just can't. We just get to be there in all our power, being our mysterious, intriguing selves."

THE DEBATE
5

"What do you mean by butch?"

"I don't know. It's real reactionary to me. I only use it in fun."

"It's hard for me to take, It's hard for me to relate to as a real thing. I guess I don't really understand it. When I think about it in terms of a relationship, I think of it as aggressiveness and passivity."

"Who's who?"

"With the more butch person being the more masculine, the more aggressive one."

"That's not my experience."

"But my experience is that a butch makes herself more available. This is not true across the board, but in a generalized statement. A butchy woman will show herself to be more available. I consider myself a butch. I very rarely make the first move. But I let the woman know that I'm out there and I'm attracted, and I'm interested and I'm available. I'm assertive to a certain degree, and I call the shots to a certain degree. But when it comes to letting the first kiss happen, she's got to do it."

"That's true butch."

. . . .

"I mean the only person that's ever called me butch to my face is JoAnn and it changed my life."

"Made your little heart go pitter patter."

. . . .

"How do you define a butch?"

"Start with what it is. It's not an imitation of a man. We all agree with that."

"In my experience, the butches that I've been lovers with, or have been close to as friends have had a strong silent way, not uncommunicative, but less direct in communication. They've also had a real soft vulnerable part that they don't show anybody at first, but is really there. So once you get close—"

"That sounds like a man to me. It does."

"I've been with men, but that wasn't my experience. Women are present. A strong silent woman is still there and present for you. As you cultivate that silence, you get something special inside that everybody else doesn't get."

"The hard shells that butches have, having had one, has to do with fighting the world out there and keeping safe. Keeping safe from the world."

. . . .

"Superficial is kind of important, you know. I purposefully wore fluffy pink clothes tonight, and I was seen as femme. I consider myself butch, and if I had worn black tonight or leather, I bet you all would have seen me as butch too."

. . . .

"I'm ambivalent."

"You're bi."

"Bi butch femme."

"Your butch is centered."

"Oh god, California!"

- -

"Can I say something about spirituality and butch-ness?"

"What is it?"

"Your observation about 12-step programs."

"That co's tend to be femmes and alcoholics tend to be butches."

"I'd say that's true."

"The alcoholic has an attitude about co's being wimpy and whiney and inferior and weak."

"That's right."

"Internalized hatred of feminine traits."

"That's true too."

"So are you assuming all those caretaking traits are identified as femme?"

- -

"When I came out at the age of eighteen, the product of a fundamental Mormon upbringing, I accompanied my new best friend to a local gay bar. I knew there were dykes from all the diesel trucks left in the parking lot. As I surveyed the scene, I noticed a short, older, and drunk dyke approaching me. She appeared, from her face, to have written the book on rough trade. She planted herself directly in front of me, looked me over from head to toe and put the question to me: 'Are you butch or femme?'

"How does one respond to a question that, to her knowledge, has never in the history of the

world been asked before? I groped for an
answer. My mind raced. I'm a girl; I've always
been a girl; I act like a girl—that's what I'll tell
her. 'I'm a femme,' I said. It was the correct
answer. She asked me to dance.

   "We danced a slow dance, and as she held
me close, head to my bosom, I thought, 'If I'm
going to be a lesbian, it will be because I want
to be with a woman, not a man, or pseudo-man,
or a woman who acts like a man, but because I
want to be with a woman who likes being a
woman. So, if this is what being a femme
attracts, I'll go butch because I want a woman.'
As a consequence of this first encounter, I wore
my daddy's sports coat to the bars, and acted
tougher than I was, believing that is what
lesbians did to attract each other. It was two
years before I realized I could just relax, be
myself and thereby become even more attractive
to other women."

"I began to realize that I had answered many of your
questions according to my image of how I would like
to be, rather than who I really am. To be specific, I
think I would like to see myself as more butch than
my behavior demonstrates. When I look at my
romantic history, I am usually more attracted to
women who seem more butch than me: older, physically stronger, more assertive, and more competent
in the left-brain department, less comfortable on
fancy straight world dressing up occasions. It's been
hard to find anyone taller than me. I certainly have
minimal homemaking skills; can't sew, not much of
a cook, after being cooked for by several of these
alleged butches.

"Why do I wish I was more butch than I think I really am? I see my butch self as independent, self-actualized, and self-assured. I see my femme persona as codependent and passive. I realize that a lot of women I peg as butch don't fit that description. Sometimes I think we classified ourselves based more on who had more feminine body characteristics. Roles never meant anything in bed—the most exciting relationship were the ones in which we could take turns being passive or aggressive in bed.

"My femme persona is also one that allows me to 'pass.' In my first few years, after I cut my long hair, I got called 'sir' at least once a week (and thought it a compliment). I always moderated my butch/femme duality according to whom I was partnered with. Today I am much more interested in integrating the two sides into a more androgynous personality. Some days I feel more butch, in some situations I feel more femme; with some women I feel more passive, and with some more assertive. I agree that the duality exists, but I defend my right to express both elements in my personality. Do I contradict myself? You bet."

"I first came out long before I became a feminist; I came up through the ranks where I was hanging out at the local women's bar. This was the bittersweet experience of walking into dark bars, with women in jeans, the smell of English Leather. And I loved it. I didn't label myself anything; they labeled me butch. I was quite fascinated by the whole thing. I swaggered like a butch and I was proud of it. I liked to court and I liked being pursued. And I responded to her butchness but yet I didn't want to be cast into the opposite role. So it was 'oh, we're just going to divide this up, I get to be over here and you get to be over there.'

"Well, you thought you'd be the woman and she'd get to be the man? See, in that instant, I think that is where myth comes in. You're saying a femme cooks and sews and does what a straight woman does. Well, I don't think that's what a femme is."

CHAPTER SEVEN

Other Rhythms

There are many rhythms for sex, many dances. Sexuality is a fluid aspect of our lives. For some of us a wide range of different sexual experiences are possible, for others a narrow range, but there are few lesbians for whom sex is totally fixed or stagnant. Lesbian sex rhythms are shrouded in silence. Just discussing butch/femme brings up great uneasiness and fear. Are we now expected to toe some other line? Did the rules change again without anyone letting us know? And if such a basic concept of lesbian eroticism got lost, then what happened to less visible styles? What I want to do here is to begin to explore the range of other sexual identifications that we have for ourselves. As I've said before, and can't say enough, language is our biggest barrier. We really don't have words for the sexual aspects of ourselves and each other that make us recognizable, if not yet identifiable. We have the feelings, but we don't have the words. What are these other rhythms? What words and categories do we have floating out there that are not yet universal language?

With help from my friends, colleagues, and lesbians throughout the country, I've come up with 25 sexual styles that I see as forces of lesbian sexual attraction and bonding. After I came up with these images, we had the idea of finding personal ads that would illustrate actual sexual attractions in our community.

Many of these sexual styles may, and in fact are intended to, overlap. And I know there are others that have not yet visibly emerged, or that I simply don't discuss. Some of these may feel to you that they have nothing to do with sex, but until we have a full-fledged lesbians erotic imagery, how can we possibly know?

These styles are about the "F" word—fun. They're to be played with, tried on, hung out to dry. My personal favorite is the Lesbian Vampire. The big taboo is that we aren't out preying on straight women. A lot of our sex is about taboos. We probably quit being silly and having fun with sex in about the eighth grade. Well, isn't it time to start again?

The styles I'm exploring here are not remotely meant to be limiting, or the final word. Because I was looking for sexual icons, for broad images, some of these styles border on stereotypes. But they do present a beginning frame for a very diverse sexuality. I suspect that if we grow into a really free lesbian sexuality, that our sexual expressions will be very fluid both in terms of identity and practice. We'll have bad girl/butch/surrender lesbians, femme/take charge/vampire lesbians, cheerleader/earth mother/ordinary gal lesbians, and the goddess only knows what else.

I've divided the different erotic styles into five categories. I did this because friends suggested that many of the concepts here really belong in distinct groups. To some extent, I've got the kumquats mixed in with the bananas. In creating the general categories, I've brought in the sexual, political, sociological and psychological aspects of the lesbian community. It's the nature of lesbians to include all these aspects within their erotic icons. It seems to be quintessentially lesbian to intertwine relationships and personality with sexuality. Instead of a purely sexual drive, lesbian sexuality embraces all the parts of our lives and becomes an expression of ourselves within our culture.

It's important when you find a style here that you don't like, are afraid of, or don't recognize, to look at how quickly you want to make it into a heterosexual or male concept. I've been working with lesbians for a long time on issues of sex, and I know that these are all lesbian configurations. We have an extremely varied sexuality and acknowledging that is the first step towards giving us a voice. *All* of us a voice.

This is just the beginning. If you have other suggestions, send them to me. I would love to hear and read what you think are lesbian erotic definitions.

Sexual Styles

The sexual styles refer to different unique lesbian sexual/emotional identities. Butch/femme is one sexual style. What I'm exploring here are the other most common sexual images. These are icons in our world that have already been given voice and will be recognizable to many. Some of them also include specific sexual activities. Each has a unique flavor and, dare I say it—taste. Eat it up, women.

THE 3

This is a concept that was new to me. The idea of the "3" is that lesbians of a particular kind are a "third" sexual identity, outside of traditional gender categories. This sexual identity is based on being *other* and powerful. There is nothing stereotypical about the 3. They are neither femme, butch, nor androgynous. The 3 is an energy that does not relate to a scale that has two ends and a middle. The 3 is not a number on a scale, but a wholly separate energy.

This sense of otherness encompasses a range of expressions. What we know of as "dyke" can be a piece of it: that outrageous lesbian energy and identity. For other 3's, it's the sense of being "outside." That's the key: outsiders in adolescence, and sometimes outsiders within lesbian culture as well.

Looking for a Few Adventurous Souls
To enhance my community of friends and lovers. I am playful, spirited, grounded, moving with a passion for living, words and open spaces. Do you share my committment to creating a life of support, exploration and laughter with lesbians who love themselves and each other? Are you willing to test the typical boundaries of relationships and and create powerful places of growth? Then write!

The 3 is a description based on Simone de Beauvoir's, *The Second Sex*. In her startling precursor to modern feminism, de Beauvoir effectively makes the case that women are treated as "other" and in many respects *are* "other." She also establishes that women are different from, but not inferior to, men—just different.

Please Write

Seeking strong lesbian with versatility for the 1990s and values from the 1960s. Social justice and meaninful work still matter most of all, but there's no dogmatism, and reality has set in. You are comfortable wearing silk blouses, Birkenstocks, or a tough leather jacket. We are both over 30, and enjoy protest rallies, downhill skiing, dogs, hottubs, trucks, dancing, good food, bookstores, long talks, or quiet massages.

The 3 is a sexual energy that could be thought of as gynandry (as opposed to the more traditional concept of androgyny). That's a combination of the female and male energy, with the female energy in the forefront (the "gyn" before the "andro"). The concept is that lesbians who identify in this way put their female energy first. They operate out of a lesbian center.

The 3 is female sexual energy that attracts other female sexual energy. The eroticism that comes from being "other" allows for exploration that can move beyond proscribed ways of seeing things. The 3 can move easily from one form of expression to another, without following either male or heterosexual images of women's sexuality.

"If men are the first sex and women are the second sex, then I'm the third sex. I started kissing girls when I was four and I never even knew it mattered. If they were girls I liked them. I've always known I was an other. I think it's more than androgyny because, for me, androgyny is the male principal first. I think that for me the attraction is entirely different."

KI-KI

This is a familiar term that was frequently used (sometimes in a perjorative sense) in the 1950s. It's still widely used in some sectors of lesbian culture to describe women who move easily from butch to femme and back again. It's a style which embodies both femme and butch sexual energy. These women have an identification with both sides of the lesbian sexual dyad.

All-American Girl-Boy

Tender, sweet butch, 23, is looking for a serious relationship, believing strongly in friendship first. I'm looking for a feminine girl 18-28 who may fall in love with the little boy in me, or maybe my femme side which is more me than my way of dress...sometimes. I enjoy bodybuilding (a real screamer), tennis, running or any sport imaginable. Interested in theology and the afterlife—let's enlighten each other. Not working but financially secure (so if this bothers you, I must ask that you do not respond). And of course nature and romance go along with my sensitive and affectionate nature. Must warn you though, I'm a little shy and don't like dancing or parties. Hopefully my crazy sense of humor will even things out. Am looking only for those who are honest and communicative. No substance abusers. Are we engaged to be engaged? Please include phone and photo.

Women first surfaced with this tag back in the '40s; when asked whether they were butch or femme, "ki-ki" became another position for women who didn't fit either role. In my opinion, this is not the same as the androgynous woman or the "3", but rather a unique identity of its own that describes moving around the butch/femme scale while still operating within this segment of the lesbian society. It is firmly a part of the butch/femme world, and perhaps a precursor to androgyny, but not the same.

> ### I Like All Different Types But...
> might go nuts if you're a woman in your 30s with strong
> butch and femme traits (depending on your mood). You
> are serious about what you want but good natured
> enough to handle relentless teasing (which I love to dish
> out). I am in my late 20s, 5'6", 120 lbs. and have dark
> brown hair and hazel eyes. During the day I work hard
> but at night I love to relax, laugh, cuddle, "do comedy,"
> movies (I'm a Woody Allen freak), theater, and anything
> else that comes to mind.

There seems to be a freedom in the eroticism of the ki-ki
woman to respond to her partner's sexual nature. Her desire is
directly connected to the style of her partner, and it increases with
the tension of opposition. The turn-on is being on the other side.
If her partner is more femme, the ki-ki woman moves into a more
butch energy. Conversely, when she is with a butch woman she
moves into her femme self. The movement can change in the
midst of a sex act, or only with the onset of a new relationship.
When she is with a partner who is also ki-ki, the movement can
be more fluid. No one needs to know who's leading in this dance;
they simply go round the floor as the spirit strikes.

"I seem to shift my identity according to my lovers.
For years, I was butch-leaning and that was very comfortable. Now, with the last two, I've been more femme.
There're no rules about all this, but sometimes I have to
laugh when I'm showing my butchier lover how to use
power tools."

S/M

I'm not going to discuss here the politics of whether or not
S/M is correct or incorrect, inherent lesbian sexuality or aping
"the boys". Just look around. Listen to discussions in your own
community. Whether you are pro- or anti- or neutral, you've got
to admit that S/M is definitely another sexual rhythm out there.
It's a rhythm not everyone may be comfortable with, but it's not
going away just because some people wish it would.

There's a lot of juice happening in the lesbian community about S/M that sounds a lot like the juice in the heterosexual community about lesbians. I want to suggest that the anti-S/M women are in a nonconsensual (nonsexual) S/M relationship with the S/M dykes. S/M lesbians are punished, publicly humiliated, and in general told that they are worthless by non-S/M dykes. It's not going to work to say, "Well, if they just stopped doing it, or being overt about it, or dressing like that, we would all be able to work together." That's just what our families tell us about our lesbianism. No, the only thing to do is admit we are all here, and try to create a loving and safe dialogue.

I Like It Rough...

Horny, smartass, crafty, butch bottom needs to be reminded who has control. Seeking experienced butch top to reduce me to the pleasures of pain and absolute submission. Push far enough, and I'll turn into the sweetest, most appreciative girl—definately worth your time. No ego-trippers please.

Given that some lesbians do practice S/M, what are the inherent *lesbian* erotic attractions in S/M? What makes the S/M lesbian sexual energy different from other types of lesbian sexual rhythms? I'm interested in the dance that these women create with one another. The dance *is* different from lesbians who don't practice S/M; what is it that shows up between S/M women when they are moving towards a sexual experience?

Most of us were socialized to play the traditional female role—don't be too assertive (*never* aggressive), but not *too* passive either. We "keep score", watch out for everyone else's feelings (even when noticing our own), making certain that everyone is treated fairly; always balancing, bargaining, ensuring that everything equals out in the end. Even as feminists, we still adhere to this role. When it comes to sex, we often continue to apply these rules. If I make love to you, you have to make love back to me. And that's where S/M lesbians differ—they don't apply these rules, at least not in the same way.

> **Brat Needs Discipline**
> Jewish, 33-yr-old bottom, new to S/M, rediscovering the
> lil' kid in me who wants to play (when the mistress is
> away...). This recovering "p.c. fascist" gets off on
> bondage, whipping & feathers; food & rubber cat
> fetishist. Need a top w/sensitivity that can make me mind
> my p's and q's. No abuse, drugs, alcohol, tobacco,
> 12-steppers *highly* preferable; Jewish wimmin most
> welcome.

The bottom is the one who lets go, lets go of control, of
responsibility; you're not afraid of being *too* available, *too* desirous;
you're present in your body, not afraid of pain or pleasure. In fact,
you're finding pleasure and pain quite connected in a way that
everyone tells you they're not supposed to be. No need to censor
the unconscious, here's the chance to indulge it. To be touched
and just be body and sensation, no judging mind. Lust and trust
and peacefulness and excitement, coexisting. You say yes to sex.
You say "These are my limits" very clearly and know you'll be
heard. You're not ashamed of voicing and asking for your desire
to be fulfilled.

The top is the one who takes control, is aggressive, assertive,
dominant, and strong. You set limits too, though yours are likely
more subtle, and always subordinate to your partner's. You are
responsible, imaginative, harsh, firm yet soft. You take, yes, but
only to give and give and give. Your primary concern is her
pleasure. You drive her wild, while part of you is gauging her
reactions, judging when to stop, when to try something new.

"What's so incredible to me is the link between us.
She's hanging on my every word, looking up at me shyly
every once in a while, but trying to stroke me so I won't
notice—she can't keep her hands off me, she keeps trying
to wiggle closer and closer, but I stay ultra-cool, forbidding,
and she just goes nuts. It's as if I'm carrying both of us down
this long road that's three-quarters magical and one-quarter
scary, but she's with me so there's no need to be afraid. I
feel powerful and strong and masterful, taking her life in my
hands as I guide her down this road, except, of course, she
is the road; I can't be here at all unless she lets me. But that's

underneath—the pavement, so to speak—right now we're
wrapped up in each other as tight as we could be."

One aspect of S/M is a verbal exchange about sexual expectations that is honest and clear. During this exchange, partners
make it clear that they are interested in one another sexually,
discuss what they want to do together, and define each other's
roles. These women have been at the forefront of openness
within our community, always trying for specificity and honesty
about sexual needs, turn-ons and turn-offs.

This overt sexual conversation in and of itself has been
threatening to our community. Throughout our history, the
majority culture has retaliated against us because of our private
acts. We have adopted a code of silence to protect ourselves. We
have unspoken pacts not to tell those outside "the life" who we
are, where we are and certainly not what we do. Out S/M lesbians
challenge all that we know about this pact.

Just as butch/femme and initiation/response exist on
continuums, so do sexual power dynamics. I talked earlier in this
book about the inevitability of unequal power and the excitement
that can follow from that. If those of us who are so critical of S/M
practices could acknowledge the existence of such a continuum,
we might stop making S/M lesbians "bad" so that we can feel
good.

CELIBACY

Many women choose with joy to have an overt love affair
with themselves. This form of erotic expression is quite common
in the lesbian world. In my *Lesbian Passion* survey, 78 percent of
the women had been celibate at one time or another (35 percent
had been for one to five years, and eight percent for six or more
years). For a lot of women, this has been "a choice", or because
"it felt right at the time."

This form of eroticism is often put down in our community.
We assume that the celibate lesbian is just waiting to become
lovers with another woman. Though celibacy may happen
"between relationships", many lesbians choose to focus on a
relationship with themselves.

The celibate woman is always ready for sex when her partner is, she and her partner like the same things, her partner always knows what she wants next. Of course, her partner is herself. You cannot find this kind of compatibility anywhere else. If a woman gives herself totally to this experience, her self-knowledge is increased by leaps and bounds. To find the nuances of what turns you on, to be left in peace when you want to spend time in contemplation, to be able to order your life without the limitations of a lover, are all compelling reasons to explore this choice of sexual expression. Celibacy can be a period of deeply satisfying sexual activity with yourself.

A Few Good Friends
I'm a transplant from the East Bay, new to singlehood, and not sure I'm ready for another relationship just yet. But I do want a few women friends to hang out with on Sunday afternoon and/or one or two evenings during the week. My interests include: dancing, going to museums and galaries, urban or rural hiking, thrift stores and flea markets, obscure foreign films, arguing about art over a few beers, etc. Please have a decent sense of humor and not be too bloody radical.

There are also lesbians who are partners with another woman yet want to be celibate as well. Some choose this as a way to heal from incest or other sexual abuse experiences. They want to put the sexual relationship on hold while they concentrate their energies on something else. Some just don't want to deal with the demands of creating that kind of intimacy with their partner.

There are celibate women who don't even masturbate. The purpose might be simply to clear your mind of sexual voices and anxieties. You might stop stimulating yourself on the physical plane and spend more of your energy on the spiritual plane. This pledge is common in certain religious or spiritual practices.

Whatever the reason for celibacy, sexual energy is still there, it's just not expressed with another person. It may not be consciously felt, but sexual drive is never absent. Holding this energy inside and not spreading it around to others is often an extremely intense and creative experience. Its power comes from the inner focus, the deep attunement that's possible with yourself.

"When my lover left me suddenly, I was shocked by the intensity of the sexual energy that surfaced. I almost couldn't get enough sex with myself. And I think the sex healed me. I got back in my body. I started to love myself for the first time in a long time. And I discovered what a profoundly sexual person I am."

TAKING CHARGE

Being a person who likes to take charge of sex is not popularly talked about within our community. However, it is one of the common steps in the erotic dance. Some lesbians like to initiate and basically run the sexual scene. The women who respond to this active approach love the license this gives them to lie back and let it happen.

Want to Get Fucked?
Lie back and enjoy hot passionate sex. Goodlooking, sexy, short, slightly kinky 34 y.o. lesbian looking for sexy/sensual woman for hot sex. Send letter describing your pleasure and phone number. Please no drugs or alcohol.

The dance here is about the power of taking charge, coupled with the power of giving in. The thrill of letting yourself really get into the desire for momentary mastery over someone else. The power of knowing what she likes and deciding how she is going to get it. Letting her know that you are going for her, and that she had better be there when you arrive. Giving her only the option of getting more comfortable, of giving in to what you know she wants, what you know will drive her crazy. Being satisfied with the knowledge that she wanted all that you gave, that your real power comes from her desire and your own attentiveness to pleasure. The erotic turn-on is very strong here. Taking the responsibility can get you very high.

> ### Highly Sexed Butch
> seeks fem who loves getting fucked. We are both very good-looking, in good shape and over 28. I am 5'8", blond/blue eyes and muscular, romantic and gentle. You are under 5'8" and looking for a long-term relationship of honesty and independence. (S.F. only).

The taking lesbian craves the woman of surrender, taking her wherever she is willing to go. This encounter may be planned or chosen, or it may occur spontaneously in the midst of making love. When a lesbian gives herself with abandon to another lesbian, part of the thrill comes from engaging in a taboo act, a secret to be kept from the lesbian thought police.

SURRENDER, LESBIAN STYLE

We believe that we should always be active, never be passive. We believe surrender has made women vulnerable and led to our oppression. Yet there are lesbians who revel in the emotional and sexual art of surrender. There is a freedom in giving in.

> ### Smartass Femme
> seeks quick-witted butch who will make her laugh. I'm tall, smart, funny and a damn good cook. Looking for a chivalrous humorous girl with personality galore—someone who will hold doors, drive on dates and lay me good. You'll get the best bran muffins in town, advice on any topic you want, and bite marks on your arms. East Bay, clean, sober, smokeless.

The act of surrender is powerful. If you don't surrender, your partner can't be her aggressive, creative self. If you don't surrender, there is a tension that is not relieved. If you don't surrender, you won't receive what is lovingly available. There are all levels of surrender. You can surrender to her way of doing dishes, you can surrender to her pedantic nature, you can surrender to her personality. You can also surrender to her in sex, giving yourself as a gift. You can allow yourself not to direct this part of the love-making, giving it over to your partner.

> ### Look No Further
> I'm interested in meeting a woman other than by going to the bars every weekend. I'm 29, White, 5'5", attractive, long dark curly hair, feminine. I'm career oriented, although not a workaholic. I love to go away on long romantic weekends or just spend the day in bed having fun! I am sexually attracted to an androgynous, aggressive woman, who enjoys taking the initiative, in her late 20s to early 30s, with a medium build, sense of humor and preferably taller than I am. She must take pride in her appearance and be career oriented. Let's have some fun and hope it goes further.

Some lesbians crave this art of surrender. The sexual excitement for them is in not knowing where things are going, letting another lead the way. They are turned on by lying passively until there is a need for active receptiveness. There is no way in which this is a woman being taken advantage of. She is strongly involved in giving in, giving it up, letting her submissive side show up fully.

Of course, the surrender can go both ways. Both partners can give themselves to each other. I'm not, however, talking about: "We each have to make love to the other—so you be passive now and I'll be active." Surrender only gains its erotic depth from a true giving over. It's an action of its own, not done to even things out. Surrender comes from a place of need on many levels—psychic, physical, and emotional.

. . . .

"When I lay back on the bed, stretch my arms over my head, spread my legs, and wait, I get more excited than any other time. I want her to want me absolutely. And I want her to take me beyond myself, and so deep into myself at the same time. It's my wanting that gets us there. If I'm not available, there's no way she can do what she wants to do."

. . . .

MACHO SLUTS

This term was made popular by Pat Califia in her book by the same name. According to Califia, the macho slut is directly connected to S/M practices. I would suggest that there are macho sluts who cross all lines of sexual style, not just S/M. In fact, there are women who celebrate being sluts; to me, this celebration is in and of itself macho. Women were not trained for this kind of bravado.

When I was discussing the whole issue of the numbering on the one to ten butch/femme scale with a friend of mine, she asked "Well, what number is slut?" I loved that. Indeed, what number *is* slut? Actually, I think it should be done with a grid. A femme could be a slut. So could a butch. And there are certainly androgynous sluts; they originated nonmonogamy.

She Slices, She Dices
She'll turn you into coleslaw in less than 30 seconds! Horny-but-shy, would-be tiger lady, 27, seeks cocky smartass for mutual sarcasm, anguished soul-searching, screwing, moderate S/M (bottom and top), and more or less serious relationship. A's fans and art snobs get special consideration. Send photo, baseball cards, and/or a really stupid joke you knew when you were ten.

The macho slut loves sex. She loves sex with her partner. She loves sex with different women. She may even love sex with men. She loves sex with herself. Sex by any other name is sex. She does sex, not just talks about it. She wants to flaunt it, try everything. (Well, maybe not everything for every macho slut, but a fair number of them are willing to try anything once.) She wants to let everyone know she is having fun with it. I think flaunting it is especially important; that is the true slut.

Control Woman From Hell
seeks sweet, innocent, young, blond woman to explore sexual boundaries. Want to control and be controlled. My tortured mind needs it. Is sex getting better and deeper?

The slut woman has been punished for centuries. The macho slut has finally reclaimed this behavior as powerful, fun, and filled with surprises. The ability to have sex when you want, with whom you want, how you want, and then to tell as many people as you want, is the dream of the macho slut.

"When I was nine, I went with my whole family to visit my very proper Southern grandmother. In one memorable battle, my grandmother told me very fiercely, 'You are not going to grow up to be a lady!' And I answered 'I don't want to be a lady, I want to be a slut!' We had to pack up and leave that afternoon. In the car, my dad asked very tersely if I knew what the 'slut' word meant. I may not have known all the connotations, but I sure had a sense of my destiny."

Coupling Styles

Within the lesbian community, it's almost impossible to talk about sex without talking about partners. Even when I ask single women at my workshops to talk about sex, they eventually get back to the relationship that ended, the relationship that is just beginning, or the relationship ideal that is just around the corner. For this reason, I decided to include some of the coupling styles that are common and easily recognizable. There are certainly other patterns, and within any coupling style, a whole range of sexual activities are possible. The possibilities for couples within lesbian culture are endless, which is one of the factors that makes our lifestyle so exciting.

TWINS

At a recent professional conference, I met a lesbian couple who were exactly the same height, both quite thin, with wild, wild hair, each talking a mile a minute. They dressed alike; they even drove alike. Neither of them ever seemed to be prepared to deal with the world: neither had enough money for the tolls, nor had they brought the right clothes. They were born in different parts of the country; one had a child, the other didn't. They had different color hair; one was a student, the other a counselor. Yet they were the same. I would get their names mixed up. I was never clear which one was talking to me. It wasn't that their faces were alike, but they were twins. They had come together like that, neither conspiring to manipulate the other. They were just truly twins.

What I Seek is Myself
in others. I want to meet other lesbians who are more like me than different. I'm flexibly domineering, adventurous, honest and sex-positive. Strong, assertive women turn me on if they have the maturity to temper their energy. Pushy child-women don't cut it! I like macabre humor, surprises and intimacy with equals. My diverse interests include archaeology, gardening, travel, prosperity-consciousness, photography and occasional juicy gossip. Sharing ourselves is effortless and exciting if the chemistry clicks. Shall we explore together? My physicals: 5'6", 37 years, 120 lbs., blond/blue, androgyne. What I seek is also what I have to offer! Your fone and foto (returnable) receive my prompt attention.

Twins are lesbians who bond with other women who look and act very much like themselves. You might think of couples you know that would fit this description. Women who can and do enjoy wearing each other's clothes, not because they wear the same size but because they truly share each other's taste and style. Women who have the same energy, not who just adjust to each other's pace. Women who actually might be mistaken for one another—the ones you always forget—which one was Sally, which one Roberta? As a couple they are attracted to the same kinds of women, and the same lesbians are attracted to both of them.

I'm not talking here about women who, as time goes on, begin to make their partner over in their own image. I think this grows out of not being comfortable with difference, rather than a true erotic attachment to similar women. In fact, the women I've seen made over in their partner's image seem not to last long in a relationship that has no room for their original and true selves.

Femme to Femme
Very femme, very pretty, single, 32, seeking to meet other like me for socializing. If you are femme, stylish, sophisticated, professional, stable, sincere, 28-38, and value friendships, I would love to meet you for fun, friendship and possibly more. Photos appreciated/will be returned.

The eroticism of the self is an exciting aspect of twinning. These women are involved with a mirror image. This is neither negative nor selfish; it's an erotic involvement of compatible energies. These women find tremendous passion for another with similar needs and wants. Sharing the same rhythm is a part of the appeal. The dance goes back and forth between them, sometimes in a very subtle way, with no one leading, no one following. The dance can include room for change, but is focused on sameness. The implosion of this passion within the twin relationship can have tremendous power.

. . . .

"I gravitate more and more towards people who are doing the same thing in their lives. Women who have similar passive and aggressive parts going on. What we share in common is some kind of psychic communication. When you're hanging around with someone who's so similar to you, you can cut through a lot real quickly."

. . . .

This coupling shows up between lesbians of any size, shape, or any placement on the butch/femme scale. There are butches who only are attracted to butches, androgynous lesbians who are only attracted to their androgynous counterparts, and femmes who are only attracted to femmes. There are also lesbians who don't identify with any of these categories, but are attracted only to remarkably similar women.

Within this configuration of twins, there can be many forms of sexual energy. Being twins does not mean that these women are completely equal in their sexual expressions or that they are always available to initiate and receive. A lesbian who chooses a partner who looks like her does not necessarily have the perfect sex life. Not even deep similarities of pace, compatibility, or rhythm will guarantee ease in the sexual arena.

When twins are together, they often exude a passionate exchange. The lust is there, the fire exponential. Though twins often have therapists who help them explore the problems of merging, this "help" may be lost on the twins. Why give up a good thing when you have it?

BOSTON MARRIAGE

This label used to refer to two "spinster" women who lived together, presumably without a sexual relationship. If these women did have sex, they were careful to hide it. The modern-day version is two women who live together as lesbians, and now what they hide is that they don't have sex. Esther Rothblum and Kathleen Brehony have described this phenomenon in, "The Boston Marriage Today: Romantic but Asexual Relationships Among Lesbians," published in *Gays, Lesbians and Their Therapists: Studies in Psychotherapy*.

Meeting My Metreya

Mature Brit artist, experienced in positive relationships and creative sexual ethics, seeks to establish a supportive heart/soul connection with emphasis on companionship and mutual growth. Rubber stamping interests not necessary. Mine are: fine arts, horses, water (in and out of boats), outdoor adventures. If you are well covered, warm-hearted, easygoing and comfortable with yourself, but want a special refinement of a woman's trusting love, write.

The modern Boston marriage is a relationship that began with sexual relating, but in which the women no longer have sex. Unlike the women of previous generations who didn't want their communities to think they had sex together, women of today *want* their community to assume they are sexual.

This is a phenomenon which is quite prevalent in the lesbian community. The minute two women are sexual together, they begin to see themselves as "lovers" and to be seen that way by their friends and community. They're expected to build a relationship after being sexual just one time. As intimacy builds between the women, the true meaning of "lover" in our lesbian culture begins to emerge, and the women form bonds that keep them together. "Lover" comes to mean two women who are building a life together. I believe the contradictions of the "lover" label put pressure on our sex lives. As soon as we are sexual together, we've formed a relationship, and then as that emotional relationship progresses, we're expected to maintain the sexual connection that was its source.

In *Lesbian Passion*, I show that lesbian couples have a 75 percent drop-off in sexual relating in the first three years they are together. There are many reasons that lesbian couples slow down or stop their sexual relationship. The role of women in society, sexual abuse, homophobia, boredom, childhood issues and, I suspect, hormones all play a part. Yet, these nonsexual couples are still called "lovers." There is an agreed subcultural silence about the fact that many lesbian couples stop having sex.

For lots of couples, sex becomes less important than the emotional bonding in the relationship. The fact that these women are not genitally sexual doesn't mean that they don't have sexual energy. They often are sexually turned on to one another. As Rothblum and Brehony point out, these women are commonly sexually affectionate in public, but once in the privacy of their own home, they do not act on those sexual feelings. They usually do not discuss the lack of sex in their relationship with one another.

I believe that these women *do* have sexual feelings which are not overtly expressed, except in situations where they know they cannot act on them. I have found that in these relationships women often masturbate in secret and can have a vivid fantasy life. The common phenomenon of lesbian couples breaking up suddenly, with one of the women becoming sexually involved with a third party, is often prompted by the slow disintegration of the sexual bond between the original twosome. Usually, if this couple comes to therapy beforehand, they don't describe the lack of sex as a problem, even though that lack may ultimately be what destroys the relationship.

Want To Come Out And Play?

I like romantic dinners by candlelight, cuddling up on the beach to watch the sunset, and brazen acts in public. I read Clavell, Rice and Zimmer-Bradley, and I write reflections on these times we live in. I'm looking for the gentle intimacy of a few friends, who like me live in the day while having dreams of the future. I prefer the sensual to the sexual and waiting for the former is worth not rushing into the latter. If you also would like to explore the newly revived concept of dating, reply with Late twenties or thirtysomething appreciated.

There are also many women who live within a Boston Marriage who don't leave. Not having sex is perfectly acceptable to both women, and there aren't other sexual temptations that they struggle with. They're happy with the affectionate connection they have. These women may have experienced trauma around sex, or they may have simply found it inconvenient, or messy. It's not a problem not to have sex; it's a relief.

I believe there is an inertia the longer the couple lives without sex, and that inertia is harder and harder to overcome. Overcoming it is just not attractive for some couples.

There is often a sigh of relief throughout my audiences when I describe nonsexual lesbian relationships as common. Many, many lesbian couples live within a "Boston Marriage." For the most part, the sexual relationship of any couple is not discussed within the community, so pretending to be sexual lovers is easy to do. The sexual energy between the two women is not fully consummated, but that is often of little concern to the couple themselves, their friends, or the community.

YES/NO

I've written about this in both *Lesbian Sex* and *Lesbian Passion*. This couple is as common as the Boston Marriage. One woman wants to have sex, and conversely her partner doesn't. At least, that's what it looks like: the "yes" woman wants sex all the time, and the "no" woman would be content with watching television for the rest of her life. The reality often is that if the "no" woman says "yes," the "yes" woman is likely to say "no." It seems as if the most important component is that there is always a "yes" and a "no" in the couple.

The dance steps seem to complement each other. You step forward and I'll step back. Then if I step forward, you have to retreat. When the "yes" woman asks for sex at the end of a tiring day, the "no" woman is in the position of stopping sex. She is the one who has to say "Not tonight, honey, I'm tired." The "no" woman is fearful of asking for sex because she is worried that if she starts initiating sex, the "yes" woman will get carried away. The dance continues in this way, and even when the "no" woman does have sex, the "yes" woman can say "Well, you're only having sex because I want to, not because you want to." It can be an endless merry-go-round. The interesting part to me is that the "yes" woman doesn't go with another "yes" woman. I always believe the "yes" and "no" are together so there will be someone to initiate, and someone to set limits.

Sex/No Sex
(This is the headline of a real ad—but you have to make up the text. We don't advertise for a push-pull dance around sex.)

This is actually a common dyad within the lesbian community and is certainly a sexual rhythm. There's a tension built between the two that can sustain a sexual passion. But if this couple begins to identify one of them as having a problem, there can be a lot of negativity—the sex maniac versus the frigid woman.

If the yes/no dance is to succeed, both positions have to be filled. The "yes" woman may be willing to concede that she doesn't always want to have sex, and is grateful that someone is stopping things. The "no" woman may be willing to admit that having a woman in her life who initiates sex is quite a gift. This surrender to what *is* can be refreshing and can, in fact, make the erotic movement between the two more recognizable.

Cultural Styles

This is a group of icons that are quite well known within the lesbian community. You may not have thought of them as sexual styles before, but there is an eroticism that is basic to each of them. I call them "cultural" styles because they fit into the sociology of the lesbian community and because they are unique in our culture. They may also appear in other sexual orientations, but the way in which they are interpreted by lesbians has a flavor all our own.

CLOSET LESBIANS

These women are familiar at least by reputation to all of us. They're not out to most people and rarely participate in overt lesbian activities. They are afraid they will lose their jobs, family ties, and neighborhood connections because of their lesbianism. Their attachments in other parts of their lives are more important than their involvement with the "out" lesbian community. These women sometimes don't like what they experience when they are in the lesbian community and prefer being involved in mainstream culture.

The sexual energy between two women who don't identify themselves or wish to be identified by anyone else as lesbian must be intense. They have to overcome their anxiety about being out in order to make a connection. These women do find each other and become sexual and emotional lovers.

> ### Play & Travel Mate
> Seeking GWF 35-45, "looks and acts straight" to play golf, tennis and any other sport you can think of. Travel the coast and country of California from Mendocino to Baja & all points in between. Love the sun & surf, camping & sightseeing. Adventurous, spontaneous, love of life & fun to be with. Has the time and $$ to go wherever & whenever.

Even when closet lesbians have had more than one sexual experience with another woman, some still believe they're not really lesbians. In fact, in the survey for this book, seven percent of the women described themselves as "a woman who fell in love with a woman." Others in the closeted group know they are lesbians, but prefer to keep their sexual orientation known only to a small group so as not to threaten their standing in the heterosexual community. I know a woman who has her friends park a block or more away from her house so her neighbors don't see the same cars there over and over. These women find each other, or find lesbians who are out in the community, and form sexual relationships.

There's a particular type of sexual energy that comes from cruising another woman without any overt indication. This smoldering sexuality must be expressed strongly but silently. Indicating to another woman that you are interested in her when there's no way to know if she's willing to become sexually involved is dangerous and exhilarating.

> ### Northern Noveau
> Is there anyone left out there, 35-45, new to lesbian lifestyle? Everyone else seems to have arrived years ago. Due to job in small community, must remain discreet. Want to meet and grow with North Bay women in same circumstances. Must have superb sense of humor, be mature and like to make up life as it goes along. Non-arrogant veteran lesbians welcome to respond.

This can be a familiar situation for lesbians who are out of the closet as well—that risk of being turned down and looking like a fool. However, closet lesbians feel they are risking their own identity, their job, or the companionship of their family. These women who are so fearful are actually taking bigger risks than "out" lesbians. Now obviously in a culture that hates women and lesbians, we all take risks to be lesbians, but I believe the hazards are lessened when you embrace the lifestyle and have friends and a supportive lesbian culture. When you try to love women with no support except perhaps from a few friends, you are on much more shaky ground.

The sexual dance that two closet lesbians do is more like the rock and roll dancing of the '60s. Each woman dances across from the other, uninvolved, acting as if in fact she is dancing alone. Through elaborate coded discussions, and finally overt overtures, closet lesbians establish their interest in one another. This can be very exciting, heightened by the fear of being found out by others or rejected by the woman you might be reading wrong. The sexual act itself might even be anticlimactic; with the courtship carrying such high stakes, the charge is heavily weighted at the beginning.

Almost half of the women in my survey said they pass for straight some of the time, and another one-third refer to their lesbian lover as their "friend" when talking to straights. This closet is filled with many of us. We use it at different times for different reasons.

WOMEN IN UNIFORM

Lesbians in uniform as an erotic rhythm may seem like a farfetched idea. However, I have heard from many women who are firefighters, police, soldiers, and doctors, that lesbians swoon over their appearance. The soldiers and peace officers may have a difficult time in certain settings since they represent what good leftist, liberal dykes aren't supposed to support. However, I know more than one very liberal lesbian who has lost it over the uniform of a woman whose politics she was at odds with. Firefighters have somewhat of an easier time, since they rescue people rather than arrest them.

The dream of a lot of girls in the Western world is of being rescued. We may all strive to rescue ourselves, but it's hard to get over the fantasy of someone else taking us away from all this.

> ### Uniformed Lesbian
> looking for similarly clad dyke to pull to the side of the Highway, interrogate at my leisure, and release on whim. Other uniform fantasies a plus. Whether as an astronaut guaranteed to take you "where no one has gone before" or a mechanic willing to make house calls, I promise you won't be bored. Your pic gets mine.

A friend wrote to me about women in uniform: "These images are attractive principally because the power they reflect is drawn from the dominant culture's validation of men in those roles. So at once this is confrontation with male-identified roles, but also a resonance with male power images." This is part of the appeal; there is no way to get around our unconscious images of power and the ways we react to them. However, these icons are additionally powerful because of the tantalizing probability that the women in these uniforms may be lesbian.

The speculation by most lesbians over whether a woman in uniform is "one of us" is universal. When she won't break composure or won't answer a direct question, the mystery keeps the sexual energy up. Is she, or isn't she?

One of the women firefighters who rode on the fire truck in the Gay Freedom Day Parade in San Francisco told me they got a tremendous amount of overtly sexualized attention. In fact, one of them was later written about in the local lesbian/gay newspaper, *Bay Times* (July, 1990) by a woman who covered the parade: "What about the dashing firefighter? Brown sparkly hair, oh so well-fitted uniform, bright coy smile; Who? Where? When? 'Oh miss?' we crooned, the gaggle of gals I sat with: 'It seems our pussy is stuck in a tree!' "

Sexualizing the uniformed image is a natural follow-up. These women are visible and approachable; they've met the strenuous physical requirements for their jobs, have obvious muscles, appear confident, and project a take-charge attitude. Many women find this a thrill. The idea that these women will take charge in bed is, I'm certain, one of the fantasies entertained at least in the unconscious mind. Whether the reality matches that fantasy or not, there is an obvious dynamic here of "You be in charge and I'll be the damsel in distress."

LESBIAN POLICE

These women are not to be confused with women in uniform. They are not truly police. They simply perform that function for our community. They police our various mores, rules, and sexual behavior. They do for us what we don't want to do for ourselves. They are the conscience of the community. Often they are not identified in the community, although we all agree that they are there. The lesbian police are the ones sure to tell the rest of us how poorly we are doing in the lesbian politically correct behavior department. They work on a national level as well, criticizing lesbians everywhere and making sure that all of us feel guilty about whatever we are doing.

The lesbian police are in fact an erotic form. You might not think so, but indeed they have taken the place of our mothers, fathers, clergy, rabbis, and the real police. They have emerged as our superego. That is, among other concerns, they help us figure out what kinds of sexual feelings are appropriate.

Angry Amazon!

Where are you? I've tried it all, but when I met you at the "Take Back The Night" protest, I knew I'd found it: love *and* politics. But I didn't get your number! Meet me at International Women's Day Demo March 8th, 4:30 PM downtown SF. I'll be wearing the Dykes From Hell T-Shirt. Honey, I "Still Ain't Satisfied"!

If we are willing to follow the strict line of the lesbian police, we won't have any stray thoughts or feelings about anything "bad." We are certain that the erotic behavior of the lesbian police is "good" behavior. If we follow their lead, there's no anxiety about whether or not we are being good lesbians. This censorship allows us to breathe a collective sigh of relief. Seriously, censorship can make some women feel more comfortable with their sexuality because they don't have to figure anything out for themselves. They can be assured this brand of eroticism is woman-positive.

The list of behaviors that are unacceptable include: fantasies about overpowering someone (being overpowered isn't even thinkable); fantasies about men (being one or being with one); using dildos; using vibrators (a 20th century tool that will get you away from hands); anal sex; S/M; and so on. For many women, this is a godsend, because trying out other kinds of sex is too distressing.

Problems arise when the lesbian police tell us they have the right to determine who is a real lesbian. If you don't follow their guidelines, you're not a real lesbian. Though there is an eroticism of sorts within the guidelines of the lesbian police, putting that out as the only standard for all lesbians is the real danger.

LESBIAN VAMPIRES

The lesbian vampire is an erotic concept that caught my attention at the "Queer Theory" conference at the University of California at Santa Cruz, in 1990. ("Queer theory" about homosexuality goes beyond gender theory. Gender theory is what is currently used to explain homophobia. Simply put, lesbians and gay men don't act like women and men are supposed to. "Queer theory" believes homophobia is created because same-sex desire transgresses the mainstream culture's view of sex.)

The lesbian vampire concept was reported in a paper by Sue-Ellen Case titled "En-Tranced Looks: The Vampire and the Lesbian." She presented information about the ancient vampire writings in literature, later expressed in movies, that included female vampires. According to Case, the lesbian vampire said, "I will take on the loathsome and revel in it." She sucked the blood of another woman, creating an extremely sexualized, erotic experience for both.

According to Case, the early use of lesbian vampire imagery was of a powerful female seducing another woman who was thrilled at being taken. She believes the vampire myth questions the meaning of existence, and adds metaphysical overtones when it is a homoerotic experience. A vampire "pierces" the living, trying to drink in the essence of life. The vampire living forever can never be of the living *or* of the dead. This metaphysical dilemma permeates vampire literature.

This concept helped me see an equivalent in the real world, the modern day "lesbian vampires." This lesbian is practiced in the art of seducing heterosexual women. We all know her—the lesbian who doesn't go for other lesbians; she's attracted to the "other" energy of women who are still in the sleep of heterosexuality. Bringing these women into the ranks of her own kind is the excitement. It's not the same as the need of a heterosexual man to keep a woman as his own. It's the thrill of finding a woman who, like a diamond in the rough, is just waiting to experience her true sexual energy. The lesbian vampire is thrilled by the swoon of the woman who has been unconsciously waiting to join her sisters. This action is shown brilliantly in Judy Grahn's title character from her book and play, *The Queen of Swords*.

The community denies that such lesbians exist. We don't want to be accused of preying on straight women. We want the world at large to believe that these women somehow wander into our world on their own, with no guidance. However, the lesbian vampire is alive and well. How many women reading this book were once straight and were brought out by an already established lesbian? Whether or not we are fearful of this act of seduction, it does exist. It's not objectification, it's an erotic exchange that serves both women involved.

Let's Get Intense

Very unusual woman, 37, intelligent, sensual, gentle, looking for a special woman 18-30 for intense relationship. I am seeking someone like myself who enjoys emotional and physical closeness in a non-possessive, non-monogamous relationship. Prefer someone who is feminine and not into roles. Okay if you are just beginning to explore with women or are bisexual. Photo appreciated.

Bringing out a heterosexual woman is a sexually exciting phenomenon for all of us. Coming out stories which recount the act of a more experienced lesbian bringing out a straight woman make our juices get going. We aren't out there preying on women, but when they come to our side, it's always a turn-on.

Yes—Yes—Yes And More Yes

Young woman—single and free—experience preferred, but will accept a wild trainee. I am a great teacher and of course you would be my pet. I am a dark and unpredictable GWF, 30s, versatile and resourceful, not to mention reliable. Please write me soon and cut out the picture from your favorite magazine that most resembles you.

PRIESTESS

Many lesbians are currently practicing the teachings of the occult and psychic worlds. There has been so much pain associated with the male-dominated religions of the world that women have returned to the pantheistic, pagan religions of matriarchal times. The women who are disseminating this information—doing the readings and teaching the ancient words—are often seen as powerful beings. There is no need for these women to be nonsexual. The earth mother and goddess images are ripe with sexualized visions. Many women expect their sexuality to enhance their spiritual growth.

These priestesses of the lesbian psychic and occult world are often seen by members of their group as holding the power of the goddess, the mother earth, and the regeneration of the spirit world. They personify a pureness of sexual desire. The priestesses themselves can see their sexuality as something of the other world. The priestess is held in high regard as the giver of a pure love which can help heal a woman's sexual self.

Mystic Female

Spiritual catalyst, let me harmonize your aura, open yourself up so you can see the light. I'm a Lover of life, my life is fun, magic, adventurous. I constantly risk, visualize, create. This feminine Aquarian is very beautiful, attractive, energetic. Loving, gentle, passionate,

romantic and I Love and accept myself. I'm looking for
a womym who can just be a friend, someone to share with,
to hit thrift stores with, who truly enjoys life and isn't
caught up in games, dishonesty—you know what I mean.
I'm not into rude city dykes, I'm allergic to negativity of
any kind, so if you don't Love yourself and abuse your
body with drink, drugs, smoke don't reply. If fear runs
your life forget it, this womyn laughs at the face of death
and doesn't believe in sickness, weakness, bitchyness.
Let your higher self guide you into meeting me, spirit
tells me you're out there. I've been guided to this city
just recently to find you. I know you're here. Come fly
with me.

THE JOCK

Lesbian jocks are a sexy and independant group. In fact, at
the first Gay Games, women got so excited by the French dyke
athletes that they auctioned off their track suits.

The sorrow that women have felt about their bodies is
legion. Almost all of us have been sexually harassed by men, 38
percent of us were sexually abused as children, one-third of us
will be raped as adults. Lost in a power struggle with men who
have tried to subjugate our bodies for their own needs, many of
us have felt almost alien to our bodies. We've abused our bodies
with self-mutilation, starvation, diets, and food binging. We've
taken harmful chemicals, smoked, had sex in ways that
endangered us, with people who have endangered us. We've
wanted to get out of our bodies.

Lesbian Into Sports!
Lesbian into sports (friends not) is looking for someone
who understands that Boggs is not a swamp and Bird
doesn't sing in a tree.

When we see a woman who has actually decided to be in
her body and honor it, she represents a claiming of self. The
lesbian athlete takes her body seriously. She takes time to train
it and takes pride in her physical abilities. The women who have
gone beyond what women are expected to do in the realm of

physical achievements are put on a pedestal. This woman who is in her body turns on other women, who may want her to be into *their* bodies.

After Martina Navratilova won her ninth straight Wimbledon singles title, becoming the woman who has won the most singles titles in its history, she ran up through the crowd to hug her lover, Judy Nelson. She put out to the world on international television that "this woman is important to me no matter what you all think about it." This famous lesbian athlete, the most successful player in the history of the sport, gives all of us more power. We know the beauty of a body as a perfect instrument, the excitement of that strength and concentration.

Talk Dirty To Me
Tall, blond Jockette, mid-thirties, seeks smart lady with good body and engaging personality. I consider myself a cross between Woody Allen, Diane Keaton, Will Clark, and Candace Bergen. I like watching movies, making movies and making love. I'd love to meet someone special, but if you're smart and funny and don't smoke, I'd be satisfied. Not a local resident, but cognizant of modern transportation.

The thrill of the jock is that she takes back control over her body. The disabled woman playing wheelchair basketball defies the proscriptions of the culture to say, "Oh yes I can!" Lesbian athletes seem as if they would be in charge of their own sexuality as well.

The fantasy (in both lesbian culture and the mainstream) is that women who are that powerful must only want to be with other women. We envision the athlete as one of our own, who has taken the risk to be different, to take care of herself, to do what women are not supposed to do. It's her power that we want for ourselves, and the beauty of her body in our hands.

"Just being able to watch her body move is like watching poetry. It's always the muscles that get me. How can a woman have such muscles? Sometimes I just can't wait to get my hands on her. I really love it that she's mine—so strong and so soft at them same time."

THE CHEERLEADER

All those athletes need cheerleaders: women who swoon over the flexing of lesbian muscles, women who wait patiently in the stands urging their friends and lovers on, women who would never enact these feats of physical prowess themselves. These are the women who make up the chants, who know how to get the crowd going. These are the women who watch game after game at the lesbian softball leagues and then organize the pot-lucks afterwards. They are the ones their lovers go to after the game to get their muscles rubbed and their egos soothed.

Fan Appreciation Day!
is where you'll find me. X-Athletic supporter loves dykes who can hit, run and steal. I'll bring the gatorade if you'll bring me out for dinner after the game. We can recap the day's big plays (I thought you were safe too), laugh a little and then??? Hurry, the season's almost over!

Cheerleaders have a sexual appeal. Cheerleaders are not going to be competitors; they revel in the competition of others. They want to receive the sexual energy of the jock coming away from the game. The cheerleader is bursting with enthusiasm. She will still be mad at the umpire at the end of the evening. She has the intensity that the athlete already spent on the game. The lesbian who has been watching is filled with sexual energy. She is ready. She can be the admiring, take-charge girlfriend any achiever wants to come home to.

. . . .

"I remember in high school always wanting the cheer-leaders to look at me like they did at football players. Now that I'm on the softball team, I have these lesbians in the bleachers looking at me. It drives me on to try to win, and it also drives my hormones crazy. I want her to see me and want me. I want her with all that wholesome, Kansas energy."

. . . .

DOWNTOWN DYKES

She's the downtown dyke, the business lesbian, the professional with a cause. She's the woman we meet in a corporate headquarters who just somehow doesn't look like she's interested in men beyond her work. She's the woman who looks you straight in the eye, who walks with assurance down the hall. She's the professional who is aching for you to take her home and take that suit off.

> ### Capture
> my imagination. Looking for complexity, courage, intelligence and a deep capacity for joy. I enjoy MTV and opera, Sondheim and Lloyd Webber, movies, tennis, evening walks, dining out during the week, dining in on the weekends, the Sunday New York Times, the south of Spain, Merlot, romance, psychology, leather jackets, eroticism and adventure. I am a busy, successful Financial District professional who seeks the company of other professional women who are over thirty and who may also be seeking new friends for fun, pleasure and a possible relationship. Women with poise, wisdom and a keen sense of the ridiculous are encouraged to reply.

This woman, with her lesbianism safely tucked inside that pinstripe (with a skirt of course), has a smoldering sexual quality. She gives off signs only to the most astute. Others spend years with her at work and never know. It's not that she is closeted at work, it's that she's *at* work, and this job is her life right at that moment. But let another lesbian move into the space, and suddenly the subtle energy exchange is electric.

There's a voice inside her saying, "Get me out of here." Lesbians crave one another, and the professional woman is no different. She may get right up from the bed and go back to work, or get dressed and go home, but when she's with you, she's filled with passion that needs release. Its containment fuels her desire.

"I love walking in the financial district in my corporate drag. I like to make eye contact with other dykes; I cruise constantly. Even though I'm out at work, lunchtime is when I get to let out the really outrageous side of myself."

OLD LESBIANS

There's a famous sex scene in June Arnold's *Sister Gin* in which one old lesbian removes her false teeth and goes down on her lover, to the intense pleasure of both. This story exploded the idea (among younger women) that old dykes don't have sex. Of course, the old dykes themselves weren't confused about this point.

Old dykes represent a powerful new vision of what it is to be old. She's a woman who's made her own choices for a lifetime, and in old age, she's not beholden to children or to family. She has all the power of her knowledge and the incredible freedom that comes at the end of life.

When post-menopausal women talk about sex, they report with some wonder that orgasms have become more frequent and more multiple (see *Lesbians At Midlife: The Creative Transition*, by Sang, Warshow and Smith). In the survey of 1500 lesbians reported in *Lesbian Passion*, there was no significant difference between any age group in how much they masturbated, had partner sex, or enjoyed sex in general. The women over 50 had as much interest in sex as the women under twenty. In fact, the general feeling was that women over 50 had more positive feelings about sex. The greatest difficulty was finding lovers their age.

Where Were You When JFK Was Shot?

If you can't remember or weren't born yet, read no further. Mature, responsible dyke seeks woman my age (50+) for friendship and possibly more. You must be emotionally stable, confident in your sexual identity, and patient—I'm just out of a 9-year relationship and am somewhat new to this "scene." Let's get together over coffee or lunch and talk. And please, no excessive alcohol or drugs.

The old woman is the teacher, the crone, the wise woman—an erotic symbol for many lesbians. Younger women hope she will show them the way, though she herself may have other fish to fry. The old dyke shares so much experience with her peers that they don't have to repeat the dance they have already done for so long. They can be adventurers, be playful, live inside the freedom that is old age. The old lesbian seems to have gotten through the vicissitudes of life; she appears less constrained by the convention of lesbian correctness.

Younger lesbians have found old lesbians very attractive, but in a patronizing way. We want them to be our teachers and our mothers. Old dykes have had to teach us that they are our lovers, not our mothers. The younger lesbian community in many ways continues to objectify old lesbians. We want to be taught by them, but we don't know how to include them in our groups.

Maybe it's their power that makes young lesbians so frightened. The old dyke isn't bound to a job, mortgage payments, a stake in the American way. She's her own woman. And she's a lover with years of experience and technique. When these women find each other, the eroticism is rich with ease and pleasure. Women are sexual until they die, and if you believe in the afterlife, the goddess only knows what comes next.

BABY DYKES

Now here's a category of lesbian that many of us are fascinated by, if not lusting after right this very moment. I'm referring to what society would call "young women"—women who are in their late teens or early to mid-twenties. You know the type. Baby dykes. These days, baby dykes can often be found in the forefront of the "bad girls", S/M dykes, or other outrageous and visible groups. Many baby dykes are also known as baby butches. It's interesting to me that I've never heard anyone refer to a young dyke as a "baby femme." Perhaps this is because of the lesbian community's devaluation of femmes in general. Or maybe we don't notice baby femmes as much because at such a young age stereotypical gender behavior is particularly well entrenched and we tend to more visibly notice those young women who challenge the status quo. In any case, "baby" seems to require a certain toughness that is definitely present in baby dykes.

What identifies a baby dyke? For many lesbians, it is the most overt qualities: a youthful physical appearance and body. Her face hasn't been through the wars. There is a romantic quality that young women create with their freshness, enthusiasm, and openness. This freshness is erotic. But the attractions are not only physical. This quality is also an attitude; a baby dyke mentality that can be equally seductive. It stems from the naivete of baby dykes and from their complete lack of boundaries. Because of their age and commensurate level of experience, many baby dykes idolize and eroticize their older sexual partners who they feel know more about life and love.

This gratification from such a beautiful young woman can be tremendously sexually exciting and empowering. One "older" woman told me a story that made it clear to me.

"I had my first relationship recently where I played a butch, and I wrote a story about it called 'The Change of Life.' Friends came up to me and said, 'How could you just change roles like that?' It's because I met a beautiful femme young woman. And all these years, I have been storing up in me the knowledge of what else I wanted done to me, or how else something should be done...and I've wanted to give it all back. I wanted my time to pleasure a woman and fill in all the spaces that were not always hooked up the way I thought they could be. She was the kindest young woman—she's in her twenties—and I say that with all respect because she didn't laugh at me. She knew *exactly* how to make me feel that what I was giving was what she needed as a femme. And I'm very grateful that I could explore that part of me."

When we look at a baby dyke we see what we wish we had been like at their age. Social mores have changed over the years and we cannot help but wonder what it would have been like to dress and act like many young lesbians do today. We also wish that we could be like them now; in a culture that so worships youth it is not surprising that we might wish we were ten or twenty years younger. There is an erotic rhythm created by our lust for these energetic young women, and it comes in part from our desire to make love to them as we wish it had been (or as it is now) made to us. And our age and experience enable us to create fantasies in which we are the experienced and perhaps initiative partner.

Making love with baby dykes can fulfill specific erotic needs for some women. There is a basic assumption that they do not know as much sexually as we do. This is very different from the anxiety we often feel with new partners closer to our own age and experience. Young lesbians represent both the past and the future. They allow us to experience feeling we have not felt in years, and their youthful energy is invigorating and enticing. Many baby dykes are conscious of their position as an object of desire within the lesbian community.

Dyke Seeks Same

I spend most of my time doing socio-political work yet PC people can nauseate me. This fun-loving, very young (but legal) Jewish assertive, energetic, nonsmoking, vegetarian, lesbosian Amazon warrior (in a socio-political sense) is seeking the company of a butch wild woman who's not in a rut. Who are you?

Another young dyke I know used to tend bar at a women's club. According to her, the best part of the job was flirting with the customers, regardless of their age. She took advantage of her position, knowing that her youth (and her sobriety) was her main attraction. The younger lesbians were pretty direct in returning her flirtations. "That felt safe. After all, no one waits up till two a.m. for the bartender to get off work." However, several older women did actively pursue her. "I thought I acted cool, but, boy, was I intimidated by a couple of them. Some of them had been out forever, and were professors at my college and stuff. I'd have fantasies of seducing them when I masturbated, but in real life I kept thinking that I was young enough to be their daughter!"

Many baby dykes can and do stick to their own age group, and two young lesbians together can have a tumultuous and volatile relationship. With little or no past and carefree attitudes, their sheer energy gives them infinite choices and distractions. This fearlessness can also create chaos, and at the same time can often be a turn-on. Needless to say, the friction between two baby dykes can make for intense and erotic sex!

Personality Styles

In addition to choices about sexual activities, relationship styles and cultural stances, lesbians approach sex with distinctive personal styles. Though obviously we're not limited to the ones below, each of these has a distinctly lesbian twist.

GOOD GIRLS

This is a sexualized term that is getting widespread use (especially in relationship to "Bad Girls", see below) in different parts of the country. These lesbians are out and are good. Not to be confused with closeted lesbians, these good girls like their lesbian lifestyle. They don't use dildos, they don't disturb the majority culture, they fit in with both lesbian and straight communities. Good girls are what really happened to the cheerleaders in your high school. Some may have tried boys for a while, but that wasn't where it was at, and they turned to girls. They came home when their parents told them to, they never smoked cigarettes, they have jobs, they don't run around on their lover, and the only leather they wear is soft, stylish jackets with no zippers.

I Would Like To Find:
Just one "nice girl" to have fun with, spoil and cultivate a relationship of substance with. Why should we let the freaks have all the fun? I'm in my early 30s, attractive, athletic and very good at making love to a woman I care about. Are you tired of flakes and dykes with sexual hangups who can't satisfy you sexually or emotionally?

The erotic dance these women do is the solid, midwestern kind of '50s thing. You go out, you like each other, you have sex, you get married, you move in together, you like each other's friends, and you have barbeques. You do not put up your tent in the rowdy camping areas at any of the women's music festivals.

Eroticism in a good girl relationship may be increased or decreased by the stability of the relationship. These women do not go for lesbian drama-rama. They don't look for another lover while they still have one. They don't break up and get back together. They pay their bills, and they don't renege on financial agreements with one another. They help one another out and are compatible.

Their sexual energy is something that can be expressed when they feel comfortable. Their sexual courting and expression are both bound to certain standards that are not out of the ordinary.

When I work with these lesbians, they do their homework. If they are working on sexual issues and I suggest they set aside a time each week to have sex, they do it. They don't come back in and say they didn't have time or they forgot. They aren't always willing to work on issues with one another, but they know they can trust each other.

Looking For A "Nice Girl"

for that special relationship we've both been preparing for. I'm hoping for a partnership with lots of tenderness and humor, honesty and affection, depth and playfulness, intellect and passion, with room to grow together and individually. Spiritual perspective essential. I'm 36, non-yuppie professional, bright, gentle, funny, more introspective than boisterous. Also 5'4", trim, nice-looking (do I sound like a "nice girl" too?). My interests: long walks, long talks, NW forests, good food, Motown, dancing, laughing, hiking, movies, occasional couch-potatoery. Turned off by cigarettes, drugs, excessive PCness, conversation hogs. So... do you have an open heart, a well-used smile and finely tuned sense of humor? Are you looking for emotional, spiritual depth in a relationship? Plus some good laughs? Perhaps two "nice girls" like us should meet!

These women sometimes have a difficult time being sexual. They don't have the friction between them that often drives couples with more differences to genital contact. The high value on being good can result in a predictable relationship.

Now of course, there are the good girls who are only attracted to bad girls. The tension in the relationship is greatly increased and sends electricity in all directions. Often the sexual energy between the two is tremendous. The good girl feels like she is taking the risk of her life, doing what she was never supposed to, getting involved with some uppity woman. The bad girl wants to corrupt the good girl and is jazzed about being able to be the outrageous one. In addition, the bad girl has the thrill of going out with the girl next door who she was supposed to become, or was forbidden to influence. Each gets to live out the part of themselves that they suppress overtly. The volatility in the relationship may be too much for either one to handle, but the sexual energy will always crackle.

BAD GIRLS

I believe this label has been used most by lesbians who came out after 1980. However, there are lesbians of all age groups who are into being bad girls. This is the dyke equivalent of the '50s rebel without a cause. Not that the bad girls don't have causes, but the bad girl image is not in and of itself politicized. Bad girls often resemble the look that James Dean made popular, even when people didn't know that he was gay. Short hair, tight jeans, short black leather jackets, fast cars, and maybe a tattoo are all parts of the scene.

As we know, "Good girls go to heaven, bad girls go everywhere." Bad girls want to do everything and be noticed while they do it. Bad girls want to be seen by other bad girls, by the culture at large, and by good girls. Shocking others is an important element. The thrill is to let the world know by stance, dress, and sometimes action that you don't follow any proscribed ideas about what women are supposed to do. Bad girls is an attitude. Unlike macho sluts, bad girls don't have to have many partners to assert their sexuality.

Catholic Girl Gone Bad
40-year-old Catholic girl gone bad. No chance for salvation. Seeks bad girls (Catholic or otherwise) for flirtation that leads to mortal sin...again and again.

The erotic dance is overt and highly charged. Though these women may or may not engage in S/M, it's often strongly hinted that they do. If S/M were an acceptable sexual expression, bad girls wouldn't make such a display of being into it. Since it's almost impossible to imagine a time when S/M will be acceptable to most lesbians, bad girls have a ready-made way of shocking the lesbian community. And they can shock the mainstream simply by being lesbians dressed in leather. Bad girls are the ones in high school who never came home when their parents told them, smoked in the girls' bathroom, and carved their initials into their arms. The good girls thought the bad girls were having sex. The bad girls made a display of looking like they were having sex, even if they weren't.

The erotic dance favored by this group has an important public component—informing the culture (lesbian or mainstream) that you aren't following prescribed rules for women. Wearing outrageous clothes with holes, showing normally hidden parts of the body, wearing leather with lots of metal on it. Cutting and dyeing hair in various creative styles. (My mother thought rollers were a mystery, she should see them now!) Wearing T-shirts that say "Dykes From Hell." Riding on motorcycles, the highlight being at Gay Freedom Day Parade in San Francisco where "Dykes on Bikes" kick-starts the parade with the thunderous display of several hundred bad girls.

Bad girl energy is highly sexualized. Being a bad girl assumes the sexual self will be expressed. The high-octane flirting of someone who acknowledges her sexual power and that of others is compelling.

> ### Bad Like Me?
> Tall, dark, aggressive, 23-year-old fem with bad attitude seeks intelligent, sexy butch with same. No Republicans, conservatives or marriage junkies.

Bad girls are often charged with the job of bringing out the sexual energy of others. When a sexual overture is made, it is often done in an offhand way, so that if rejected or ignored, the bad girl can easily recover. In fact, the persona of the bad girl is to be chilled at all times. Hysterics in the crowd love that supposed detachment and are drawn like moths to the flame. The bad girl loves the focus and increases the erotic tension by flaunting her mastery of every situation, appearing not to care about the outcome. Why shouldn't she? She's a bad girl.

THE EARTH MOTHER

This image, long in our archetypal heritage, is that of the mother who feeds us, nurtures us, and loves us best. These lesbians are the ones who always have room at their table, who will always listen to what we have to say. These are the women who give us their breasts to be suckled in an act that is both sexual and life-giving. These are the women with whom we sleep deeply.

Earth mothers suggest a woman with large hips and breasts, soft flesh and strong muscles. For some of us, the lesbian earth mother is a woman we seek. She is the softness between our uniforms, our working out, our independence. She's the one who says, "Come here, I will wrap you up, I will rock you and listen." She is the one who carries that powerful mothering tradition down through the ages.

"The only way that I can describe myself is by what I seek in the other that I can love. There is a hunger for me for a kind of nurturing. It's something that I never got as a child, and that I never could ever find in men. I just hunger for it, and I don't have enough of it myself. I'm always looking for that other. And I truly have found that in women. When I think of the women I've been with, they've always been very nurturing, very tender, very deep women that I can sort of fall into. They're endless. It's very female to me, that's how I look at it. It is sexual and emotional. It doesn't matter to me whether the woman is butch or femme, if she has that in her, then that's what I'm searching for. It's like someone opens a door, and there's light there, and that's what I go toward."

Mothering behaviors are often put down as "co-dependent." This is the woman who loves to nurture, is fed herself by nurturing, who is connected to the giving of the universe in a way that we want to share. This giving is not always from co-dependence; it is a positive, powerful woman gift, that is never ending. Yes, these women may need to learn to care for themselves as well, but their caretaking is not sick or wrong. This care-giving is part of the life force, and it *gives* the earth mother power.

The big business of turning "co-dependence" into a money-making proposition is a painful process to watch. It is another variation of woman hating, and making women despise themselves for the very thing that separates women from men and makes them powerful. Yes, there is such a thing as co-dependence. However, not every woman is co-dependent, and not every female life-giving characteristic is sick. Women do not have to drain themselves to feed others. The ability of a woman to give life, to sustain and to nurture, is a powerful gift that women need to cultivate and to keep alive.

Older, Wiser Woman

At 35, I have a life full and magical. I'm ready now to fall in love with a strong, gentle, wise woman. A woman of extraordinary heart and mind, probably older than I am. I am beginning to long for a woman who can be a spiritual and sensual teacher to me, as I have for so long been a teacher to others. I live fully and intensely and am most often attracted to women who are, like me, lovely and graceful, whose touch is exquisite, whose words are real. Write me a long letter.

The eroticism of this kind of lesbian is legend in any community. Her fecund, round appearance (not necessarily relating to her size), her fertility (not necessarily about childbearing), and her nurturing attract many lesbians who are more sharp and detached. Sex with the earth mother is both the act of making love and the act of regeneration. These two parts may not be distinct, but are always there. We crave to be mothered. In fact, lesbians are often accused of this. I say, who doesn't want to be mothered? Heterosexual women are the only ones who may miss out on being mothered in their sexual relationships. We're lucky.

THE WAIF

Although we lesbians have the reputation of being independent and able to take care of ourselves without help, there are some of us who don't fit that mold. Waifs are lesbians who want to be cared for in a particular way. They are young acting no matter what their age. They don't give their opinions easily, and they are often dependent on a stronger personality for guidance. The waif sometimes appears as if she were abandoned.

Conversely, there are lesbians who over and over seek to rescue waifs. The erotic bond these women form can be very strong. The waif's partner wants to be the one who will direct all her movements. She wants to show her how to have sex and to teach her the ways of the world. The waif's air of naivete, feigned or not, can be a real attraction. Part of being teachable is an openness to sensual experiences. The waif wants to be discovered, and her erotic self is open to the ministrations of her lover. The waif may turn out to be quite a performer, thrilling you by turning you on and filling you up.

Sugar Mommy Sought

I'm looking for a sugar mommy to house, clothe, and feed me so that I may cherish her, and finish my doctorate. I'm honest, witty, well travelled, attractive, and—alas—poor.

She's happy to go to your house or hers, but you have to decide. She eventually moves in with her lover. She is content to be protected and loved in a way that makes her feel secure.

This dependence makes many of us uneasy and is often seen as wrong. We always assume that each woman in the couple should be equally powerful in all ways. This is an ideal that will flatten each of our beautiful differences. In fact, if we were honest, who among us wouldn't like to be taken care of, maybe not always, but at some point in our lives? Who wouldn't like someone to make all the decisions, at least for awhile? Just saying "All right, dear" could seem very restful. Some of us may have less tolerance for that than others, but the fantasy is one that appeals to many.

ORDINARY GALS

Lesbian "ordinary gals" are the women who claim "I'm just like heterosexual women, only I have sex with other women." These women are not attached to the movement. They are not necessarily closeted, but might be. They aren't identified as lesbians like the "good girls" are, but they don't seem to be as tortured as the closeted lesbians can be. The distinguishing feature seems to be the "humanistic leveling" quality, as my friend called it. "We are all just the same and I like it that way."

> ### Old Fashioned Girl Who
> believes in love, family, good friends and taking care of each other is seeking non-butch/femme over 30 with similar beliefs for a relationship. Your mother would be delighted that I am well educated, well dressed, financially stable, professional in the corporate world, dependable, non-butch and have good manners. You might be interested that I am well travelled, have many cultural and sports activities, am affectionate, romantic and a little zany. If you or your mother wish to meet me, please write back about yourself.

The erotic dance these women do is a simple two-step. No need for extras, no need to make a statement. No need to wear sequins to the prom, I'm just taking my lover. We order Cokes, not even Diet Cokes, and we eat the potato chips that are on the table. We don't need creme brulée; in fact, we don't even know what it is. We like the kind of sex where you make love to me and then I make love to you, or it might be vice versa and we don't even keep track of whether it was equal. We don't stand out, we don't embarrass each other. Sex is fun, and we like to have it. We wouldn't drive a red car—too flashy. We wouldn't buy a dildo because our fingers work just fine. Anyway, it's too overt. Subtlety is the name of this dance. Easy listenin' rock.

> ### I'm Gay But...
> ...being a lesbian is not my life. There's so much else to do. Trips to Japan, evening strolls, family visits, playing in the music industry, tennis, ashrams, London, helping people, dressing to the nines, laughing a lot, the rain forests, old movies, board games, world peace, putting love into practice. Kindness and gentility: at 31 it's been a rough road but...oh, what a wonderful life. Don't miss it. And don't have me look for you in a bar. Write and tell me where you are.

When I first had the idea for an "Other Rhythms" chapter in this book, I could only think of a few sexual styles. What's become clear from my own experiences and from talking with many lesbians, is that our sexuality represents a rich mixture of specific activities, personal identity, relationship styles, and more. We have the opportunity now to claim and reclaim within ourselves that sexual mix: to know ourselves as butch, femme, androgynous or "3"; to recognize desires about receptivity and initiation; to act on core attractions in an infinite variety of ways. Understanding the real erotic history of lesbian culture gives us the possibility of enlarging that culture today, embracing flexibility instead of a new set of rules, and accepting each other for our true natures.

I've talked a lot throughout this book about the interconnections between language and culture. Most of lesbian history has been shrouded in secrecy. Stolen kisses, stolen lives. Yet, we have always been defiant. We've found each other, become lovers, created underground cultures.

My hope is that now, twenty years into a more open rebellion for gays and lesbians, we will make that culture more visible and complex. The curious invisibility of lesbians today provides it's own opportunity to create our culture without censorship. We can say almost anything to each other, and no one else in the world will know. And when we do decide to let the straight world in on our culture, we can do so on our own terms, from within our own vibrant, proud, exciting emotional and erotic frameworks.

What "Other Rhythms", and this whole book, is about is telling more of the truth of our sexual lives. I hope we will enlarge the discussions, the language, the images and the possibilities for lesbian sexuality. That we can know multiple aspects of our own desires, and can listen lovingly to those of others. Our hearts and our bodies don't lie, if we are willing to listen without preconceptions. And we have the right to be loud and proud about those desires, to announce ourselves to each other and the world.

Our similarities give us power; our diversity is our promise for the future. We need to not leave our erotic lives to guessing and hiding. Our truth is all we have, really. Because of this, I am driven to give a voice to our heritage and a nudge to our future. Because I know the price I paid for hiding the femme part of my nature, I feel we all must consider the hidden places. We need our truths, multiple and diverse. We need to talk and to create language. With ourselves, with a lover, with friends, throughout our communities, and out into the whole world.

THE DEBATE
6

"There are people left out of this conversation. I feel left out. I do not relate to butch or femme, even though I feel that within myself I have both of those parts. But when this conversation goes on, and we're talking about butch or femme, I feel like, what about me? I am somewhere in the midst. I feel like an other. That's what I claim."

"Sometimes I feel like I'm another sex altogether. If I had to choose, of course I would choose butch, but really it isn't about butch *or* femme for me. "

"What do you mean by another sex? Isn't that just being a dyke?"

"Not really. I have friends who really identify as butch or femme, it's real essential to who they are. But I've always seen myself as an outsider. When I was growing up, I didn't fit either gender. I wasn't a girl or a boy."

"I have a question. Do you think that we use these terms 'butch and femme' sort of as points on a spectrum?"

"Which is not defined."

"Which we will not talk about."

"Why don't we make it a wheel?"

"Okay. So we have a wheel that goes through various stages and phases. Now do you think that similarities or more closeness on the wheel makes for less attraction? Somehow we naturally tend to be attracted to people who are further away?"

"When you live together, you share. You just sort of balance things out."

"For me, it's not that at all. In a home setting, I think it's important to have a balance that comes from opposites."

"—because I think, my experience of being named anything is to be limited."

"Does that mean being named a lesbian?"

"Well, I was thinking about that before I said anything, and I call myself a lesbian and I call myself a dyke, but I do that within the community where that is a very rich word. I hate it when a straight person calls me that because they don't know the meaning of the word."

"Lesbian or dyke, or both?"

"They're using it as a put down."

"As a label, a flattener. And the fact of the matter is, as soon as I get my hair long, I shave my head. When I shaved my head I felt absolutely wonderful but began to feel labeled and confined. Don't box me in. Like that fundamentalist church that gave me so little room. It's really a thing to me to be named anything by anybody but myself."

"You're saying that being labeled butch or femme is pejorative?"

"Lesbian and dyke I'm fine with within the community. Butch and femme feel flattening to me, although at times I've claimed to be one, taken it to the max, and then go to the other one. I've done that nine or ten times in twelve years. I claim the right to the spectrum, don't call me anything because I may be on the opposite end tomorrow and it's still me."

"If I look at the women I'm attracted to, there is kind of a pattern. But then it's more style and aesthetics than anything else."

"There's people that open and close the door about their sexuality and there are other's for whom it is more fluid."

"And move on that scale."

"Yeah, move."

"That's what I find interesting."

"There's some spark to it."

"The high femme and the high butch, that doesn't interest me. It's this in-between. When you move about here and there and you get it all."

"I haven't been able to come up with other words yet, but the concept I think of that is a much more positive and non-restrictive one is the concept of yin/yang, within which the idea of the feminine/masculine polarity is merely a small part. Thinking about this complementary of opposites in a holistic framework can help us to conceive more positive and flexible terms which reflect our diversity."

CHAPTER EIGHT

The Dish: What 589 Lesbians Say

Because butch/femme is an abiding interest of mine, I wanted to find out what other lesbians have to say about it today. I wanted to know the dish. I'm not a researcher by training, what I am is a chronicler of lesbian culture. I have the good fortune to travel the country talking with a lot of lesbians and listening to their feelings and ideas. Some of the women who filled in this questionnaire were excited to share their experiences. Many more thought I was asking *all* the wrong questionss. The epigraph of this book says, "Every word has a charge on it, either positive or negative. There is not a neutral word in the lesbian community." And that was certainly true with this study! I found the disagreements enormously valuable and want to share the full range of that information here. There's no new party line, folks. I'm not out trying to convert the non-believers.

So this is it. The dish on androgynous women, butches, femmes and none of the above, from 589 lesbians all across America.

Lesbian demographics

I call these "lesbian demographics" because I think it's important to distinguish between the general questions asked on many surveys from those which are specific to lesbians. As lesbians we are so infrequently asked about our culture that there is little information that is concrete, and so much more that should be asked. I want to encourage lesbian graduate students and researchers to "be brave, be bold," as Kate Clinton says, and study our own kind. We need information about ourselves and the mainstream culture needs information about us as well.

EARLY SEXUALITY

Information about our first lesbian sexual experiences and what they meant to us, is almost never discussed. I find these early experiences very important to the development of self-image and lesbian identity. I purposefully did not ask women questions about childhood sexual abuse. In this survey, I wanted to emphasize the positive influences on our lesbian erotic nature.

I wanted to know when these lesbians started having consenting sex with other females. For some, consenting sex may be kissing, fondling, and necking; others may believe that consenting sex is having genital contact. Typically, lesbians discover who they are attracted to during adolescence, just like all other sexual orientations. There is no great mystery, no woman preying on them in the locker room, no older women hanging around playgrounds luring them into dingy bars, giving them cigarettes so they'll come out. Lesbians begin to explore their sexual feelings as children (even if they don't know they are sexual); as adolescents they are likely to start acting on those feelings. The majority of the women surveyed here were sexual with women as young adults.

Once lesbians are sexual with women or with other girls, we enter a world with which our heterosexual counterparts don't have to contend. Heterosexuals have many words to describe their feelings. They know what to call their relationships and have a language to describe the nuances of their love life. There are songs on the radio, images on television and in the movies. They can read literature about themselves, and are even taught about birth control and sex in schools.

LESBIAN LANGUAGE

The lesbian has no such experiences. We enter a world with few words to describe ourselves, our sexual feelings and our relationships. The words we do have are wooden and simplistic. Humans developed language to describe what is within and without, so we can communicate that with one another. Language is the key to what is going on inside another. The words we use to define ourselves and our relationships are crucial in creating our culture.

We lesbians have hidden our culture from the scrutiny of others for our own safety. This has resulted in a watered-down language that is vague and neutral. Our lesbianism is awash with words that do not begin to define us. When we neutralize words, we give up on and co-opt our own culture. When we do this for centuries, our culture itself becomes vague and ill-defined. We don't know who we are and we find that confusion stressful. When we don't have words for something, we begin to believe it is wrong. I think this is most dramatically shown when we look at the words we use to label our lesbianism.

The overwhelming majority of the women who answered this survey were lesbians, with a very few bisexuals and undecided women. Let me briefly address bisexuality since it is a word that does not appear again in this text. There are always women who say, "Why don't you talk about bisexuals?" Well, very simply, I just don't. Not that I think bisexuals don't exist, or that they don't have a viable sexual orientation; it's just that bisexuals aren't lesbians. I write and talk about lesbians. No one says to me, "You talk about lesbians, why not gay men?" Just because female bisexuals have sex with women doesn't mean that I should automatically include them in discussions about lesbians. It's rather like comparing apples and oranges. Inevitably, bisexuality includes a discussion of sex with men. I'm really only interested in women having sex with other women.

When it comes to the words lesbians do use in public, we have made our culture palatable to the heterosexual mainstream. We don't like to use the words "dyke" and "queer"; we frequently use words like "gay" and "woman-loving" to make our language more acceptable. There's more than a little homophobia in this process.

Perhaps the most vague are the women (a small group in this study) who say they simply "fell in love with a woman." Many of us started off that way, but to keep that label for ourselves when we have had more than one female lover is a way to excuse ourselves. Sort of like "I can't help it, it just happened to me on the way to the grocery store." What does this mean? That she fell in love with a woman, but other women don't interest her at all? I'm suspicious of women who are unwilling to label themselves in a way that addresses their woman-loving head on. What is the fear (except the obvious) of claiming the label of the sexual outlaw? After all, Random House Dictionary describes lesbianism as "homosexual relations between two women." Pretty simple. As a friend of mine is fond of saying: "If you eat the cat, honey, then you eat the cat. No way around it." Yet somehow if we "fall in love", maybe our straight sisters and co-workers will understand. After all, everyone wants to fall in love.

"Gay woman" was a phrase that became popular in the 1970's after the Stonewall rebellion. This has been a way for some women to be able to celebrate their homosexuality while still avoiding the word "lesbian." "Gay" is also a sweet word that has some charge to it, but not as much as lesbian. I think one of the major attractions of this word is that is continues to tie us to male privilege; it connects us to the gay male movement. It provides us some shelter when the word "gay" is on the cover of *Time* magazine with a photo of two men holding hands. There may be strong reaction to it, but at least it's there. The word "lesbian" isn't on the cover of *Time* magazine.

Using the words "queer" and "dyke" was quite popular in the late 1970s in many lesbian communities. These words were taken back from the mainstream culture that had used them for so many years to put us down. We reclaimed them not unlike the feminists reclaimed the word "cunt" so that no one could use it against us anymore. Dyke and queer in this context became our power words. Most of us do define ourselves as lesbians, however. This is our word; it means that we are connected with other women in a sexual, emotional, and cultural way. The more we use the word, the less oppression there will be towards us.

Most of the women answering the survey found "queer" the most uncomfortable for them. "Queer", according to Random House Dictionary, is defined as "strange, odd, unusually different; of questionable nature or character, mentally unbalanced; slang for homosexual." According to "Queer Theory," the dominant notion of "natural" is what is transgressed by queers. We don't have babies when we have sex, we don't create generations of ourselves, we are ethereal and phantom.

"Dyke" followed close behind as a word that many women didn't like being used to describe them. It is the radical members of our movement that feel most comfortable with these words since they are so shocking to the mainstream culture. They are words rarely heard and used in the course of daily conversation. However, they are also powerful words that describe a certain proud lesbian energy.

ARE LESBIANS MADE OR BORN?

We've all had to answer that age old question "So Sally, how'd you get that way?" Why are we lesbians? I like to answer that question with, "Who cares?" Actually, I do care, I just don't care to discuss it with hostile heterosexuals. I asked the women taking this survey what they thought, and almost half thought it was a combination of heredity, environment and a chosen way of being. Well, that's what I'd say, since I think there are all different ways of ending up with a particular sexual orientation. I don't think this issue of who do we find attractive and who would we risk everything to love is a simple one.

There are lesbians who believe their connection to women is genetic and that no matter what century, what culture, no matter what circumstance, they could not be with a man. Other lesbians find the environmental factors most significant in their identity. The feminist movement, negative experiences with men, the way they grew up, living in a woman hating culture, and other factors make them lesbians. Then there are those who believe their choice to be a lesbian is positive and conscious, but they could also choose to be with men.

Some of us are just born that way. It probably *is* genetic; homosexuality does run strongly in some families. I know a woman who has six brothers and sisters and all but one are gay. Recently I met a woman who told me she and her husband had raised eight children, one of whom was adopted. She and her husband had both come out and all of their children except two are lesbian and gay as well. The adopted child is bisexual and one of the biological children is heterosexual. Her child who got heterosexually married was afraid she was letting the family down. Nice twist.

Studies show that a gay man has twice the chance of having a gay brother as does a heterosexual man. Most of us can find a family member we suspect of being gay. However, we run right into the problem of centuries of closeting—we really don't have a record of our homosexual relatives. It will be a few more generations before we can prove this genetic component. Meanwhile, we can depend on the stories like those above to prove that yes, one of the components is our DNA.

The current position taken by many of those trying to get legal rights established for homosexuals is that we don't have a choice about our orientation, that it's genetic. I'm sure that's true for many, but I don't see what's wrong with the truth that some women *choose* to be lesbians. It's a wonderful lifestyle and nothing to be ashamed of. Choosing it seems just as powerful and just as important as being born that way. In fact, one-third of the women in this group *did* choose their lesbianism.

I understand that if everyone thinks we're born that way they might feel sorry for us and stop persecuting us. But I don't think this is the tack to take. It's almost as if we are saying: "We don't really want to be lesbians, but we can't stop our DNA." It keeps the blame off our parents for making us queer. It takes the heat off a woman hating culture. But it also makes it sound like lesbianism is some sort of genetic defect. Being a lesbian is *not* pathological, so let's celebrate however we got here.

COMING OUT

After dealing with ourselves, the next issue is dealing with others. How do we tell the world out there that we are lesbians? The way we approach this tells a lot about how we feel about our lesbianism and what power the mainstream culture has over us. There are plenty of women who have little economic power, are in danger of losing their children, and still come out. There are young teenagers who come out while living at home with strict parents. There are women in very powerful positions in business who come out. There are famous people who come out. What is it internally that allows these women to risk so much, to come out against all odds? And what is it that stops women who have seemingly the economic and social freedom to come out yet cannot do it? What makes someone doubt their own ability to deal with adversity to the point that they cannot buck the system? These questions have something to do with self esteem, with an ability to differentiate from others' reactions, and with ego strength.

Everyone in this survey has come out to someone, although there are lesbians out there in the world who live with that gnawing feeling all their lives and never tell anyone. That must be the definition of hell on earth. If you have a hard time coming out to others and want a conversation opener, you might try wearing the popular button that says "Don't die wondering."

Coming out is always difficult. Every time we turn around we have to decide if we are going to come out to this or that person. There are those who say, "We don't have to make a big deal about being lesbians. Why bother coming out? If people figure it out so be it, but you don't have to shove it down their throats." Others say, "We have to come out. The only way to secure gay rights is if everyone knows how many of us there are." I would suggest perhaps a more personal approach—looking honestly at the toll it takes on us *not* to be out.

Staying in the closet is a stress some women don't consider. Many believe the strain of coming out is greater than not coming out. On the surface, this appears true. What is not considered is the terrible price we pay by not being ourselves. We don't ever have an honest day, which eventually contributes to shutting off our feelings, increasing our low self esteem, and forcing us to compromise our integrity. This price is not small. Day to day we may be able to live with these choices, but we accommodate ourselves to being less and less alive. Over a lifetime, there is considerable pain and loss in having lived life on the outskirts of our hearts.

The connection between mother and child is powerful. Most of those in the survey were willing to be out to their mothers and their children (if they had them). Almost all of the mothers in the survey were out to their children. This may give some support to the women who haven't yet come out to their children. Others have done it and survived. Their children survived as well. You know how tied you are to your parents even if they don't do what you want them to? Your children are in the same boat. They want your approval almost no matter what. They may have problems with your choices, but they will still be there.

Two-thirds of the sample were out to their mothers. The traditional mom role of helping children grow up (even if she didn't do such a hot job), leaves a deep bond. Most of us continue to let her in on what we are doing with our lives. We may even wish afterwards we hadn't told her, but somehow she got it out of us. Sometimes she just knows, a sixth sense. Just like I know when my son is doing something that I should take note of, even if I am nowhere near him. There's a knowing that moms and kids have together.

Being out to one's father seems not as important as being out to one's mother. We have come to believe that men are not as easy to be intimate with as women. That's the cultural rap and it's been corroborated by the results of this survey. I think certainly men contribute to this. Not quite half the women were out to their fathers. Also, far more were out to their sisters than their brothers.

The notion of not being out to those that we grew up with may or may not be a painful experience for us. We lived with these people probably longer than anyone else in the world, and that they don't know about our love creates a chasm. Not being out to them may be a contributing factor in why we aren't close to them. It's always interesting to me when lesbians tell me they aren't out to their family members because the family might stop speaking to them. I wonder how much they "speak" to these people? I wonder how close you could possibly be to someone who doesn't know about your heart? What if you knew nothing about your sister's boyfriend or your brother's wife? What if you didn't know your parents got a divorce? If these thoughts are preposterous to us, why isn't it just as preposterous for us to continue to hide our lives from them?

We spend most of our waking hours at work, yet a third of us are not out to our straight co-workers. Some are not even out to gay co-workers. Sometimes this comes from working with flamboyant lesbians who make more closeted lesbians nervous. Maybe the closeted lesbian is worried she'll be lumped into the same category: "Oh yeah, this is how all lesbians are." Maybe you are the boss and feel you can't let your employees know because of what you perceive as higher stakes. You may not want your co-workers to have power over you, knowing this vulnerable detail about your life.

I'm amazed at the toll it takes to spend so much of our lives not being lesbians. This trains us how not to feel, how not to include our lover and friends, and how to keep our thoughts secret. The impact of this is discussed with great insight by Lee Zevy and Sahli Cavallaro in "Invisibility, Fantasy, and Intimacy: Princess Charming is not a Prince," *Lesbian Psychologies* (University of Illinois Press, 1987). As they state: "...because the lesbian's process of making herself into a hollow copy is unconscious, she frequently cannot cease doing it when with another lesbian." I would add that not only is the process unconscious, but *constant*, which enormously increases the impact of this hiding and silencing.

There are lots of subtle ways we can avoid being out, like not telling our children's teachers. Some say, "What difference can it make?" Well, if you and your lover split up, it might impact your children's behavior at school, and their teacher ought to know. We also might not let our children's friends or their parents know about our sexuality. This could deprive you of a conversation like the one I had with my son and his friend when they were seven. We were driving to a soccer game and I misspoke and called them "you gays" instead of "you guys." My son's friend spoke up: "We're not gay, you are!" I said, "I know I am." He said, "And you are the only one who is!" Whereupon my son piped in, "Oh no, my dad is too." End of conversation, no one uptight, just a little clearing of the communication waves.

Another factor that influences coming out is whether we think others know we are a lesbian. I suppose most people don't think about lesbians. Which in and of itself doesn't make me happy. Why don't they? We have to think about straight people all the time. Well, maybe not all the time, but we are well aware that they are in our lives. Most of us pass through their lives unnoticed, which is why they get so freaked out when we point out to them that we are lesbians and not who they thought we were.

NAMES FOR OUR LOVERS

Another way that our homophobia shows up and directly impacts our lives is in the language we use to refer to the woman

with whom we are closest. The problem shows up, of course,
when talking with straight people. We most frequently refer to
our lover as our "friend." Now, don't trot out the "but she *is* my
friend" line. I know that. (Although I also know a fair amount of
lovers who aren't really friends.) What's important here is that we
call our most treasured companion, our heartmate, our partner,
our main squeeze, the one we are building a life with, our
"friend." How many other women could be called "friend" in
your life? I bet a lot. In writing this, I'm not trying to make women
who do this feel bad. I just want you to think about what it does
in your life and the life you share with your lover to keep putting
her in the category of "friend."

The next most frequently used word is "roommate." These
two words are used by more than half the women in this survey.
No charge, no sexual component, no heart connection, no psychic
impact. Roommate. Friend. How sad. Then there is the word
"partner"—a term that we could use with a business associate,
someone with whom we bought an investment, an old pal from
childhood. And a few of us still disguise our lesbianism with the
pronouns of "he and him" used to describe our lover. Many of us
also use vague pronouns so that no one knows what sex our
partner is.

But no wonder our lesbian culture is so quiet about sex. No
wonder we have so many rules about what is right and what is
wrong. We have no everyday basis even for a language that has
us romantically connected to one another. We may start by being
lovers, but we end up being what we call ourselves: roommates
and friends.

The good news from this survey is that we are overwhelm-
ingly comfortable being seen in public with our lover. We are
willing to be out there with her, even if we aren't for the most
part telling anyone. But we know. And, we recognize our own
kind when we see two women in public who have some charge
together. (I think everyone recognizes even if they aren't
conscious of it.)

PASSING

I asked a number of questions about each woman and her
lover passing or not passing for straight. When asked how they

felt about passing, most of the women surveyed were either not concerned with other's opinions, or they were angry that they even felt the need to pass. These women did not, for the most part, feel proud or happy to be putting something over on straight people. I think this shows that the issue of passing is imposed on us by external pressures. It's not something we prefer. Lesbians who didn't pass were either not concerned with others' opinions, or were proud of not passing. On the other hand, these same women were also concerned that they might be discriminated against because of their lesbianism. Shocking straights was not a concern of most women. These are pretty simple and clear answers. This whole issue is a drag and why is it in our lives all the time?

The series of questions about one's lover passing or not passing brought similar answers. We are all tired of this issue, yet we are caught by it. When their lover passed, the respondents most frequently had no feelings or were angry they even felt she had to. If their lover didn't pass, they again were angry that passing was an issue, or they were completely at ease with others knowing that their lover was a lesbian. For the majority, it did not pose a problem to be seen with their lover in straight settings. These women had plenty of feelings about passing themselves or their lover's passing, provoking both anger and an indifference to what the outside world thinks.

General demographics

I contacted the women who filled out this survey primarily at my speaking engagements throughout the country. The basic profile of the respondents is: white, middle-class, Protestant, college graduate, between 30-39 years of age, earning over $21,000 a year, able-bodied and not a mother. There are obvious problems with this profile: not enough women of color, disabled women, or old women. In Appendix A, I describe the outreach methods used. Suffice it to say that once again, statistics are skewed in these directions.

Almost half of the women responding to the survey were raised in the middle-class. But there were also sizeable numbers of working-class and upper middle-class women, and small numbers of women from poverty and upper-classes. These numbers were representative of the general population.

As in my last survey (published in *Lesbian Passion: Loving Ourselves and Each Other*), the level of education was substantially above the national average for women. Over two-thirds of the women had either bachelor's or master's degrees. I feel this partly reflects the need lesbians have to earn their own living. The women answering this survey are forced to do as much as possible to be employable. There is no cultural support that aids lesbians economically. Perhaps more of these women got degrees as well because they are not as influenced as straight women to quit school because of childrearing or pursuing the affections of a man. Clearly this level of education is also related to the overal privilege of the sample.

This group was primarily raised Protestant and Catholic, which is representative of the culture of the United States today. In all my surveys there are always a lot of us lesbian Catholic girls. (Do you think it has anything to do with the long tradition of paganism and the cult of Mary within the church? Just let the pope hear about that idea, I'll be excommunicated for sure.) I feel it is safe to assume that the influence of Christianity and its accompanying negativity towards homosexuality is significant.

A little under one-tenth of these women were raised as Jews, probably the religion that shows the most tolerance towards homosexuals.

When asked about their body types, about half of the women described themselves as medium height, though almost one-fifth saw themselves as either short or tall. A small minority thought they were thin, another small group saw themselves as fat or muscular. Few of the women surveyed considered themselves disabled.

Less than one-fifth of the women were parents. In my sample, this may be influenced by the difficulty of getting to an evening event when you are a parent, but I think it safe to say that there are fewer lesbian than heterosexual moms.

I asked the mothers in this survey what kind of role they had in their children's lives. The vast majority saidg they were either mothers or both mother and father to their children. A tiny group thought they played a fathering role with their children.

Why are there so few women who are parents in this community? Why is it that lesbians choose not to have children? Perhaps this is a true reflection of what all women would do if given the real chance to choose. We certainly don't have children by accident, unless we have done so in the past in heterosexual relationships. The lesbian community accepts childless women with ease. Does the lesbian community also discourage women from having children? The reality of having to deal with men in either a cursory or ongoing way may keep some lesbians from having children.

Especially in large cities in the United States, some lesbians today are choosing alternative insemination, adoption, and foster care. The National Center for Lesbian Rights, in San Francisco, has been quite instrumental in this area. Among other ways of supporting lesbian families, they represented two women who were successful in their bid to both adopt and become legal mothers of a child. Some co-mothers are now using this as a possible way to become legally recognized parents of their lover's children.

Butch/Femme/Androgyny or None Of The Above

I asked a number of questions to find out what respondents thought about the concepts of butch, femme, and androgyny. I've already reported a substantial amount of this information throughout the text of this book, so this analysis will be limited. In all my questions, there was always a category for "none of the above" (from now on designated as n.o.t.a.), to accommodate the women that do not resonate with any of these labels.

Lesbians balked at this whole section, with many feeling forced to answer questions that didn't relate to them. Some women said they hated the whole idea of labels. Others said they just wanted to be themselves.

I believe that labels give order to our lives. To assume we can escape the ones that make us uncomfortable is to kid ourselves. In fact, I think our greatest struggle as humans is learning to be ourselves, and that labels assist us in doing just that. They give us a picture, something to relate to.

One-third of this group identified as either butch or femme. The butch/femme concept is probably the most difficult lesbian label to actually define. Only a minority of women accept that lesbians actually have identities within lesbianism. When I asked these women how they understood the concept of butch/femme, over 40 percent saw it as "male/female role-playing" or a "gender identity within lesbianism". Another 40 percent saw it as "mannerisms" or "sexual energy differences", concepts which are more neutral and less stigmatized. Of course, there can't really be gender identities within lesbianism, since there is only one female gender. But the constructs for a butch lesbian and a femme lesbian are different to the point of being almost as separate as two genders. This separation makes for interesting and exciting combinations, but ones that have been taboo for so long within the lesbian community that it is difficult to imagine how to make the designations dynamic and not stereotyped. Of the women who felt that butch/femme characterization was important to them, only a small percentage replied that they are willing to overtly show that in the community.

It is not surprising that well over half of the women surveyed identified as androgynous or n.o.t.a. Most of the women answering this survey came out as lesbians in the feminist era when androgyny was the preferred identity, and it was not acceptable to identify as butch or femme.

It is also not surprising to me that more women were attracted to femmes than butches. It is safer to be attracted to women that we can bring home, take out in public, and who are likely not to embarrass us. It is hard to be objective and wonder if indeed this is really who we find more attractive, or just who we find more acceptable.

The butch/femme scale presented interesting results. The women, rating themselves and rating their lovers, were distributed on a perfect bell curve. The majority were in the middle, with a sloping down to each end that was almost equal in terms of self and completely equal in terms of one's lover. The center and those "femme-of-center" and "butch-of-center" represented the vast majority of lesbians.

In an experiment with some friends, we rated ourselves on two different scales, one for our femme aspects, and the other for our butch aspects. I asked the respondents to do the same thing on two matching one to ten scales. True to the rest of the survey, two-thirds of the group saw themselves between 4 and 7 on each of the scales.

About half the women said their rating on the main butch/femme scale had changed since they had come out. I wanted to know what accounted for this. For three-fourths of the respondents, their ratings changed according to different situations (which they did not elaborate on). Such situations might be jobs, styles of dress, being with family of origin, traumatic or exciting events in life. Maybe it's that one's rating changes throughout the day given where you are: at the opera, at work, cleaning out your gutters, fixing your car, going to the bank, grocery shopping.

What surprised me was that for three-fourths of the respondents their partner's rating on the scale did not affect their own rating. It is my feeling that we dance in relation to our partner. Sometimes they move and change, sometimes we do. To find that so many women felt that "situations", and not their lovers, impact their movement on the butch/femme scale fascinated me. Again, I can't help commenting on the desexualizing of our culture. Over and over, I see ways in which our sexuality is something that is denied, not seen, ignored. However, other actions in our lives are very much recognized as having an influence on us.

Predictably, the majority of women surveyed saw butch/femme as a dyad that "somewhat" relates to the heterosexual male/female model; only one-fifth didn't see that as so.

The surveyed group was also similar to many of my audiences, where the majority of women had conversations about butch/femme at least occasionally, but most also found it "not at all" important to their identity. Once again, I find this fascinating. "Yes, it's common in my life, but no, it's not important to me."

The group was almost evenly divided as to whether they believed that androgyny or butch/femme were more valued in the community. In light of the reluctance of the butch/femme women to be visible in the community, I was surprised by this response.

Goddess identification

I used the images aptly described by Jean Shinoda Bolen in her book *Goddesses in Every Woman: A New Psychology of Women.* I asked each woman to identify herself and her most recent lover as one of the goddesses mentioned on this list.

Clearly, Artemis and Aphrodite were the goddesses of choice. Artemis, the goddess of the hunt and the moon, was the identification of both one-third of ourselves and our lovers. She is the independent, achievement-oriented feminine spirit. This is certainly how we present our lesbian nation to the world, and it showed up here as well. Aphrodite is the goddess of love and beauty, the "alchemical" goddess governing a woman's enjoyment of love and beauty, sexuality, and sensuality, who impels women to fulfill both creative and procreative functions. This idea of embodying different energies and different aspects of self is certainly a wonderful image.

Athena, the goddess of wisdom and craft, represents the logical, self-assured woman who is ruled by her head rather than her heart. She, almost equally with Hestia (the goddess of the hearth embodying the patient and steady woman who finds comfort in solitude and exudes a sense of intactness and wholeness) got the next highest number. Again, these archetypes give wonderful strong images of women who are not exactly the traditional female roles and who present us with valuable identities.

Persephone is the maiden and queen of the underworld, who expresses a woman's tendency toward compliancy, passivity and a need to please and be wanted by others. She was one of three that were not embraced by this group. Interestingly though, twice as many saw their lover as Persephone than saw themselves. Not surprisingly, Hera (the goddess of marriage who stands for the woman who considers her roles as student, professional, or mother secondary to her essential goal of finding a mate and being married) and Demeter (goddess of grain and the maternal archetype, representing a woman's drive to provide physical and spiritual sustenance for her children) were the least popular. This is certainly due to their traditional heterosexual female flavor.

Correlations with Butch, Femme, Androgynous and None of the Above Identities

The most significant finding throughout this survey was that there were very few differences between these four groups. It seems as though the identity each woman claimed was based more on internal process than with externalized activities, characteristics, or looks. This directly contradicts most of our stereotypical assumptions about butch/femme identity.

There is a good deal of speculation about what is a butch, femme or androgynous woman. Many will say it is how she is built, how much she weighs. Some will say it has to do with how she walks or dresses. Still others believe that it has to do with an attitude in the world, and especially in lovemaking. When it comes to the sexual aspect of the discussion, there are pretty strong ideas that butches are aggressive and femmes are passive, while androgynous women believe in total equality.

I decided to cross-correlate the questions in this survey according to whether the women identified as butch, femme, androgynous, or none of the above ("n.o.t.a."). I poured over the information trying to find if our stereotypes are confirmed by how we saw ourselves, by our activities, or by objective facts about ourselves. Some readers may find it interesting to compare the numbers throughout this section to the numbers for the whole sample which you will find in Appendix B.

The whole discussion which follows needs to be within the context of acknowledging how deeply and vociferously lesbians balked at being identified with any of the categories. One of the things I asked was if we could create new categories and new words, what would they be? Over and over, women said, "I just want to be me", "No labels", "Women", "I'm myself—no categories." My personal favorite was "I dunno."

It's a lifelong project to become authentically ourselves, especially in a woman hating and lesbian hating culture. But to then let our lovers be separate and different from ourselves is fearsome. This nest may be the only safe haven many of us have.

I'm reminded in all this of what in kids is labeled the "terrible twos." The only thing terrible about that two-year-old is that she is trying for the first time ever to establish a separate identity from her parents. And we can't stand that separation. This we is cultural and widespread. Separation is very frightening.

Though parents of teenagers may not always agree, acting out and being outrageous is a really healthy stage towards independence. And I think this psychological concept translates to lesbians. That there is a kind of authenticity we can't get to, unless we're willing to tolerate (or heaven forbid, go through ourselves) the outrageous. Describing oneself as "me", "a

woman", "who I am", and so on, is about as bland and undifferen-
tiated as one can get. Yet over and over, lesbian relationships
break up because they are too merged, because we lack differentness.

I think it's time we begin to really look at this fierce resistance to categories, to names, to the outrageous. Not just butch/
femme, but all the ones in "Other Rhythms" and all the ones we
have yet to name. In fact, if what we really want is to "just be
ourselves" this process is essential.

Over two-thirds of the women in this survey identify as
androgynous or none of the above. Yet even with such an overwhelming vote, androgyny doesn't really describe a lot of the
women who chose it. For some, androgyny has male connotations,
for others it's just what's left over. We don't have very many
choices about where to stand. Two thirds of these women are not
all the same, and perhaps we can find ways to describe their
realities, their distinctions, their choices.

Interestingly, far more of the androgynous women and the
n.o.t.a.'s would be attracted to femmes than butches, if they had
to choose. Femmes could get elected president with a margin like
that. I suspect that femmes seem more attractive because they
seem familiar to us as women, they are not "other" in the same
way butches are. What's striking though, is how much lesbian-
feminism has been butch-leaning in its looks, attitudes, choices
about work, and yet how clearly androgynous women embrace
femmes (when forced to choose).

Another thing that struck me as noteworthy was that when
there were differences in the data, more often than not, the
androgynous responses correlated with the femmes, and the
n.o.t.a.'s correlated with the butches. The responses of these
groups were remarkably similar.

I continue to see how profoundly we de-sexualize our
culture. I talk about this more in the section on words later on.
What came up in this section was that 44 percent said their
identity had changed since they came out, but 77 percent thought
this had nothing to do with their lovers. Okay girls, what do you
think *did* change your identity, your stance about Nicaragua? I'm
not doubting that we believe what we report, but I also know we
really want to think that we don't get changed by our girlfriends.
Now, we move in together, wear the same clothes, throw out our

dishes, change all our friends, start dancing and give up movies—
but no, we aren't changed by our girlfriends.

I'm reminded a bit here about how we all talk about butch/
femme but we almost universally think it's an unimportant topic.
When is it going to be okay for lesbians to be sexual beings? For
us to have strong desires and attractions, to acknowledge and to
claim them. I'm not talking just about butch/femme here. I'm
talking about claiming and owning the full range of our sexuality,
whatever it is.

This silence around sex is really not surprising. We have no
safe space within mainstream culture in which to sexualize
women without the taint of objectification. And because of homophobia, the sexualization of lesbians is equally co-opted. But the
denial of sexuality and eroticism that grows out of this silence
comes at a very high price. It's hard for me not to connect the
belief that our lovers don't influence our identity, with the reality
that lesbian couples have very little sex after the third year of a
relationship. These are complicated questions, and I'm not trying
to pose simple solutions. But there is a real danger when we stifle
discussion and dissent that we keep repeating patterns in our sex
lives and in our relationships.

When I say that there are "no differences" in this survey
between butch, femme and androgynous women, I mean that:

- there are no significant differences in bed (though femmes
  penetrate their lovers more frequently than anyone else!)—
  not in orgasms, enjoyment, initiation, or other practices;
- there are no class differences—middle-class and upper-class
  women are as likely as working-class women to identify butch
  or femme;
- there are no body types specifically associated with any one
  identity;
- there's no correlations between motherhood and identity;
- and here's no connection between roles in domestic life and
  identity.

Yet so many women have written or spoken movingly about
the differences they experience. So what really are butch and
femme? This central question was answered in this survey as
much by what they aren't as by what they are. If we can drop our
stereotypes about butch/femme, our categories of assumptions,

and our beliefs, can we start to give these attractions deeper names?

In this context, I also noticed that androgynous women and n.o.t.a.'s were more likely to label butch/femme as "male/female role playing"—to make butch/femme "other". Butches and femmes themselves are more likely to say these identities concern "sexual energy differences" or "mannerisms"—concepts that seem to come from *within* lesbian culture.

There are a few other general observations I want to make about points of similarity among the four identities.

The questions I asked about passing were awkward and sometimes difficult to answer. It struck me as I wrote them, that passing is something every lesbian deals with, and yet virtually every straight person is oblivious to. They don't know the price we pay either for passing or not passing. The confusion this whole issue raises within us showed up when the two most common feelings about passing were "not concerned with other's opinions" and "feel like I'm living a lie."

Almost the entire survey reported being comfortable being seen in public with their lover. I have to wonder how much this comfort is associated with assuming nobody identifies you as a lesbian. In the *Lesbian Passion* survey, 75 percent said they don't hold hands in public. In this study, 24 percent were "relieved" or "proud" that their lover passes.

Not surprising, perhaps, given our self-image as lesbians, the majority of each group saw themselves as initiating household, relationship and sexual activities. Very few women identified themselves, as "responsive" in any activities at all. This matches with choices of characteristics on the Bem scale, where "yielding" and "conventional" got the lowest scores. But "aggressive" was down near the bottom as well. (Curiously, we see ourselves as always initiating but never being aggressive.) What this rejection of responsiveness also leaves out is the longing to be nurtured and cared for, which nearly everyone experiences sometimes. Is there something about lesbian-feminism that makes it difficult to "yield" to care, to "respond" to nurturing?

With this general discussion in mind, what follows is more specific survey information, focusing on the areas in which the four identities showed some differences.

Demographics for Identity Groups

There were no significant differences in height and weight among the four categories. There were slightly more androgynous women who were over 5'10" and there were slightly more butches over 161 pounds, but not enough percentage points to be considered statistically significant.

Other writers have often suggested that differences in class background are what sets the lesbians who identify with butch and femme apart from those who identify as androgynous or n.o.t.a. As reported earlier in this book, I found no such correlation in comparing five levels of socioeconomic class. I looked at class from three angles: 1) how many women from each of the four groups identified with one of the five classes; 2) what percentage of the whole sample fit into categories such as working-class femme, middle-class butch or upper-class androgynous; 3) how did each of the five classes correlate with each of the four identifications. The two largest groups were androgynous middle-class and androgynous working-class women. The rest of the numbers were evenly divided. Upper-class women identified as butch, femme, androgynous and n.o.t.a. in the same percentages as those from poverty, working-, middle-, and upper middle-class. The same percentage of femmes were from poverty, working-, middle-, upper middle-, and upper-class, and so on. Again, none of this analysis showed any differentiation that was statistically significant.

The sample used in this survey was not random, so I don't know the distribution outside of these demographics. However, this sample is quite large and does represent the public lesbian community in some respects. I think it's valuable to use this information to break through the mythology that divides us over class. These identifications of butch, femme, androgyny and n.o.t.a. are more complex than we originally thought. These women are engaged in a sexual, erotic identity that obviously is not strongly attached to class.

Surprisingly, there were also no significant differences in the four groups in relation to motherhood. Most of the mothers were biological mothers, with femmes being the smallest group of co-mothers. Butches and androgynous women were almost as likely to be biological mothers as were femmes. Femmes were also the highest number of foster moms, but had no adopted children. Sexual identity seems to have no significant impact on the decision to mother.

LESBIAN DATA

Of the most common lesbian questions, "Are you out?" and "Who are you out to?" there were no differences in the responses from all four categories of identity. The rest of the lesbian data showed some slight variation, but again, throughout this section there were only small differences between the four groups. Commonality of attitude and experience appears to be the norm for this group.

When asked to identify themselves, butches used "lesbian" slightly more often than the other three groups, although this label was the primary choice of all the respondents. About one-tenth of the femmes used "woman who fell in love with a woman" to describe themselves. This calls to mind the stereotypes that femmes are just glorified straight women who came here by accident and are on a round trip ticket, or that a butch being more willing to use the term "lesbian" shows her inability to pass for a woman who just fell in love with a woman. But the differences are really quite small when you study the actual numbers.

When asked what words made them most uncomfortable, all four groups again had the same response: "queer." However, butches were noticeably more uncomfortable with this word than others were. Perhaps that is because this word had been used more maliciously against butches than other women.

In the decision about what to call your lover to non-lesbians, the groups again were practically the same. The femmes were slightly more likely to call them "girlfriends" and butches were slightly more likely to use the word "roommate". This again may reflect what we are able to get away with in the mainstream culture. Femmes perhaps look like a woman that would have a "girlfriend," while butches are more likely to have a "roommate." When talking to a lover on the phone, the n.o.t.a.'s were most likely to use "code" so that co-workers weren't aware of who they were talking to. Perhaps this reflects the homophobia of someone who prefers not to be labeled. One-third of the total group talks in code to their female lovers. This may change for different women in different settings, though over half of the women don't deny their lover in that way.

PASSING

Passing is a painful topic in the lesbian community. The fact that we even need to be concerned with whether we pass or not is an outrage. Why should anyone care whether or not we are lesbians? Yet, whether we are out or pass, whether we are complicit in this or it is against our will, the topic is heartbreaking. In fact, not only do we have to be concerned with passing, but sometimes we are mistaken for a man as well. In this survey, the butches were the most likely to have been seen as men.

I discuss passing more fully in other sections of this book; however it is important to note that we all do it in some situations (or wish we could, if only for our own safety). There are always lesbians who cannot pass, and butches were more likely to be in that category. The femmes, perhaps predictably, were the most likely to be able to pass. When asked how they felt when they passed, the femmes were most likely to say they were "relieved." Butches were the most likely to feel like they were living a lie if they did pass. That makes sense since butches more commonly aren't used to passing and must find it unnerving to do so. But plenty of femmes, androgynous women and n.o.t.a.'s as well felt like they were living a lie and were angry about the need to be concerned with passing.

Feelings about not passing again had very similar percentages for all four identifications. The few differences were, in my mind, predictable. The butches were slightly more relieved; femmes were slightly more angry and "happy to shock straights"; n.o.t.a.'s were most concerned with their own safety; and the androgynous women were most concerned with discrimination.

Butches were the most likely to have a lover who passed for straight (two-thirds of them), while only half of the femmes and androgynous women have a passing lover. Once again, femmes were more likely to be relieved if a lover passed. However, one-fifth of the femmes were also angry that a lover would have to worry about passing. The androgynous women and n.o.t.a.'s were the most likely to have no feelings about their lover passing.

When asked what their least frequent feeling was about their lover passing, femmes were the least concerned with safety. This again makes sense if we extrapolate that the femmes were the most likely to pass. A concern for safety because of looking like a dyke probably doesn't come up as much for femmes.

Conversely, femmes were the most likely to have a lover who didn't pass for straight. All groups again were similar in their feelings about this. However, androgynous women were the least likely to be proud. There seemed to be equal division within the androgynous group between being angry and being at ease and proud. Oddly enough, given they were relieved when lovers did pass, femmes were the most likely to be proud of a lover who *didn't* pass.

BUTCH AND FEMME

This has been discussed in great detail in the rest of the book; I will only report data here that hasn't been reported elsewhere. When asked, "What phrase best describes your understanding of the butch/femme concept?" the androgynous and n.o.t.a women were more likely to choose "male/female role-playing." Femmes and butches were more likely than androgynous women to see it as "sexual energy differences." I think these results are understandable, given that androgynous women and n.o.ta.'s are observing from the outside, while butches and femmes are living it.

Responses to the question about changes in identity on the butch/femme scale were very similar between the four groups. I had expected the androgynous women and n.o.t.a.'s to be more fluid in their movement on this scale, but in fact, all of the groups were. The majority of each group felt their rating changed in different settings, as we saw in the sample as a whole; only a minority felt their rating changed as a result of the influence of their lover.

When asked if their rating had changed since they had been out, the n.o.t.a.'s were the least likely to have changed. This is perhaps a somewhat predictable stance of, "I don't identify with any of this, and my rating has always been the same." The rest of the respondents were pretty evenly divided between having changed and not changed.

Most of all four groups felt their identification was chosen or was a combination of heredity, environment and chosen. The femmes were the most likely to feel their identification was hereditary, though this was still a minority.

When the question of attraction was raised, almost half the femmes were attracted to butches; almost half of butches were attracted to femmes; two-thirds of androgynous women were attracted to other androgynous women; and almost half of n.o.t.a.'s were attracted to others who identified as they did. However, one-third of femmes were attracted to other femmes; one-fourth of the butches were attracted to butches; one-fourth of the androgynous women and one-third of the n.o.t.a.'s were attracted to butches or femmes. So, none of the rules about "opposites attract" or "like with like" are hard and fast.

ACTIVITIES

I asked a series of questions about what role each woman played in different activities with her lover: whether she was the initiator, the responder, or if her actions depended on the situation. The responses to these questions were interesting. In the survey, the butches were the highest percentage of "initiators" in paying bills, working in the yard, working on the car, and dancing. Femmes were the highest percentage of "initiators" in cleaning house, decorating the house, childcare, organizing social activity, and socializing. Androgynous women were in the highest percentage of "depends" in paying bills, organizing social activity, cooking, working on the car, and dancing. The n.o.t.a.'s had the highest percentage in the "depends" category on cleaning house, decorating the house, working in the yard, childcare, and socializing.

One might conclude from this that butches are taking over male roles, femmes female roles, with the androgynous and n.o.t.a. women vying for the position of being the most likely to split responsibilities with their mates. But a closer look at the numbers in this part of the questionnaire shows that the differences are not very great between the four categories.

However, there remains the persistent question, "Does this have anything to do with male and female roles?" Not really! Daily tasks don't belong in immutable roles. At the very least, 30 percent of each group were in the "depends" category for each question, and more often than not, 40 to 50 percent chose this answer. This definitely shows a lack of hard and fast rules as to who does what. Not surprisingly, the smallest number of women in any group was in the "responders" role. We just don't like to be passive, do we?

SEX PRACTICES

The age that the respondents first had consenting sex with a woman showed only one significant difference. The femme women were slightly more likely than the others to have had this kind of sex under the age of ten.

When asked about being the initiator in sex, most of the women were comfortable with this role. Femmes had the highest percentage (half) who said they initiated "sometimes." The butches were the most likely to "often" and "always" initiate sex. The four groups were pretty evenly paired in other questions in this category. It seems that we are able to initiate and respond to sex similarly. Butches were slightly less likely to be the responder in sex, but only slightly. One-third of the other three groups said they were "often" the responder.

In this sample, almost half "often" or "always" initiate and receive oral sex. Femmes led the way in "always" initiating oral sex, although only slightly. Butches led the way by a small margin in both the "never" and "always" receiving oral sex responses.

Orgasm questions also showed few differences. Butches had the highest percentage of those who "never" had orgasms, although the numbers were quite small. Femmes, on the other hand, had the highest percentage of those who "always" had orgasms. When asked if their lover had orgasms, half the n.o.t.a.'s said their lovers "always" had orgasms. The other groups reported slightly lower percentages. The rest of the orgasm questions showed that all four groups had about the same experiences with their own and their lover's orgasms.

There are stereotypical views that in butch/femme relationships, the butch is the one who penetrates, not the femme. When I asked who did what to whom in the arena of penetration, there were clearly responses that did not uphold this theory at all. Butches were the most likely to "never" vaginally penetrate their lover. N.o.t.a. were the most likely to "always" vaginally penetrate their lover. While butches were the largest category of "never" being penetrated by a lover, one-quarter of butches said their partner "always" penetrates them. Femmes were slightly higher in "always" being penetrated by a partner.

One third of the sample used dildos. Of those, the spread is equal through the four groups as to whether they or their lovers used dildos. Just as many femmes used dildos when making love to their partners as did butches, androgynous women and n.o.t.a.'s. There were slight increases for femmes to have their lover use dildos on them rather than vice versa, but again this difference was only slight.

The majority of the sample never fantasize about themselves or their lover being a man during sex. The only exception to this was that more butches "occasionally" fantasize being a man, although the others are close behind. When asked about fantasies of one's partner being a man, butches again were slightly higher in the "occasional" category, though again the others were close behind. So, butches were slightly higher in both categories. Now how are we supposed to interpret that? Perhaps that the outlaws of lesbianism also have more ability to have outlaw fantasies. I still want to emphasize that the difference is very small.

There were four sexual activity questions in which all groups had an equal distribution: French kissing, using vibrators, anal sex to a partner, and anal sex from a partner. Since French kissing is done by virtually everyone, the numbers are evenly distributed. Anal sex is done by about one third and crosses all four of the groups equally. Vibrators are also used (by one-third, at least occasionally) by all four groups.

The results from the questions about sucking breasts once again showed only slight differences. When asked whether they liked to have their breasts sucked, all groups were virtually the same, except in the "always" category. More than half of the n.o.t.a.'s and femmes always like it, while only one-third of butches said they always like it. When asked whether they liked to suck their lover's breasts, n.o.t.a.'s again were the highest with two-thirds "always" liking it (versus somewhat over one-half for the others).

When asked if they like giving sex, the four groups were the same; 80-90 percent said "often" and "always." When asked if they liked to receive sex, 80-90 percent said "often" or "always." Clearly, we have a group that likes sex. And we have a group that does not have many differences across the four categories.

GODDESSES AND US

These same similarities held true in the questions that involved the goddesses. When describing themselves, the following groups most identified with specific goddesses, but all other groups were very close behind.

Artemis: androgynous and n.o.t.a.'s
Athena: butches
Hestia: n.o.t.a.'s
Hera: androgynous
Demeter: androgynous
Persephone: butches and femmes
Aphrodite: femmes (this was the widest variance, with a fourteen percent difference between femmes and the next category, n.o.t.a.'s)

When asked what identification they gave their most recent lover they responded:

Artemis: femmes (again, with a eleven percent spread between them and the next group, androgynous)
Athena: androgynous
Hestia: butches
Hera: butches
Demeter: butches and androgynous
Persephone: androgynous
Aphrodite: butches

Words Used To Describe Ourselves

Perhaps the most striking characteristic of the words these lesbians chose to describe their identities, is the degree of unanimity. When butches describe butches, femmes describe femmes, androgynous women describe androgynous women, they do so with exactly the same words that outside groups use to describe them.

There's a theory in linguistics that it's tremendously difficult to transform the cultural concept of a word and give it new meaning. You have to chose a new word to change the meaning.

When we were called "girls" (though we were adults) or "ladies", there was no way those words could incorporate the energy of feminism. They could not be transformed. So we reclaimed "women" in order to embrace our reality.

When all four groups spontaneously choose the word "dominant" to describe butches, we have a similar situation. "Butch" as we know it can't stretch to incorporate soft. Conversely, "feminine" was the most commonly chosen word for femmes (86 percent of femmes describe themselves that way).

Each of the identity groups (femmes, butches, and androgynous women) see themselves from inside the cultural framework. It is terribly difficult to change the meaning attached to the words. sometimes, we can enlarge them with modifiers, like baby butch, faggot butch, femme butch and so on. But by themselves, they don't stretch to include all of how we see ourselves.

This language, this framework, grows out of something real—differences of energy, style, stance, manner. Many of us recognize something that we try to describe with these words, butch, femme, androgynous. Not unlike how feminism has had to overcome stereotypes about women, lesbians are now in a position to enlarge our sexual concepts. These concepts are neither as stereotypical nor as fearful as the words would make us feel.

When lesbians describe themselves outside of the role (when I ask "What characteristics describe you?" instead of "What characteristics describe butches?") a different picture emerges. For many of us, the labels are both liberating—giving name—and confining—creating expectation.

When women who identified as butch earlier in the survey described themselves, to a greater degree than any other group, they saw themselves as: sympathetic, sensitive to the needs of others, understanding compassionate, loyal (100 percent!), tender, gentle, adaptable, and friendly.

Femmes, while not the leader in these categories were still right up in the top numbers, for: self-reliant, defends own beliefs, assertive, strong personality, has leadership abilities, self-sufficient, ambitious, and acts as a leader.

Yet, when we ask what lesbians find erotic, the top words are that they want "strong" butches and "soft" femmes. It seems as though we want all of it, the differentness and the similarity. As though we long for both poles, find wholeness in synthesis. No matter how often friends of mine talk about how the butches they know are cream-puffs and pushovers (and look at how many quotes in this book attest to that), that is not what they find erotic. Almost no one says that soft butches is what attracts them.

The question for us now is what lesbian language can stretch to embrace, still keeping a sense of differentness. Can we enlarge, reclaim, and transform words to more nearly fit our deepest experiences, and to make those experiences manifest in the world?

The other really striking thing about the words chosen, is that even when lesbians are explicitly asked to chose erotic words, they choose relationship words. These are not the words that show up in *On Our Backs* or in erotic literature. When asked to name what's erotic, not one single lesbian wrote "wet vagina" or any equivalent of it. Not one. Think about it.

I discuss the specifics of all these choices immediately below, and in other parts of the book as well. I encourage you to read the entire lists in Appendix E—maybe even out loud. These choices are a beginning of both enlarging the frame, and seeing what we currently have inside it.

BEM SURVEY RESULTS

Because I've already reported some of the information from the Bem Sex Role Inventory in other chapters, I won't repeat that information here. You can see the entire Bem list and how women self identified in Appendix D)

In this inventory (originally conceived in the mid-1970s), Sandra Bem believed that certain words were perceived as having male, female and androgynous characteristics. She also believed that these assignments reflected the sexism of society at large, and were not really characteristics of one sex or another. What Bem set out to do was to establish a middle ground of androgyny, unrelated to either sex.

When Bem originally did this work, the concept of androgyny became widespread; it was an exciting concept that challenged the traditional roles of men and women in society.

The results of using this sex role inventory to describe butch, femme, and androgynous women were that they fell into the same three roles traditionally assigned to male, female, and androgynous people, respectively. The majority responded that butch women had "male" characteristics, femme "female" ones, and androgynous women "androgynous" ones. I report the detailed lists in Chapter Three.

There were remarkably few deviations from traditional sex roles. The androgynous women were assigned the "male" characteristics of "self-reliant", "defends own beliefs", "independent", "willing to take a stand", "individualistic", "willing to take risks", and "self-sufficient." These characteristics were all positive ones in the lesbian community. Androgynous women were never assigned a traditionally "female" characteristic over the others.

The butches were given the "male" characteristics (including "dominant", "aggressive", etc.) that are seen as less acceptable in the lesbian community. They only moved outside the traditional "male" roles when given "moody" and "jealous" from supposedly androgynous characteristics and "loyal" from the supposedly female characteristics.

The femmes were *never* assigned anything but female characteristics, which is remarkable. Here you have it, femmes are like heterosexual women and butches are like men Once again, the androgynous women are the good people. This showed up again in the survey, as you will see later in this discussion.

However, when you break down the group into butch, femme, androgynous and n.o.t.a. women, they report very different results when describing themselves. To begin with, as in most other sections of the survey, there is almost no statistical difference between the four for any of the 60 sex role characteristics suggested by Bem. For example, if femmes saw themselves as independent, so did each of the others in almost equal numbers.

Only nine of the 60 words had more than a ten percentage point spread between any of the groups. Those words (followed by the abbreviation of the group that most identified with it) are: feminine (F), dominant (B), likeable (F), masculine (B), solemn (A), aggressive (B), childlike (B), and competitive (B). The rest of the 51 characteristics were pretty much evenly divided. The only two deviations from traditional expectations were that the butch women saw themselves as "childlike" (which both Bem and the women in my survey assigned to females and femmes respectively), and that the femme women saw themselves as "likeable" (which is androgynous).

There were several questions throughout the survey that asked women to choose words either from the Bem Sex Role Inventory list or from the English language in general. The first question addressed the issue of defining butch, femme, and androgyny. The second asked what attracts you to women in these different groups. The third group of questions asked what physical, intellectual, emotional, and spiritual aspects of lesbians you found erotic.

The most striking thing about all the answers was that the range of the words was so far reaching. Many of the words chosen do not usually have erotic connotations. When asked to list words that describe what attracts them, lesbians said: empathic, complex, attentive, balanced, esoteric, truthful, responsible, harmony, caring, compassionate, and agreeable. From the words chosen, it appears that we have our own standards and our own beliefs. Lesbian erotic systems are grounded in relationships and in what women want from a long-term partner. Because these words seem to represent the beginnings of a lesbian erotic language, I've listed all of them in Appendix E.

Women were also asked to choose three words from the Bem inventory to describe butch, femme and androgynous women. I wanted to see what butches said about themselves and the other two groups, what femmes said about themselves and the other two, and what androgynous women would say about themselves and the other two.

Below I list the four words most frequently used by each group. Because these are words that are suggested by a list, this may skew the results, but the differences and similarities between the groups is very interesting.

When asked to describe butches (in order of preference) femmes said, dominant, masculine, athletic, forceful; butches said, self-reliant, athletic, assertive and dominant; androgynous women said, masculine, dominant, aggressive, and a strong personality. The picture is obvious—even butches said they were dominant—and all the other words chosen by others had similar connotations.

When asked to describe femmes, femmes said, feminine, gentle, affectionate, and warm; butches said, feminine, gentle, warm, and affectionate; androgynous women said, feminine, gentle, tender, and helpful. It is fascinating to me that femmes and butches used exactly the same four words, just in different order of preference. It seems extremely unlikely that all three groups would use "feminine" and "gentle" as the two most frequently used words. Since even femmes evaluated themselves the same as the others, one can hardly believe that others are simply stereotyping.

True to form, when asked to describe androgynous women, the same words came up as well. Femmes said, individualistic, yielding, adaptable, and shy; butches said, individualistic, adaptable, independent, and self-sufficient; the androgynous women saw themselves as independent, self-reliant, individualistic, and assertive. Again, everyone used "individualistic" and two used "independent." All the characteristics were very much in keeping with the idea that androgynous women rebel against traditional expectations.

These results seem remarkable to me. All three groups not only identified themselves in particular ways, but the other two groups saw them in the same way. I think this shows how much our community does have clear ideas about who we are. I think this also shows that words in a culture take on a meaning and that there is almost no way to change that meaning until new words are found. In fact, the women who identify as butch, femme or androgynous cannot shake the stereotypes that the lesbian culture has prescribed.

I thought it important as well to create a set of questions that allowed the women to freely describe what characteristics they find erotic in each of the three groups. I wanted there to be an opportunity for the women to choose their own words. Since you can see the entire list of words in Appendix E, I will only cite the most popular here.

"If you identify as butch, choose three words to describe aspects of femmes you find erotic." (Since the majority of butch women are attracted to femme women, this turned out to be the right way to ask this question.) The words butches most frequently chose were: soft, gentle, sensual, sexual/sexy, beautiful, and "the way they dress."

"If you identify as femme, choose three words to describe aspects of butches you find erotic." (Once again, femmes were most attracted to butches.) The femmes chose: strong, confident, assertive, muscles, independent, tough.

"If you identify as androgynous, choose three words to describe aspects of women you find erotic." (In this survey, they found other androgynous women most attractive.) Interestingly, androgynous women chose words that showed up on both the butch and femme lists, as well as new ones: strong, soft, intelligent, sensitive, tender, independent, assertive, gentle. The words chosen by the androgynous women were much more varied, and there were smaller percentages of the group that chose any one word.

The last group of questions asked the respondents to report what characteristics they found erotic on the physical, intellectual, emotional and spiritual levels. The complete list of the words used by the respondents is in Appendix E.

The words most commonly used for erotic physical characteristics were: breasts, eyes, muscles, soft, strong, hair, dark skin, ass/hips, athletic, and smooth skin.

Those most commonly used for the erotic intellectual aspects were: intelligent, humor, witty, analytical, articulate, well read, creative.

The erotic emotional characteristics were: sensitive, compassionate, gentle, tender, warm, caring, loving, and open.

Finally, the spiritual aspects they found erotic were: open, searching/seeking, loving, and honest. There were many words used for this category and few were used frequently. The combination of sexuality and spirituality seems to be an area that may not be commonly recognized.

Conclusion

A study like this is a never-ending process. With so little information available about lesbians, I really enjoy being able to put these pieces together. The entire survey results are reported in Appendix B for the intrepid or the scholarly to follow.

There is so much to glean from this survey. Perhaps most significant of all is that our stereotypes about role identity just don't hold true. From class identification to specific sexual activities, you cannot find any significant correlations with the choosing of one role over another.

There were very few differences between those who identified as butch, femme, androgynous or none of the above. What differences that did show up were not that significant. Though minor inferences could be made that follow the stereotypes we have of those four groups, there were also big surprises. There were virtually no differences in the arena of sexual activity. The most significant difference was in the goddess identification, not exactly a high point for roles.

In addition, what emerges is a lesbian eroticism that is at its core fluid, in terms of initiation and response, and in terms of specific activities. This eroticism seems grounded as well in relationships and characteristics that are not traditionally seen as sexual. The words we choose for our attractions, the things we actually do and desire, seem to be the starting point for a more open and complex lesbian sexuality.

THE DEBATE
7

The following excerpts from two articles present diametrically opposed analyses of butch/femme lesbian relationships. In "Butch and Femme: Now and Then," Sheila Jeffreys asserts her belief that butch/femme relationships can be seen as the reproduction of traditionally unequal heterosexual alliances. She is distressed by a butch/femme tendency to eroticize power differences leading, she says, to forms of communication that can be sado-masochistic or polarized into the dominant and the submissive.

Sue-Ellen Case, in "Toward a Butch-Femme Aesthetic," accuses heterosexual feminist critics of devaluing butch/femme while attempting to make lesbianism more acceptable to the heterosexual mainstream. In the process, Case argues, core lesbian identity and the validity of butch/femme is often obscured.

As far as I can tell the two women do not know each other and were unaware of each other's articles at the time that they were written; still they use many of the same quotes from lesbian material. Their compelling arguments and differing perspectives make for a good debate and I have arranged excerpts from their articles by name so that the reader will understand their positions. Although it may appear to be a dialogue, it is not; it is simply the debate going on in another form.

Jeffreys: It was a shock to many lesbians in the 1980s to find that some lesbians in the U.S. who could be seen as leaders of their community were identifying themselves again as butch and femme. They were not only adopting roles cheerfully, but reclaiming roleplaying as lesbian history as well as the lesbian present as revolutionary and positive....

It is a basic building block of feminist theory that women's oppression is maintained by the social construction of masculine and feminine roles.

Case: ...[Teresa] de Lauretis [states]...that the previous [academic political writing about] the female subject assumes, but leaves unwritten, a heterosexual context for the subject and this is the cause for [the female subject's] continuing entrapment.

...De Lauretis' conclusion is my starting place. Focusing on the feminist subject, endowed with the agency for political change, located among women, outside the ideology of sexual difference and thus the social institution of heterosexuality, it would appear that the lesbian roles of butch and femme, as a dynamic duo, offer precisely the strong subject position the movement requires.

Jeffreys: I am not neutral in this debate and see the reclamation of roleplaying as a dangerous political development for lesbians....I see that [these] patterns of lesbian relating and identifying based on dominance and submission and gender fetishism are certainly present in the lesbian community today.

Case: ...The butch-femme couple inhabit the subject position together. They are not split subjects....They are coupled ones that do not impale themselves on the poles of sexual difference....

Jeffreys: The contemporary proponents of roleplaying are offering a romaticised version of the lifestyle of 50's roleplayers. According to writers like [Joan] Nestle roleplaying was a form of erotic preference. It does not seem from the accounts we have available that roleplaying in the 50's was positively chosen for its erotic advantages. It is clear that both the butch and femme roles had serious disadvantages attached to them which make the revalidation of these roles today particularly difficult to understand.

...It would seem that Nestle is then distorting lesbian history in stating that it is mainly feminists who have found roleplaying unacceptable. Her writings suggest that she is hostile to feminism and it suits her therefore to attribute any discomfort with roleplaying only to feminists.

Case: Nestle describes it: [butch women] did announce themselves as tabooed women who were willing to identify their passion for other women by wearing clothes that symbolized the taking of responsibility.... This courage to feel comfortable with arousing another woman became a political act.

Jeffreys: For [Nestle] the main attraction seems to be a masochistic sexual response to the power and privilege of the butch.

Case: In other words, the butch, who represents by her clothing her desire for other women, becomes the beast—the marked taboo against lesbianism dressed up in the clothes of that desire. Beauty is the desired one and the one who aims her desirability at the butch.

Jeffreys: The implication of Nestle's writing is that somehow feminists imposed egalitarian forms of relationship upon lesbians...from outside the lesbian community.... In fact roleplaying and dress were an issue for lesbians long before feminism introduced its own critique.
Del Martin and Phyllis Lyon write in *Lesbian Woman* about the Daughters of Bilitis [D.O.B.] lesbian organization which predated this wave of feminism.... "...One of the D.O.B.'s goals was to teach the Lesbian a 'mode of behavior and dress acceptable to society....' We knew too many Lesbians whose activities were restricted because they wouldn't wear skirts...."

Case: ...Homophobia...is an outgrowth of the typical interaction between feminism and lesbianism since the rise of the feminist movement in the early 1970s. Del Martin and Phyllis Lyon describe...in... *Lesbian Woman* the way in which the DOB moved away from the earlier bar culture and its symbolic systems to a more dominant identification and one that would appease the feminist movement. DOB's goal was to erase butch-femme behavior, its dress codes, and lifestyle from the lesbian community and to change lesbians into lesbian feminists.

"...One of DOB's goals was to teach the Lesbian a mode of behavior and dress acceptable to society.... We knew too many lesbians whose activities were restricted because they wouldn't wear skirts."

The description of [a rebellious butch, which immediately follows], portrays her as uncivilized, recalling earlier, colonial missionary projects. [She] is portrayed as similar to the inappropriately dressed savage whom the missionary clothes and saves.

Jeffreys: Joan Nestle's effeminised lesbian would have fitted quite well into this scene since it was clearly butch rather than femme clothing which was criticised.

Case: If butches are savages in this book, the femmes are lost heterosexuals who damage birthright lesbians by forcing them to play the butch roles. The authors assert that most femmes are divorced heterosexual women who know how to relate only to men and thus force their butches to play the man's role....

Jeffreys: ...We are reduced to understanding this contemporary glorification of butch and femme in terms of sadomasochism. The writings of [Cherrie] Moraga and [Amber] Hollibaugh [in "What We're Rollin' Around in Bed With: Sexual Silences in Feminism"] demonstrates

the connection…. "I think the reason butch
/femme stuff got hidden within lesbian-
feminism is because people are profoundly
afraid of power in bed. And though everybody
doesn't play out power the way I do, the question
of power affects who and how you eroticize your
sexual need."

Case: …[The] compulsory adaptation of lesbian
feminist identification [by women such as Del
Martin and Phyllis Lyon] must be understood as a
defensive posture, created by the homophobia that
operated in the internal dynamics of the early movement….

[Moraga and Hollibaugh] described [in the same
article cited above by Jeffreys] the feminist reception
of lesbians this way: "The first discussion of
lesbianism among feminists was: '…when we're just
learning how to be friends with other women, you
got to go and sexualize it' …they made men out of
every sexual dyke…. In our involvement in a
movement largely controlled by white middle-class
women, we feel the values of their culture…have
been pushed down our throats…."

Jeffreys: As the radicalism of gay liberation died
and lesbians deserted in large numbers for lesbian feminism, gay male theorists of liberation
turned around and began to promote as revolutionary practices based upon internalized homophobia, gender fetishism, eroticised power
imbalances and sexual objectification…. It is
from such male gay sexual politics that contemporary lesbian promoters of roleplaying get such
theoretical support as exists.

Case: ...The lesbian has been assigned the role of the skeleton in the closet of feminism; in this case, specifically the lesbian who relates to her cultural roots by identifying with traditional butch/femme role-playing.... Several factors are responsible for this ghosting.... The first is the growth of moralist projects restricting the production of sexual fiction or fantasy through the anti-pornography crusade.

> **Jeffreys:** It is difficult to reconstruct our sexuality when we have been raised, and learned our emotions and sexual feelings, in a heteropatriarchal context of dominance and submission. But this is the feminist project...the real pleasures of a sexual relationship in which two lesbians...seek to meet each other and make love without roles.
>
> "Male-female polarity" is so fundamental to the way we conceptualize and experience sexual desire, i.e. in the form of eroticised sexual imbalance, that those of us who criticise this form of sexuality are constantly accused of being anti-sex.... Is there any other form of sex? Can we have homo sex, based on sameness, mutuality, equality?

Case: ...The female body, the male gaze, and the structures of realism are only sex toys for the butch-femme couple.... The butch-femme couple can...move through a field of symbols...playfully inhabiting the camp space of irony and wit, free from biological determinism, elitist essentialism, and the heterosexist cleavage of sexual difference. Surely, here is a couple the feminist subject might perceive as useful to join.

Cross-Correlations

For the research-minded, this appendix contains the data discussed in Chapter Eight, along with my methodology. The entire questionnaire and its results are in Appendix B.

Hypothesis

It is my experience that there are different erotic designations within lesbianism, butch and femme being two of the earliest and most well known. An androgynous category, now quite popular, was created with the influence of feminism in the 1970s. It is my contention that in addition to these three, many others exist, but that we do not have the vocabulary to express our unconscious concepts of the different lesbian erotic identifications.

Because of internal and external homophobia, I believe we stereotype the designations we do have and are frozen in our attempts to create a new language that more fully describes lesbianism. This is true with lesbian culture in general, and more specifically in regards to sexual and erotic differences within lesbianism.

In this study, my hypothesis was that the respondents would for the most part not identify with butch and femme, and that they would have few other words to describe any differentiations within lesbianism. It was my assumption that those who do identify as butch, femme, androgynous or none of the above would not differ much from one another in actual behavior (e.g. who uses a dildo on whom, who takes care of the kids, etc.).

I believe there really are differences in the four groups and differences in how that energy is expressed. Yet I believe we are at a loss to describe it. I believe that once we are able to describe those differences in a way that is both accurate and positive, we will be able to move away from the stereotyping of behavior.

Methods

The questionnaire used in this research consisted of 166 questions, including multiple choice questions and single word or short answer questions to be supplied by respondents. The questionnaire also included the Bem Sex Role Inventory to be used by the respondents to rate themselves and others. The purpose of using Bem's inventory was to have a standardized form (already accepted in sociology and social psychology) with which to compare results about gender assignment of sex-role characteristics.

It is impossible to get a random sample of lesbians. Because this culture is so homophobic, all lesbians cannot be open about their lesbianism. Therefore, it was necessary to contact lesbians who were already attending an event that either catered primarily to lesbians or which lesbians would be likely to attend. This narrowed the group to lesbians who would be at a publicly known lesbian event, or would willingly pick up a questionnaire at a non-lesbian event.

The following are the distribution sites along with the number of questionnaires passed out and returned at each site: the West Coast Women's Music and Comedy Festival, September 1989,(400 with 253 returned); public lectures and workshops of mine, September 1989 through February 1990 (600 with 407 returned); the Dynamics of Color Conference in San Francisco, November 1989, (250 with ten returned); a lesbian Latina gathering, November 1989, (150 with five returned); an African-American lesbian gathering, November 1989, (100 with seven returned). An additional 100 were given out by friends specifically to women of color with five returned. All those distributed at some site other than at a lecture, had self-addressed stamped envelopes attached. Of the 687 returned, 589 were analyzed. The other 98 were not analyzed because they were returned too late, or the response sheet was not filled out correctly, or only partially filled out. The majority of the respondents were from California

(206), Colorado (57), Minnesota (54), New Mexico (72), Ohio (66), Oregon (38), Texas (61) and Washington (six). The other states which had smaller representation (22) included: Florida, Georgia, Idaho, Indiana, Iowa, Kansas, Kentucky, Missouri, New York, and Tennessee. A few (seven) came from Australia, Canada, and West Germany.

I made an effort to get more representation from women of color than I had achieved in my previous survey (published in *Lesbian Passion: Loving Ourselves and Each Other).* Six hundred were distributed at black, Latina and other women of color conferences and through personal networks. There were 27 returned from those settings. Some women of color have said that they thought the return was so poor because women of color found it offensive that one more white woman was asking for help from women of color to create a product that was essentially white-oriented.

Several Latina women commented that the use of "Hispanic" rather than "Latina" in the race question was not their preferred designation. Some respondents were offended because a designation for Jews was not made under race, but only in the religion question.

There was a significant effort made by a a colleague of mine to distribute questionnaires at an older lesbians' conference, but the organizers would not let her. This was unfortunate, because the information would have been quite valuable. A few friends gave 50 questionnaires specifically to older lesbians, but none were returned from that group.

There were no specific designations or categories of disabilities included in the survey. The question about whether or not a woman was disabled was general. All of my events were wheelchair accessible, most were signed and at a few, women who attended were asked not to wear scents.

Education and sophistication in regard to testing was needed to answer this survey, which did not make it accessible to the whole community. One of the drawbacks of this questionnaire was that I used a vocabulary that was difficult for many people. In addition, there were problems with the layout of the response sheet, which was not a standardized test form. Finally, it took 30-60 minutes to fill out. Women seemed, in general, to be more motivated to finish if I had just given a talk, gave out the questionnaires, then waited for them to be completed.

It continues to be a struggle to get responses from a true cross-section of the lesbian community. The most problematic issue is that there is no easy way to find a random sample of lesbians. In addition, it's clear that women from all facets of the lesbian community need to be included in the design of the questionnaire, as well as its distribution. While this book itself includes feedback from women of different backgrounds, races, and abilities, most of this information came from personal contacts, interviews and conferences, and not from the questionnaires. I changed some of my distribution techniques this time, with better overall return, and with a better ethnic and age distribution than in my last survey. However, there were fewer disabled lesbians than before, and there were fewer lesbians in the oldest age category. It isn't a simple process, but since I am bound and determined and stubborn, I'll keep trying.

There were a few other comments on the methods I used that are valuable to report. There were many other questions I would have liked to ask, but didn't because the survey was already too long. More open-ended questions would have been useful as well, but again, the length would have become prohibitive.

Topics purposefully left off included questions about childhood sexual abuse, early same-sex consensual activities, family history of gayness, and so on.

The ten point "butch/femme" scale is a scale that is used informally in the lesbian community. It is a common practice to choose the middle as a self-description in an effort to dis-identify from the butch or femme designations, but a ten point scale does not have a true middle unless fractions are used. Assuming that women would rate themselves as a 5 because they thought it was the middle, I used a nine-point scale to correct for that common error.

Results

These are listed in the order in which they are discussed in Chapter Eight, and not as they are in the questionnaire itself. The number in front of the question refers to its number in the questionnaire. The entire questionnaire and the results for the whole sample can be found in Appendix B, immediately following.

LESBIAN DEMOGRAPHICS
EARLY SEXUALITY

(19.) *What age were you when you started having consenting sex with females?* never have (1%); under age 10 (4%); 11-15 (7%); 16-20 (34%); 21-25 (30%); 26-30 (12%); 31-35 (7%); 36-45 (5%); over 46 (1%).

LESBIAN LANGUAGE

(42.) *What word/phrase do you most commonly use to identify yourself in relation to your sexual/emotional connection to women?* bisexual(1%) other (1%); queer (1%); woman-loving-woman (4%); dyke (6%); woman who fell in love with a woman (7%); gay woman (15%); lesbian (64%).

(43.) *What word makes you the most uncomfortable when others describe you?* queer (37%); dyke (17%); bisexual (17%); none (12%); gay woman (7%); lesbian (6%); a woman who fell in love with a woman (4%); woman loving woman (.5%).

ARE LESBIANS MADE OR BORN?

(18.) *Why do you have the sexual orientation you do?* environmental (2%); none of the reasons given (9%); genetic (10%); chosen (33%); all of the reasons given (46%).

COMING OUT

(20.) *What age were you when you first came out (to yourself)?* never have (1%); under age 10 (2%); 11-15 (7%); 16-20 (27%); 21-25 (30%); 26-30 (16%); 36-45 (9%); 36-45 (7%); over 46 (1%).

(23.) *What age were you when you came out to anyone besides yourself?* never have (0)%; under 10 (1%); 11-15 (4%);16-20 (27%); 21-25 (33%); 26-30 (16%); 31-35 (11%); 36-45 (8%); over 46 (1%).

(24.) *Who are you out to?* lesbian/gay friends (98%); straight friends (86%); lesbian/gay co-workers (70%); mother (68%); straight co-workers (60%); sisters (56%); brothers (50%); father (46%); extended family (36%); boss (31%); neighbors (30%); children (15%); grandparents (9%); children's friends (7%); teachers of your children (5%); no one (0%).

(27.) *Do you assume most people know you are a lesbian?* yes (39%); no (42%); unsure (19%).

(28.) *Do you think that you pass for straight unless you tell people otherwise?* yes (45%); no (10%); sometimes (40%); unsure (5%).

NAMES FOR OUR LOVERS

(33.) *How do you* most often *refer to a lesbian lover to non-gay people?* friend (35%); roommate (22%); partner (16%); lover (13%); girlfriend (12%); other (2%); mate (1%); wife (.2%); companion (.2%).

(34.) *When speaking of your lesbian lover to a non-gay person, what pronouns do you most often use?* she, her (69%); neutral ones so the sex of the person is vague (30%); he, him (1%).

(41.) *Do you feel comfortable being seen with your lover in public?* very comfortable (67%); comfortable (30%); uncomfortable (2%); very uncomfortable (1%).

PASSING

(29.) *If you pass for straight, what is your* most *frequent feeling about this?* this is how I look, not concerned with others' opinions (38%); angry to feel I have to do so (19%).

(30.) *If you pass for straight, what is your* least *frequent feeling about this?* proud (32%); happy I'm putting something over on straight people (20%).

(31.) *If you do not pass for straight, what is your* most *frequent feeling about this?* this is how I look, not concerned with others' opinions (24%); concerned I may be discriminated against (22%); proud (19%).

(32.) *If you do not pass for straight, what is your* least *frequent feeling about this?* happy to shock straights (26%); no feeling (20%).

(37.) *If your lover passes for straight, what is your* most *frequent feeling about this?* no feeling (25%); angry to feel she has to do so (23%).

(38.) *If your lover passes for straight, what is your* least *frequent feeling about this?* ashamed to be seen with her in lesbian settings (21%); no feeling (20%).

(39.) *If your lover does not pass for straight, what is your* most *frequent feelings about this?* angry that this is an issue (19%); at ease (19%).

(40.) *If your lover does not pass for straight, what is your* least *frequent feeling about this?* ashamed to be seen with her in straight settings (29%); no feeling (21%).

(36.) *Do you think your current or most recent lover passes for straight unless she tells people she is a lesbian?* yes (54%); no (28%); unsure (18%).

GENERAL DEMOGRAPHICS

(2.) *What is your ethnic designation?* Pacific Islander (.2%); Asian (.5%); Native American (2%); African American (2%); Latina (6%); and Caucasian (89%).

(9.) *What is the class background in which you were raised?* poverty (3%); working (27%); middle (45%); upper- middle (23%); upper (1%).

(4.) *What religion were you raised in?* Mormon (1.2%); Jewish (8%); Protestant (45%); Catholic (31%); other (6%); n.o.t.a. (10%).

(10.) *What level of education have you completed?* less than high school (1%); high school (6%); trade school (2%); some college (19%); B.A. (37%); M.A. (28%); PhD. (3%); M.D. (2%); J.D. (2%).

(1.) *What is your age?* under 25 (8%); 25-29 (17%); 30-39 (50%); 40-49 (21%); 50-59 (3%); 60 or over (.5%).

(11.) *What is your yearly income from all sources?* Under 10K (12%); 1-20K (22%); 21-35K (41%); 36-50K (17%); 51-75K (5%); 76-90K (2%); over 91K (1%).

(3.) *Are you disabled?* (5%)

(13.) *Are you a parent?* yes: (17%); no: (82)%

(14.) *If yes, mark all that apply:* biological (72%); co-parent (18%); foster (6%); adoptive (5%).

(7). *Mark all the answers that apply to your body type:* medium (44%); short (23%); tall (19%); average build (6%); muscular (5%); fat (3%); thin (1%).

BUTCH/FEMME/ANDROGYNY

(113.) *What do you most identify with?* femme (18%); butch (15%); androgynous (48%); none of the above (19%).

(104.) *What phrase best describes your understanding of the butch/femme concept?* mannerisms (27%); male/female role-playing (27%); gender identity within lesbianism (16%); state of mind (11%); sexual energy differences (10%); archaic lesbian language (5%); other (3%).

(17.) *Are you more attracted to women who are:* androgynous (44%); femme (25%); butch (19%); none of the above (12%).

(105.) *Where would you place* yourself *on butch/femme scale?* 1 (2%); 2 (5%); 3 (14%); 4 (16%); 5 (26%); 6 (19%); 7 (13%); 8 (3%); 9 (1%).

(110.) *Where would you place your* most recent lover *on a butch/femme scale?* 1 (2%); 2 (6%); 3 (17%); 4 (15%); 5 (22%); 6 (15%); 7 (17%); 8 (6%); 9 (2%).

(111.) *Where would you place yourself on a scale that rates only your femme aspects (#10 being the ultimate femme)?* 4 (15%); 5 (22%); 6 (14%); 7 (16%).

(112.) *Where would you place yourself on a scale that rates only your butch aspects (#10 being the ultimate butch)?* 4 (15%); 5 (21%); 6 (14%); 7 (13%).

(108.) *Since you have come out has your rating changed on the butch/femme scale?* yes (44%); no (55%).

(106.) *Does your rating vary in different situations?* yes (72%); no (27%).

(107.) *Is your rating influenced by where your lover is on the butch/femme scale?* yes (22%); no (77%).

(119.) *Do you feel butch/femme relates to the heterosexual male/female model?* somewhat (44%); yes (28%); no (19%); not sure (8%).

(109.) *If you rate yourself #5 on the scale and had to choose either butch or femme to identify with, which would it be?* butch (46%); femme (52%).

(124.) *How often do the concepts of butch/femme/androgyny come up in conversation with other lesbians?* always (2%); often (19%); occasionally (69%); never (10%).

(123.) *How important is a butch/femme characterization to your personal identity?* very (4%); somewhat (30%); not at all (66%).

(126.) *Do you feel there is more value placed on being androgynous in the lesbian community than on being butch or femme?* yes (40%); no (19%); not sure (41%).

GODDESS IDENTIFICATION

(165.) *Which of the above (Goddesses) best describes you?* Artemis (35%); Athena (15%); Hestia (16%); Hera (2%); Demeter (3%); Persephone (5%); Aphrodite (24%).

(166.) *Which of the above (Goddesses) best describes your most recent lover?* Artemis (30%); Athena (17%); Hestia (13%); Hera (5%); Demeter (3%); Persephone (10%); Aphrodite (23%).

CORRELATIONS BETWEEN BUTCH, FEMME, ANDROGYNY AND NONE OF THE ABOVE IDENTITIES

What is presented here and discussed in Chapter Eight are any of the differences that showed up between the groups. The rest of the data showed that there were no significant differences between the different identities.

General Demographics:

(9.) *What is the class background in which you were raised?* (These were explained in three different ways in the discussion section and are all given here.):

(a.) What percentage of the identifications were from each class (e.g., How many femmes were from the working class?) Poverty class (F-4%; B-3%; A-3%; N-4%); working class (F-24%; B-29%; A-27%; N-29%); middle class (F-43%; B-42%; A-47%; N-46%); upper-middle class (F-27%; B-24%; A-23%; N-19%); upper class (F-2%; B-1%; A-1%; N-1%).

(b.) The percentages of each category within the sample as a whole were: Poverty class (F-1%; B-.5%; A-1%; N-1%); working class (F-4%; B-4%; A-13%; N-5%); middle class (F-8%; B-6%; A-23%; N-9%); upper-middle class (F-5%; B-4%; A-11%; N-4%); upper class (F-.3%; B-.1%; A-.3%; N-.1%).

(c.) When we consider the percentages of each identity within the class background, the distribution is as follows: Poverty

(F-22%; B-17%; A-39%; N-22%); working (F-16%; B-16%; A-47%; N-20%); middle (F-17%; B-14%; A-50%; N-19%); upper-middle (F-21%; B-15%; A-48%; N-15%); upper (F-33%; B-17%; A-33%; N-17%).

(14.) *If you are a parent, mark all that apply:*

Biological mothers: femmes and n.o.t.a. (76%); butches and androgynous (69%).

Co-mothers: femmes (10%); butches and n.o.t.a. (19%); androgynous (21%).

Foster moms: femmes (14%); butches (6%); androgynous (4%); n.o.t.a. (0%).

Adoptive mothers: butches and androgynous (6%); n.o.t.a. (5%); femmes (0%).

Lesbian Data

(43.) *Which word makes you the most uncomfortable when others describe you?*

Queer: butches (44%); androgynous (39%); femmes (34%); n.o.t.a. (27%).

(42.) *Which word/phrase do you most commonly use to identify yourself in relation to your sexual/emotional connection to women?*

Lesbian: butches (78%); n.o.t.a. (66%); androgynous (65%); femmes (62%).

Woman who fell in love with a woman: femmes (12%); n.o.t.a. (8%); butches and androgynous (6%).

(33.) *How do you most often refer to a lesbian lover to non-gay people?*

Girlfriend: femmes (15%); n.o.t.a. (13%); androgynous (12%); butches (8%).

Roommate: butches (30%); androgynous (24%); n.o.t.a. (17%); femmes (15)%.

(35.) *At work or around straight people, do you talk in code on the phone to your female lover so that no one knows to whom you are talking?*

Yes: androgynous (14%); butches (13%); femmes (10%); n.o.t.a. (8%).

No: n.o.t.a. (67%); femmes (56%); butches (54%); androgynous (52)%.

Passing

(122.) *Are you ever mistaken for a man?*

Yes: butches (36%); n.o.t.a. (27%); androgynous (25%); femmes (4%).

No: femmes (88%); butches (30%); androgynous (54%); n.o.t.a. (52%).

(28.) *Do you think you pass for straight unless you tell people otherwise?*

Yes: femmes (79%); androgynous (42)%; n.o.t.a. (38%); butches (23)%.

No: femmes (1%); butches (19%); androgynous (10%); n.o.t.a. (9%).

(29.) *If you pass for straight, what is your most frequent feeling about this?*

Relieved: femmes (12%); butches (7%); androgynous (6%); n.o.t.a. (3%).

Living a lie: butches (34%); femmes and androgynous (19%); n.o.t.a. (26%).

Angry I have to: androgynous (20%); femmes (19%); n.o.t.a. (18%); butches (17%).

(27.) *Do you assume most people know you are a lesbian?*

No: femmes (56%); androgynous (41%); n.o.t.a. (40%); butches (30%).

Yes: butches (56%); androgynous (40%); n.o.t.a. (36%); femmes (28%).

(36.) *Do you think your current or most recent lover passes for straight unless she tells people she is a lesbian?*

Yes: butches (71%); femmes (46%); androgynous and n.o.t.a. (53%).

No: femmes (41%); androgynous (30%); n.o.t.a. (21%); butches (13%).

Butch and Femme

(104.) *What phrase best describes your understanding of the butch/femme concept?*

Male/female role playing: n.o.t.a. (32%); androgynous (31%); femmes (20%); butches (18%).

Sexual energy differences: femmes (17%); butches (15%); androgynous (7%); n.o.t.a. (5%).

(117.) *Are you more attracted to women who are:*

Butch: femmes (40%); butches (24%); androgynous (12%); n.o.t.a (11%).

Femme: butches (45%); femmes (35%); n.o.t.a. (24%); androgynous (14%).

Androgynous: androgynous (69%); femmes and n.o.t.a. (22%); butches (21%).

N.o.t.a.: n.o.t.a. (42%); butches (11%); androgynous (5%); femmes (3%).

Activities

In *the following behaviors, are you the initiator, responder, depends?*

(135.) *Paying bills:*

Initiator: butches and n.o.t.a. (53%); femmes (47)%; androgynous (42)%.

Depends: androgynous (46%); femmes (40%); n.o.t.a. (39%); butches (30%).

Responder: butches (16%); femmes (13%); androgynous (12%); n.o.t.a. (11%).

(136.) *Cleaning house:*

Initiator: femmes (45%); androgynous (40%); butches (35%); n.o.t.a. (34%).

Depends: n.o.t.a. (51%); butches (43%); androgynous (42%); femmes (39%).

Responder: butches (21%); androgynous (19%); femmes (17%); n.o.t.a.15%.

(141.) *Cooking:*

Initiator: n.o.t.a. (40%); butches (39%); femmes and androgynous (36%).

Depends: androgynous (42%); n.o.t.a. (41%); femmes and butches (40%).

Responder: femmes (24%); androgynous (22%); butches (21%); n.o.t.a. (18%).

Sex Practices

(19.) *What age were you when you started having consenting sex with females?*

Under the age of ten: femmes (8%); n.o.t.a. (6%); butches and androgynous (2%).

(145.) *Are you the initiator in sex?*

Never: n.o.t.a. (2%); androgynous and butches (1%); femmes (0%).

Occasionally: n.o.t.a. and femmes (17%); butches (13%); androgynous (12%).

Sometimes: femmes (54%); androgynous and n.o.t.a. (41%); butches (28%).

Often: butches (51%); androgynous (42%); n.o.t.a. (39%); femmes (28%).

Always: butches (6%); androgynous (4%); n.o.t.a. (2%); femmes (1%).

(146.) *Are you the responder in sex?*

Never: butches (2%); femmes and androgynous (1%); n.o.t.a. (0%).

Occasionally: butches (21%); femmes (13%); androgynous (12%); n.o.t.a. (9%).

Sometimes: androgynous (54%); n.o.t.a. (51%); butches (49%); femmes (47%).

Often: n.o.t.a. (35%); femmes (33%); androgynous (28%); butches (21%).

Always: butches and femmes (7%); n.o.t.a. (6%); androgynous (5%).

(147.) *Do you initiate oral sex?*

Never: androgynous (9%); femmes and butches (8%); n.o.t.a. (7%).

Occasionally: femmes and butches (20%); androgynous and n.o.t.a. (15%).

Sometimes: n.o.t.a. and androgynous (27%); femmes (26%); butches (21%).

Often: n.o.t.a. (43%); androgynous (39%); butches (35%); femmes (30%).

Always: femmes (16%); butches (15%); androgynous (9%); n.o.t.a. (8%).

(149.) *Are you orgasmic?*

Never: butches (6%); n.o.t.a. (4%); androgynous (2%); and femmes (0%).

Occasionally: n.o.t.a. (8%); femmes (7%); androgynous (6%); butches (5%).

Sometimes: androgynous (15%); butches, femmes and n.o.t.a. (7%).

Often: butches (39%); femmes and n.o.t.a. (31%); androgynous (29%).

Always: femmes (54%); n.o.t.a. (50%); androgynous (48%); butches (44%).

(150.) *Is your lover orgasmic?*

Never: butches and femmes (3%); androgynous and n.o.t.a. (2%).

Occasionally: n.o.t.a. (9%); butches (7%); androgynous (6%); femmes (3%).

Sometimes: butches (14%); androgynous (12%); femmes (8%); n.o.t.a. (4%).

Often: femmes (41%); butches (36%); androgynous (35%); n.o.t.a. (32%).

Always: n.o.t.a. (53%); femmes and androgynous (45%); butches (39%).

(151.) *Do you practice vaginal penetration with your lover?*

Never: butches (98%); androgynous and femmes (95%); n.o.t.a. (2%).

Occasionally: androgynous (11%); n.o.t.a. (10%); femmes and butches (8%).

Sometimes: androgynous (20%); femmes (19%); butches (13%); n.o.t.a. (10%).

Often: n.o.t.a. (42%); butches (41%); androgynous and femmes (37%).

Always: n.o.t.a. (36%); femmes (31%); butches (29%); androgynous (27%).

(152.) *Does your lover penetrate you?*

Never: butches (13%); androgynous (6%); n.o.t.a. (2%); femmes (1%).

Occasionally: butches (14%); n.o.t.a. (12%); femmes (11%); androgynous (9%).

Sometimes: androgynous (19%); femmes (11%); butches and n.o.t.a. (14%).

Often: n.o.t.a. (41%); butches and femmes (38%); androgynous (37%).

Always: femmes (39%); n.o.t.a. (36%); androgynous (29%); butches (25%).

(155.) *Do you fantasize being a man while having sex?*

Never: femmes (74%); n.o.t.a. (71%); androgynous (68%); butches (61%).

Occasionally: butches (24%); androgynous (18%); n.o.t.a. (15%); femmes (14%).

(156.) *Do you fantasize your partner being a man while having sex?*

Never: n.o.t.a. (77%); androgynous (73%); butches (71%); femmes (70%).

Occasionally: butches (20%); femmes (18%); androgynous (16%); n.o.t.a. (14%).

Sometimes: femmes (10%); androgynous (9%); n.o.t.a. (6%); butches (2%).

Often: n.o.t.a. (4%); femmes, butches and androgynous (2%).

Always: butches (2%); androgynous (1%); femmes and n.o.t.a. (0%).

(161.) *Do you like to have your breasts sucked?*

Never: butches (4%); femmes and androgynous (1%); n.o.t.a. (0%).

Occasionally: n.o.t.a. (8%); butches and androgynous (7%); femmes (5%).

Sometimes: butches (21%); femmes (16%); androgynous (15%); n.o.t.a. (13%).

Often: butches (34%); androgynous (30%); femmes (26%); n.o.t.a. (25%).

Always: n.o.t.a. (54%); femmes (53%); androgynous (47%); butches (35%).

(162.) *Do you like to suck your lover's breasts?*

Never: androgynous (.3%); femmes, butches, and n.o.t.a. 0%).

Occasionally: n.o.t.a. (4%); androgynous (2%); femmes and butches (1%).

Sometimes: butches (15%); femmes and androgynous (10%); n.o.t.a. (7%).

Often: femmes (35%); butches (31%); androgynous (30%); n.o.t.a. (23%).

Always: n.o.t.a. (66%); androgynous (57%); femmes (55%); butches (53%).

(163.) *Do you like giving sex?*

Never: femmes (2%); androgynous (1%); butches and n.o.t.a. (0%).

Occasionally: femmes and n.o.t.a. (2%); butches and androgynous (1%).

Sometimes: femmes (8%); androgynous (7%); butches (5%); n.o.t.a. (3%).

Often: n.o.t.a. (35%); femmes and androgynous (32%); butches (28%).

Always: butches (67%); androgynous (60%); n.o.t.a. (59%); femmes (56%).

(164.) *Do you like getting sex?*

Never: femmes and androgynous (1%); butches and n.o.t.a. (0%).

Occasionally: butches (5%); femmes (3%); androgynous (2%); n.o.t.a. (1%).

Sometimes: butches and androgynous (9%); n.o.t.a. and femmes (4%).

Often: femmes and n.o.t.a. (33%); androgynous (31%); butches (28%).

Always: n.o.t.a. (62%); femmes (60%); butches (59%); androgynous (57%).

GODDESS IDENTIFICATION

(165.) *Which of the above (Goddesses) best describes you?*

Artemis: androgynous and n.o.t.a. (37%); butches (35%); femmes (27%).

Athena: butches (21%); androgynous (16%); n.o.t.a. (15%); femmes (9%).

Hestia: n.o.t.a. (19%); femmes (17%); androgynous (15%); butches (13%).

Hera: androgynous (3%); n.o.t.a. (2%); femmes (1%); butches (0%).

Demeter: androgynous (4%); femmes (2%); butches and n.o.t.a. (1%).

Persephone: butches and femmes (8%); n.o.t.a. (5%); androgynous (3%).

Aphrodite: femmes (36%); n.o.t.a. (22%); androgynous and butches (21%).

(166.) *Which of the above (Goddesses) best describes your most recent lover?*

Artemis: femmes (41%); androgynous (30%); n.o.t.a. (25%); butches (21%).

Athena: androgynous (18%); femmes (17%); n.o.t.a. (16%); butches (15%).

Hestia: butches (16%); n.o.t.a. (15%); femmes and androgynous (12%).

Hera: butches (6%); androgynous (5%); n.o.t.a. (5%); femmes (4%).

Demeter: butches and androgynous (4%); n.o.t.a. (3%); femmes (1%).

Persephone: androgynous (11%); butches (10%); n.o.t.a. (9%); femmes (8%).

Aphrodite: butches (29%); n.o.t.a. (27%); androgynous (21%); femmes (18%).

WORDS USED TO DESCRIBE OURSELVES

Bem Survey Results

(128.) *Characteristics that describe butch:*

Femmes: dominant and masculine (40%); athletic (39%); forceful (30%).

Butches: self-reliant (40%); athletic (24%); assertive and dominant (23%).

Androgynous: masculine (41%); dominant (38%); aggressive (28%); strong personality (18%).

(129.) *Characteristics that describe femme:*

Femmes: feminine (62%); gentle (29%); affectionate (28%); warm 26%).

Butches: feminine (35%); gentle (28%); warm (25%); affectionate (18%).

Androgynous: feminine (41%); gentle (23%); tender (18%); helpful (17%).

(130.) *Characteristics that describe androgynous:*

Femmes: individualistic (30%); yielding (24%); adaptable (21%); shy (20%).

Butches: individualistic and adaptable (21%); independent and self-sufficient (13%).

Androgynous: independent (26%); self-reliant (25%); individualistic (22%); assertive (15%).

(114.) (76 words were given, some multiply used with a total of 206 replies.)*If you identify as butch, choose three words to describe aspects of femmes you find erotic:* soft (26%); gentle (16%); sensual (14%); sexual/sexy (13%); beautiful (10%); the way they dress (8%).

(115.) (79 words were given, with a total of 210 replies.) *If you identify as femme, choose three words to describe aspects of butches you find erotic:* strong (34%); confident (16%); assertive (13%); muscles (8%); independent (6%); tough (6%).

(116.) (124 words were given, with a total of 321 replies.) *If you identify as androgynous, choose three words to describe aspects of women you find erotic:* strong (11%); soft (6%); intelligent (4%); sensitive, tender, independent, assertive, and gentle (each 3%).

(131.) *List three words which describe* physical *characteristics which you find erotic (arousing or satisfying sexual desire) in women:* breasts (11%); eyes (9%); muscles (9%); soft (7%); strong (6%); hair (6%); dark skin (5%); ass/hips (5%); athletic (4%); and smooth skin (4%).

(132.) *List three words which describe* intellectual *characteristics you find erotic in women:* intelligent (9%); humor (7%); witty (6%); analytical (5%); articulate (5%); well read (4%); creative (3%).

(133.) *List three words which describe* emotional *characteristics you find erotic in women:* sensitive (10%); compassionate (8%); gentle (6%); tender (6%); warm (5%); caring (5%); loving (4%); open (4%).

(134.) *List three words which describe* spiritual *characteristics which you find erotic in women:* open 5%); searching/seeking (3%); loving (2%); honest (2%).

································

APPENDIX B

································

JoAnn Loulan's Questionaire for Lesbians, 1989-90

For each of these questions, mark *one* response (unless otherwise indicated) on your answer sheet that represents what you feel is most true. When the question calls for a response about your lover, it is meant to indicate your current lover. If you do not have a lover at this time, base the response on your most recent lover. For women who have never had a lover, these questions will not be relevant.

    1. *What is your age?* under 25 (8%); 25-29 (17%); 30-39 (50%); 40-49 (21%); 50-59 (3%); 60 or over (0.5%).

    2. *What is your ethnic designation?* African American (2%); Caucasian (85%); Hispanic (6%); Asian (5%); Native American (2%); Pacific Islander (0.2%).

    3. *Are you disabled?* yes (5%); no (95%).

    4. *What religion were you raised in?* Jewish (8%); Catholic (31%); Muslim (0%); Mormon (1.2%); Hindu (0%); Protestant (75%), Native American (0%); no religious background (10%); other (6%).

5. *What is your height (round fractions up)?* under 5 feet (2%); 5'-5' 2" (14%); 5'3"-5'5" (39%); 5'6"-5'8" (36%); 5'9"-5'11" (9%); over 6' (1%).

6. *What is your weight?* under 100 lbs. (1%); 101-125 (24%); 126-140 (28%); 141-160 (25%); 161-180 (12%); 181-200 (6%); 201-220 (2%); 221-240 (1%); 241-260 (1%); over 260 (0.5%).

7. *Mark all that applies to your body type:* tall (19%); medium (44%); short (23%); muscular (5%); fat (3%); thin (1%); average build (6%).

8. *Mark all that applies to your hair:* buzz cut (2%); short (61%); shoulder length (27%); long (6%); curly (3%); straight (1%); spiked (1%); braids (0%) dreadlocks (0%).

9. *What is the class background in which you were raised?* poverty (3%); working (27%); middle (45%); upper middle (23%); upper (1%).

10. *What level of education have you completed?* less than high school (1%); high school (60%); trade school (2%); some college (19%); Bachelor's degree (37%); Masters (28%); PhD (3%); MD (2%); J.D. (2%).

11. *What is your yearly income from all sources (salary, investments, etc.)?* under 10,000 (12%); 11,000-20,000 (22%); (21,000-35,0000 (41%); 36,000-50,000 (17%); 51,000-75,000 (5%); 76,000-90,000 (2%); over 91,000 (1%).

12. *Where do you live now? Fill in the blanks on the answer sheet.*

13. *Are you a parent?* yes (17%); no (82%).

14. *If yes, mark all that apply:* biological parent (72%); adoptive parent 5%; co-parent (18%); foster parent (6%).

15. *What roles do you play in your childrens lives?* mothering (50%); fathering (3%); both (35%); none (12%).

16. *According to Elizabeth Kubler-Ross, there are four basic feelings, which are you most prone to?* happy (65%); angry (12%); sad (10%); scared (13%).

The following questions are related to your lesbian self. Please choose one answer unless otherwise indicated.

17. *Are you:* heterosexual (0.5%); lesbian (92%); bisexual (5%); undecided (3%).

18. *In response to your answer in #17, do you feel this is:* genetic (10%); chosen (33%); environmental (2%); all of the above (46%); none of the above (9%).

19. *What age were you when you started having consenting sex with females?* never have (1%); under age 10 (4%); 11-15 (7%); 16-20 (34%); 21-25 (30%); 26-30 (12%); 31-35 (7%); 36-45 (5%); 46-55 (0.5%); 56-65 (0.2%); over 65 (0%).

20. *What age were you when you came out (in this case, identified to yourself that you were a lesbian)?* never have (1%); under age 10 (4%); 11-15 (7%); 16-20 (34%); 21-25 (30%); 26-30 (16%); 31-35 (9%); 36-45 (7%); 46-55 (1%); 56-65 (0.2%); over 65 (0%).

21. *Where did you come out (to yourself)?*

Northeast (9%); Southeast (5%); Midwest (37%); Northwest (6%); Mid-South (3%); Southwest (22%); West Coast (15%); Alaska/Hawaii (1%); Other Country (3%).

22. *What year did you come out to yourself?* before 1940 (0%); 1941-1950 (1%); 1951-1960 (3%); 1961-1965 (4%); 1966-1970 (39%); 1971-1975 (19%); 1976-1980 (26%); 1981-1985 (26%); 1986-present (13%).

23. *What age were you when you first came out to anyone besides yourself?* never have (0%); under age 10 (1%); 11-15 (4%); 16-20 (27%); 21-25 (33%); 26-30 (16%); 31-35 (11%); 36-45 (8%); 46-55 (1%); 56-65 (0.2%); over 65 (0%).

24. *Who are you out to (mark all that apply)?* your children (15%); mother (68%); father (46%); sisters (56%); brothers (50%); grandparents (9%); extended family (36%); straight friends (86%); lesbian/gay friends (98%); straight co-workers (60%); lesbian/gay co-workers (70%); neighbors (30%); teachers of your children (5%); your children's friends (7%); boss (31%); no one (0%).

25. *Have you discussed you lesbianism explicitly?* yes (87%); no (12%).

26. *If you have discussed your lesbianism explicitly, mark all with whom you have done this.* your children (15%); mother (68%); father (46%); sisters (56%); brothers (50%); grandparents (9%); extended family (30%); straight friends

(86%); lesbian/gay friends (98%); straight co-workers (60%); lesbian/gay co-workers (70%); neighbors (30%); teachers of your children (5%); your children's friends (7%); boss (31%); no one (0%).

27. *Do you assume most people know you are a lesbian?* yes (39%); no (42%); unsure (19%).

28. *Do you think that you pass for straight unless you tell people otherwise?* yes (45%); no (10%); sometimes (40%); unsure (5%).

29. *If you pass for straight, what is your most frequent feeling about this?* relieved (7%); proud (32%); like I'm living a lie (8%); scared I'll be found out (3%); angry to feel I have to do so (5%); happy I'm putting something over on straight people (20%); this is how I look, not concerned with straights (29%); no feeling (20%).

30. *If you pass for straight, what is your least frequent feeling about this?* relieved (8%); proud (32%); like I'm living a lie (8%); scared I'll be found out (11%); angry to feel I have to do so (5%); happy I'm putting something over on straight people (20%); this is how I look, not concerned with straights (9%); no feeling (8%).

31. *If you do not pass for straight, what is your most frequent feeling about this?* relieved (7%); proud (19%); concerned I may be discriminated against (22%); afraid for my safety (3%); angry that this is an issue (20%); happy to shock straights (1%); this is how I look, not concerned with straights (24%); no feeling (6%).

32. *If you do not pass for straight, what is your least frequent feeling about this?* relieved (11%); proud (7%); concerned I may be discriminated against (6%); afraid for my safety (8%); angry that this is an issue (7%); happy to shock straights (26%); this is how I look, not concerned with straights (16%); no feeling (20%).

33. *How do you most often refer to a lesbian lover to non-gay people?* friend (35%); lover (13%); roommate (22%); girlfriend (12%); partner (16%); companion (0.2%); mate (1%); wife (0.2%); other (2%).

34. *When speaking of your lesbian lover to a non-gay person, what pronouns do you most often use?* she, her (69%); he, him (1%); neutral ones so the sex of the person is vague (30%).

35. *At work or around straight people, do you talk on the phone in code to your female lover so that no one knows whom you are talking to?* yes (12%); no (56%); sometimes (32%).

36. *Do you think your current or most recent lover passes for straight unless she tells people she is a lesbian?* yes (54%); no (28%); unsure (18%).

37. *If your lover passes for straight, what is your* most *frequent feeling about this?* relieved (7%); proud (3%); concerned she will be discriminated against (2%); afraid for her safety (2%); angry to feel she has to do so (23%); happy she's putting something over on straight people (2%); ashamed to be seen with her in lesbian settings (1%); at ease (35%); no feelings (25%).

38. *If your lover passes for straight, what is your* least *frequent feeling about this?* relieved (6%); proud (18%); concerned she will be discriminated against (5%); afraid for her safety (7%); angry to feel she has to do so (6%); happy she's putting something over on straight people (9%); ashamed to be seen with her in lesbian settings (21%); at ease (7%); no feelings (20%).

39. *If your lover does not pass for straight, what is your* most *frequent feeling about this?* relieved (2%); proud (16%); concerned she may be discriminated against (17%); afraid for her safety (5%); angry that this is an issue (19%); happy she shocks straights (1%); ashamed to be seen with her in straight settings (5%); at ease (19%); no feeling (16%).

40. *If your lover does not pass for straight, what is your* least *frequent feeling about this?* relieved (12%); proud (5%); concerned she may be discriminated against (3%); afraid for her safety (6%); angry that this is an issue (5%); happy she shocks straights (11%); ashamed to be seen with her in straight settings (29%); at ease (7%); no feeling (21%).

41. *Do you feel comfortable being seen with your lover in public?* very comfortable (67%); somewhat comfortable (30%); uncomfortable (2%); very uncomfortable (1%).

42. *What word/phrase do you most commonly use to identify yourself in relation to your sexual/emotional connection to women?* lesbian (64%); a woman who fell in love with a woman (7%); dyke (6%); woman loving woman (4%); bisexual (1%); queer (1%); gay woman (15%); other (1%).

. . . .

43. *What word makes you the most uncomfortable when others describe you?* lesbian (6%); a woman who fell in love with a woman (4%); dyke (17%); woman loving woman (.5%); bisexual (17%); queer (37%); gay woman (7%); none (12%).

(Note: the next section, which covers Sandra Bem's Sex Role Inventory is fully reported in Appendix D)

The following are personality characteristics from Sandra Bem's Sex Role Inventory. How well do each of these words describe you? Rate yourself on a scale of 1 (never or almost never true) to 7 (always or almost always true)?

44. self reliant	45. yielding
46. helpful	47. defends own beliefs
48. cheerful	49. moody
50. independent	51. shy
52. conscientious	53. athletic
54. affectionate	55. theatrical
56. assertive	57. flatterable
58. happy	59. strong personality
60. loyal	61. unpredictable
62. forceful	63. feminine
64. reliable	65. analytical
66. sympathetic	67. jealous
68. has leadership abilities	69. sensitive to the needs of others
70. truthful	71. willing to take risks
72. understanding	73. secretive
74. makes decisions easily	75. compassionate
76. sincere	77. self-sufficient
78. eager to soothe hurt feelings	79. conceited
80. dominant	81. soft spoken
82. likeable	83. masculine
84. warm	85. solemn
86. willing to take a stand	87. tender
88. friendly	89. aggressive
90. gullible	91. inefficient
92. acts as a leader	93. childlike
94. adaptable	95. individualistic

96. does not use harsh
    language
98. competitive
100. tactful
102. gentle

97. unsystematic

99. loves children
101. ambitious
103. conventional

The following are a group of questions about butch, femme and androgyny. Please choose one answer unless otherwise indicated.

104. *What phrase best describes your understanding of the butch/femme concept?* gender identity within lesbianism (16%); mannerisms (27%); state of mind (11%); male/female role playing (27%); sexual energy differences (10%); archaic lesbian language (5%); other (3%).

105. *Where would you place yourself on a butch/femme scale (#1 being ultimate femme, #9 being ultimate butch)?* 1 (2%); 2 (5%); 3 (14%); 4 (16%); 5 (26%); 6 (19%); 7 (13%); 8 (3%); 9 (1%).

106. *Does this rating vary in different situations?* yes (72%); no (27%).

107. *Is your rating influenced by where your lover is on the butch/femme scale?* yes (22%); no (77%).

108. *Since you have come out, has your rating changed on the butch/femme scale?* yes (44%); no (55%).

109. *If you rate yourself #5 on the butch/femme scale now, and had to choose either butch or femme to identify with, which would it be?* butch (46%) femme (52%).

110. *Where would you place your most recent lover on a butch/femme scale(#1 being ultimate femme, #9 being ultimate butch)?* 1 (2%); 2 (6%); 3 (17%); 4 (15%); 5 (22%); 6 (15%); 7 (17%); 8 (6%); 9 (2%).

111. *Where would you place yourself on a scale that rates only your femme aspects (#10 being the ultimate femme)?* 1 (2%); 2 (4%); 3 (9%); 4 (15%); 5 (22%); 6 (14%); 7 (16%); 8 (13%); 9 (4%); 10 (3%).

112. *Where would you place yourself on a scale that rates only your butch aspects (#10 being the ultimate butch)?* 1 (3%); 2 (8%); 3 (14%); 4 (15%); 5 (21%); 6 (14%); 7 (13%); 8 (8%); 9 (2%); 10 (2%).

113. *Which do you most identify with?* femme (18%) butch (15%); androgynous (48%); none of the above (19%).

(Note: The words listed for Questions 114 - 116 are given in full in Appendix E)

114. *If you identify as butch, what three aspects of femmes do you find erotic ?*

115. *If you identify as femme, what three aspects of butches do you find erotic?*

116. *If you identify as androgynous what three aspects of women do you find erotic?*

117. *Are you more attracted to women who are:* butch (19%); femme (25%); androgynous (44%); none of the above (12%).

118. *Do you believe that your identification is:* genetic (9%); environmental (9%); chosen (28%); all of the above (43%); none of the above (11%).

119. *Do you feel butch/femme relates to the heterosexual male/female model?* yes (28%); no (19%); somewhat (44%); not sure (8%).

120. *How do you feel about being called butch?* very comfortable (8%); comfortable (35%); uncomfortable (40%); very uncomfortable (17%).

121. *How do you feel about being called femme?* very comfortable (10%); comfortable (39%); uncomfortable (42%); very uncomfortable (10%).

122. *Are you ever mistaken for a man?* yes (23%); no (57%); sometimes (20%).

123. *How important is butch/femme characterization to your personal identity?* very (4%); somewhat (30)%; not at all (66%).

124. *How often does the concept of butch/femme/androgyny come up in conversation with other lesbians?* always (2%); often (19%); occassionally (69%); never (10%).

125. *If the butch/femme characterization is very important to you, do you demonstrate that in obvious ways in the lesbian community?* yes (22%); no (76%).

126. *Do you feel there is more value on being androgynous in the lesbian community than butch or femme?* yes (40%); no (19%); not sure (41%).

(Note: answers to Questions 127-130 have been covered in the text itself.)

127. *If the butch/femme characterization is not at all important to you, what other word or phrase would you use as an alternative characterization that does have importance to you?*

Please choose three words from Sandra Bem's characteristics list (see questions #44-103) to describe the words below.

Write the numbers of the characteristics on the answer sheet.

128. Butch.

129. Femme.

130. Androgynous.

Please use your answer sheet to record the words that best describe your answer to the following questions.

(Note: Words listed for Questions 131-134 are shown in Appendix E.)

131. *Please list three words which describe* physical *characteristics of women which you find erotic (arousing or satisfying sexual desire)?*

132. *Please list three words which describe* intellectual *characteristics of women which you find erotic?*

133. *Please list three words which describe* emotional *characteristics of women which you find erotic?*

134. *Please list three words which describe* spiritual *characteristics of women which you find erotic?*

As part of a couple, how do you react when you are in the following situations? Answer the following questions by choosing (1) initiator (2) responder (3) depends on situation

	Initiate	Respond	Depends
135. *paying the bills*	46%	12%	41%
136. *cleaning the house*	39	18	43

137. *decorating the house*	36%	25%	39%
138. *working in the yard*	39	28	32
139. *caring for children*	32	17	51
140. *organizing social activities*	35	22	33
141. *cooking*	37	21	31
142. *working on the car*	35	33	33
143. *socializing*	36	19	35.
144. *dancing*	40	22	38

In the following section, all questions relate to sex practices. Please indicate your response according to a 5 point scale: (1) Never (2) Occasionally (3) Sometimes (4) Often (5) Always

	Never	Occasionally	Sometimes	Often	Always
145. *Are you the initiator in sex?*	1%	14%	41%	40%	3%
146. *Are you the responder in sex?*	1	13	51	29	6
147. *Do you initiate oral sex on your lover?*	8	17	26	38	11
148. *Do you receive oral sex from your lover?*	6	19	29	34	12
149. *Are you orgasmic?*	3	6	11	31	49
150. *Is your lover orgasmic?*	2	6	11	36	46
151. *Do you practice vaginal penetration with your lover?*	5	10	17	38	30
152. *Does your lover practice vaginal penetration with you?*	5	11	14	38	32
153. *Do you use dildos with your lover?*	65	16	12	5	2
154. *Does your lover use dildos with you?*	66	17	11	4	2
155. *Do you fantasize being a man while having sex?*	69	18	9	4	1
156. *Do you fantasize your partner being a man while having sex?*	73	16	8	2	0.2
157. *Do you french kiss?*	1	3	8	32	56
158. *Do you use vibrators?*	47	18	16	14	5

159. *Do you practice anal sex with your lover?*	58%	23%	13%	5%	2%
160. *Does your lover practice anal sex with you?*	60	22	11	5	2
161. *Do you like having your breasts sucked?*	1	7	16	29	48
162. *Do you like sucking your lover's breasts?*	0.17	2	10	30	58
163. *Do you like giving sex?*	11	6	32	60	0
164. *Do you like getting sex?*	0	52	7	31	59

The following is the goddesses from Jean Shinoda Bolen's book *Goddesses in Every Woman: A New Psychology of Women.* (1984, Harper and Row; N.Y.) Answer the questions below by using this list.

1) *Artemis—goddess of the hunt and the moon, personifies the independent, achievement-oriented feminine spirit:* yourself (35%:) your lover (30%).

2) *Athena—goddess of wisdom and craft, represents the logical, self-assured woman who is ruled by her head rather than her heart:* yourself (15%); your lover (17%).

3) *Hestia—goddess of the hearth, embodies the patient and steady woman who finds comfort in solitude and exudes a sense of intactness and wholeness:* yourself (16%); your lover (13%).

4) *Hera—goddess of marriage, stands for the woman who considers her roles as student, professional, or mother secondary to her essential goal of finding a mate and being married:* yourself (2%); your lover (5%).

5) *Demeter—goddess of grain and the maternal archetype, represents a woman's drive to provide physical and spiritual sustenance for her children:* yourself (3%); your lover (3%).

6) *Persephone—maiden and queen of the underworld, expresses a woman's tendency toward compliancy, passivity, and a need to please and be wanted by others:* yourself (5%); your lover (10%).

7) *Aphrodite—goddess of love and beauty, the alchemical goddess governing a woman's enjoyment of love and beauty, sexuality, and sensuality, impels women to fulfill both creative and procreative functions:* yourself (24%); your lover (23%).

165. *Which of the above best describes you (choose one number)?* (see answers above)

166. *Which of the above best describes your most recent lover (choose one number)?* (see answers above)

Thank you for spending the time filling out this questionnaire.

Main Survey Graphs

Percentage of Lesbians Who Think They Pass

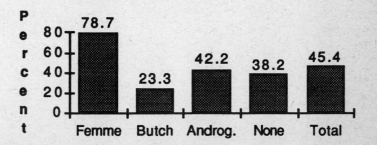

Role Identification of Total Survey Group

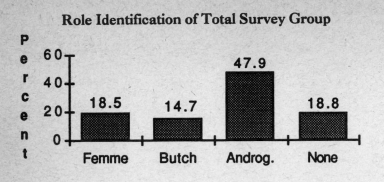

Role Identification of Lesbians Who Came Out Before 1981

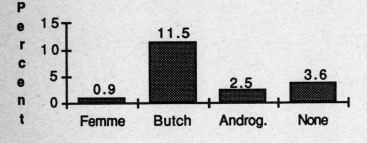

Percentage of Lesbians Who Feel Publically Visible

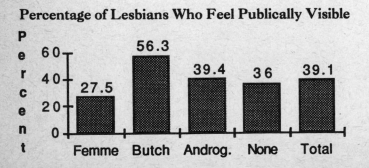

Where Androgynous Place Selves on Butch-Femme Scale

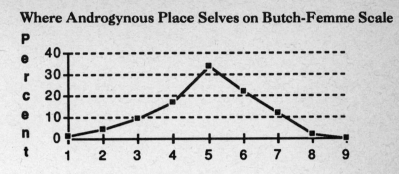

Where N.o.t.a.'s Place Selves on Butch-Femme Scale

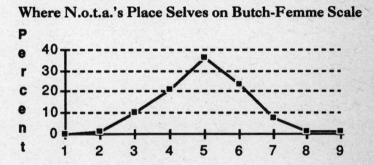

Where Femmes Place Selves on Butch-Femme Scale

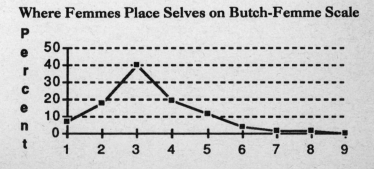

Where Butches Place Selves on Butch-Femme Scale

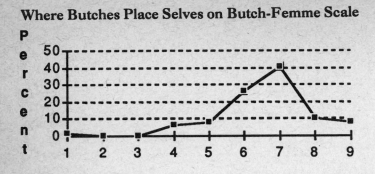

Where Total Group Places Most Recent Lover on Butch-Femme Scale

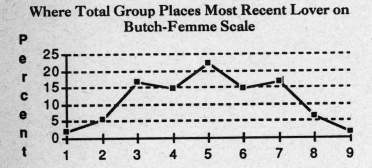

Where Androgynous Place Most Recent Lover on Butch-Femme Scale

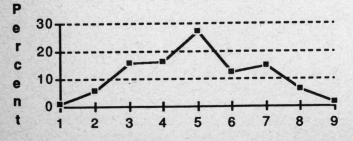

Where Femmes Place Most Recent Lover on Butch-Femme Scale

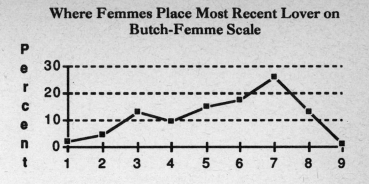

Where Butches Place Most Recent Lover on Butch-Femme Scale

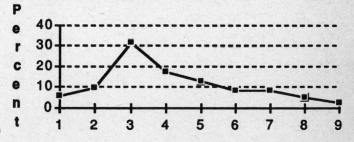

Where N.o.t.a.'s Place Most Recent Lover on Butch-Femme Scale

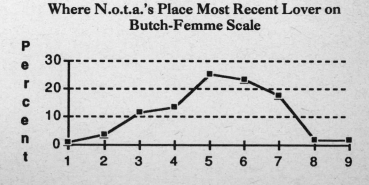

Sandra Bem's Survey and JoAnn Loulan's Survey Compared

The following is the Bem Sex Role Inventory as it was included in the survey. It gives 60 characteristics, which Bem has evaluated according to mainstream assumptions about sex roles. Immediately after each word is Bem's assessment of whether it is traditionally an androgynous (A), feminine (F), or masculine (M) characteristic.

I asked each woman in the survey group to rate themselves on a scale of one (never or almost never true) to seven (always or almost always true). I wanted to know how they saw themselves, without any role identities involved. Do you feel you are self-reliant, cheerful, shy, and so on? In the percentages below, I've combined all the women who answered with a five, six, or seven for each characteristic—those who said that characteristic was usually, frequently or always true for them. What is presented below is the cross-correlation between the role women identified with earlier in the survey and what they said about themselves here. What's amazing to me is that how we see ourselves consistently defies all the stereotypes about identity.

The following are words as they are listed on the BSRI. The columns to the right of the words represent: I: the assignment of the characteristic "masculine (M)," "feminine (F)," or "androgynous (A)" according to the BSRI ; II. the mean (the average) of all the respondents' self-rating (median, which is the middle, being 4); and the last three columns represent the number of respondents who assigned each particular BSRI word or phrase to III. Butch; IV. Androgynous; V. Femme.

	Butch	Androgynous	Femme	N.o.t.a.
Self-reliant (M)	92%	90%	91%	91
Yielding (F)	22	30	33	35
Helpful (A)	91	86	83	86
Defends own beliefs (M)	79	82	83	86
Cheerful (F)	72	72	70	73
Moody (A)	31	32	35	40
Independent (M)	92	90	85	92
Shy (F)	41	36	30	40
Conscientious (A)	81	91	88	84
Athletic (M)	74	58	37	55
Affectionate (F)	84	83	92	86
Theatrical (A)	36	29	46	31
Assertive (M)	77	70	75	73
Flatterable (F)	51	46	54	44
Happy (A)	76	77	71	83
Strong personality (M)	84	79	88	89
Loyal (F)	100	93	93	98
Unpredicatable (A)	21	20	24	29
Forceful (M)	47	40	40	39
Feminine (F)	16	42	86	47
Reliable (A)	89	94	94	95
Analytical (M)	74	77	77	82

Sympathetic (F)	85	85	80	83
Jealous (A)	29	33	35	35
Has leadership abilities (M)	86	82	88	86
Sensitive to needs of others (F)	94	88	87	89
Truthful (A)	94	87	93	95
Willing to take risks (M)	70	71	66	70
Understanding (F)	92	89	85	94
Secretive (A)	32	22	25	26
Makes decisions easily (M)	64	47	57	53
Compassionate (F)	92	87	84	87
Sincere (A)	92	91	96	91
Self-sufficient (M)	91	92	89	91
Eager to soothe hurt feelings (F)	74	75	77	74
Conceited (A)	14	14	18	18
Dominant (M)	66	44	44	47
Soft-spoken (F)	25	33	27	29
Likeable (A)	80	83	92	81
Masculine (M)	59	25	3	17
Warm (F)	87	85	88	82
Solemn (A)	40	28	20	30
Willing to take a stand (M)	82	82	83	84
Tender (F)	87	85	87	88
Friendly (A)	89	83	87	84
Aggressive (M)	60	46	36	43
Gullible (F)	29	28	39	37
Inefficient (A)	11	8	7	5
Acts as a leader (M)	71	70	79	77
Childlike (F)	44	35	34	37
Adaptable (A)	77	74	66	65
Individualistic (M)	85	81	80	80
Does not use harsh language (F)	35	32	21	32
Unsystematic (A)	23	14	12	14
Competitive (M)	70	60	53	60
Loves children (F)	59	58	57	62
Tactful (A)	60	59	64	55
Ambitious (M)	64	69	76	67
Gentle (F)	88	83	83	83
Conventional (A)	24	24	27	23

The Words We Use For Lesbian Eroticism

Aspects of femmes that butches find erotic:

adaptable	aggressive	ass
assertive	attractive	
beautiful	breasts	
caring	compassionate	confident
curvy		
delicate	dependent	dominant
dress		
elegant	energetic	eyes
face	feminine	flashy
flirtatious	fluffy	friendly
full	fun	

gentle   giving   good looking
graceful

hair   hot   huggable
humane

independent   initiator   intelligent

legs   lips   loyal

motherly   mysterious

non-athletic   noncompetitive nurturing

open

passive   personality   pretty
provocative

responsive

scent/smell   self-confident sensitive
sensual   sexy   skin
skirts   sleek   slender
small   smile   smokey
soft   stable   strong
surrendering   sweet

teasing   tender   thin

voluptuous   vulnerable

warm   witty

yielding

Aspects of butches that femmes find erotic:

active   aggressive   appearance
assertive   athletic   attitude

beautiful   boyish   brave

capable   clean   clothes
comforting   confident   considerate
consistent   controlled   coordinated
courageous

dark   different   dominant
dykey

emotionally stable   energetic   eye contact

fair   felling   firm
forceful   friendly

good body

handsome   hard

in control   independent
individualistic

kind   kinky

larger   leader
lean
lost

moody   muscles

nontraditional

orgasmic

patient   penetrating   positive
powerful   protective   proud

searching   secure   self-confident
sensitive   sensual   sexy
slick   smooth   solid

straightforward   strong   stubborn
supple

tall   tender   touching
tough

unhappy

voice

well-built   well-dressed   willing to risk

Aspects of androgynous women that like-minded women find erotic:

acrobatic	active	affectionate
aggressive	amazon	androgenous
animated	appealing	assertive
athletic	attentive	attractive
beautiful	bonding	breasts
bright	butch	
capable	caring	committed
communicative	compassionate	complex
confident	connected	creative
cuddly	curvy	cute
direct	dresses well	
emotional		empathic
		empowered
esoteric	eyes	
feminine	flesh	flirtatious
friendly	fun	
gentle	gentle touch	girlie
graceful	grounded	

hair	hands	happy
healthy	hips	honest
hot	humorous	
imaginative	imposing	independent
initiator	intelligent	intense
intimate	intriguing	
kind		
lips	lost	loving
mature	mysterious	
older	outgoing	
passionate	passive	playful
positive	powerful	pretty
protective	provocative	pubic hair
quiet		
receptive	regal	respectful
responsive	round	
scent/smell	searching	self love
self-contained	sensitive	sensuous
shapely	sharp dresser	shy
simple	sincere	skin
smart	smile	sober
socially conscious	soft	soft spoken
spiritual	stance	strong
successful	supportive	sweet
tender	thin truthful	
understanding	unhappy	unique
voice	volatile	vulnerable

warm   whole   witches
womanly

Which physical characteristics do you find erotic in women?

abdomen   active   adventurous
aggressive   alluring   androgenous
ass/hips   athletic   attractive

beautiful   blond   bodacious
body shape   boyish   breast
broad shoulders   butch

calves   carriage   clean/groomed
clitoris   clothes   coloring
coordinated   cunt   curvy
cute

dark   delicate   desirable
dress

ears   energetic   eyes

face   feminine   figure
firm   full

gentle   good looking   graceful

hair   hands   handsome
happy   healthy/well   humor

impish   in shape

muscular

jeans

labia   large   lean
legs   lips/mouth   lithe
long limbs   loving

manners	medium build	movement/walk
mysterious		
natural	neat	neck
nipples		
overbite		
passionate	perfume	pink
posture	pretty	
reliable	responsive	round
self assured	sensitive	sensual
sexy	shapely	short
shoulders	slender/thin	small
smell/scent	smile	smooth skin
soft	sold	straight looking
strong	stylish	supple
sweet		
tall	tattoos	teeth
tender	thighs	touching
trim	truthful	
victorian	voice	voluptuous
warm	weight	well-built
wet	womanly	

What intellectual characteristics do you find erotic?

able to negotiate	adaptable	adventurous
aggressive	agile	agreeable
ambitious	amusing	analytical
articulate	artistic	assertive
aware		
bright		
capable	caring	challenging

childlike

committed

compassionate

complex

considerate

cultured

clear

common sense

competent

confident

conversive

curious

clever

communicative

competitive

conscientious

creative

decisive

diplomatic

deep-thinking

direct

diligent

diverse

educated

exciting

emotional

expressive

ethical

feminist

funny

flexible

forthright

glasses

growing/learning

goal oriented

grounded

happy

humor

healthy

humble

imaginative

independent

independent thinker

individualistic

intelligent

interesting

inventive

informed

insightful

introspective

ironic

inquisitive

intense

intuitive

judgment

knowledgeable

leader

logical

liberal

listener

motivated

multilingual

musical

open

open-minded

opinions

patient

perceptive

personality

philosophical	playful	poetic
political	probing	problem solver
professional	pronunciation	
questioning	quick	
rational	reader	reasonable
receptive	reflective	responsive
risk-taking		
seeking	self reliant	self-loving
sensitive	sets limits	sexual
smart	socially aware	spiritual
spontaneous	stimulating	straight-looking
streetwise	strong	successful
theoretical	thoughtful	truthful
unconventional	understanding	unimpressionable
uninhibited		
varied	verbal	visionary
warm	well-informed	well mannered
well-read	well rounded	willful
wisdom	witty	worldly

Which emotional characteristics do you find erotic?

able	able to negotiate	able to set limits
accepting	adaptable	adult
affectionate	aggressive	analytical
approachable	appropriate	assertive
attentive	attitude	available
balanced	big-hearted	
calm	care-free	caring
centered	challenging	changeable
charming	cheerful	childlike
clear	comforting	communicative

compassionate complimentay confident
connected conscientious conscious
dangerous daring decisive
deep thinking defensive dependable
desirable dominant dramatic

educated emotional empathic
energetic enthusiastic exciting
expressive

faithful feeling feminine
friendly funny

gentle giving growing

happy healthy honest
humor

impulsive independent inquisitive
insightful integrity intense
intimacy
introspective Italian

kind knowledgeable

listener lively loving
loyal lusty

mad mature modest
moody morals/values mysterious

nice nurturing

open

passionate patient perceptive
physical playful positive
powerful practical present
psychic

real	recovering	reliable
responsive	risk taking	romantic
sad	secure	seductive
self assured	self aware	self reliant
sensitive	sensual	serene
sharing	sincere	soft
spiritual	stable	strong
supportive	sympathetic	
teasing	tender	thoughtful
touching	trusting	truthful
understanding		
varied	vulnerable	
warm	willing	
yielding		

What spiritual characteristics do you find erotic?

able to be alone	accepting	adaptable
adventurous	agnostic	alert
ambitious	analytical	anti-patriarchal
articulate	artistic	atheist
aware		
balanced	belief system	
calm	caring	centered
changing	clairvoyant	clear
common experience	compassionate	compromising
connected	conscientious	consistent
contemplative	contributes	cosmic
creative	curious	
decisive	dedicated	deep-thinking
diverse		
earthy	embracing	emotional

empathic
experimental
fair
feminine
free thinking

enlightened
exploring
faithful
flowing

ethereal

feeling
free spirit

gentle
global

genuine
goddess worship

giving
grounded

happy
holistic
humanist

harmony
honest
humble

healing
hopeful
humor

imaginative
individualistic
intense

inclusive
inner strength
intuitive

independent
integrity

Jewish

joyous

judeo-christian

keeps journal

learning

loving

loyal

meditates
musical

mercy
mysterious

moral

nature loving

nonchurch

non-
denominational

nondogmatic

nontraditional

open

optimistic

pagan
peaceful
powerful
present

passionate
philosophical
practical
private

patient
positive
prayerful
psychic

questioning

quiet

receptive	recovering	relaxed
religious	risk-taking	rituals
safe	seeking	self aware
self respect	self assured	self loving
sensitive	serene	sharing
sincere	sober	soft spoken
spiritual	stable	sympathetic
tender	thinking	thoughtful
tolerant	true to self	trusting
truthful		
unconventional	understanding	uninhibited
values	visionary	
willful	wise	woman-identified
worldly		

▨ spinsters book company

Spinsters Book Company was founded in 1978 to produce vital books for diverse women's communities. In 1986 we merged with Aunt Lute Books to become Spinsters/Aunt Lute. In 1990, the Aunt Lute Foundation became an independent non-profit publishing program.

Spinsters is committed to publishing works outside the scope of mainstream commercial publishers: books that not only name crucial issues in women's lives, but more importantly encourage change and growth; books that help to make the best in our lives more possible. We sponsor an annual Lesbian Fiction Contest for the best lesbian novel each year. And we are particularly interested in creative works by lesbians.

If you would like to know about other books we produce, or our Fiction Contest, write or phone us for a free catalogue. You can buy books directly from us. We can also supply you with the name of a bookstore closest to you that stocks our books. We accept phone orders with Visa or Mastercard.

Spinsters Book Company
P.O. Box 410687
San Francisco, CA 94141
415-558-9655